CITIES
RAC

Task Forces as Agents of
Race-Based Policy Innovations

Richard T. Middleton, IV

Foreword by
Judith A. Winston

University Press of America,® Inc.
Lanham · Boulder · New York · Toronto · Plymouth, UK

Copyright © 2008 by
University Press of America,® Inc.
4501 Forbes Boulevard
Suite 200
Lanham, Maryland 20706
UPA Acquisitions Department (301) 459-3366

Estover Road
Plymouth PL6 7PY
United Kingdom

All rights reserved
Printed in the United States of America
British Library Cataloging in Publication Information Available

Library of Congress Control Number: 2008926472
ISBN-13: 978-0-7618-4109-8 (paperback : alk. paper)
ISBN-10: 0-7618-4109-1 (paperback : alk. paper)

∞™ The paper used in this publication meets the minimum
requirements of American National Standard for Information
Sciences—Permanence of Paper for Printed Library Materials,
ANSI Z39.48—1984

This book is dedicated to my family and friends for the loving and steadfast support they have given me during my academic and research endeavors.

Table of Contents

Foreword by Judith A. Winston   vii

Acknowledgments   ix

Chapter 1   Introduction   1

Chapter 2   Factors Affecting Race-Based Policy Innovations   15

Chapter 3   Research Approach   33

Chapter 4   Madison, Wisconsin Mayor's Race Relations Task Force   61

Chapter 5   Columbia, Missouri Mayor's Race Relations Task Force   89

Chapter 6   Kansas City, Missouri Mayor's Race Relations Task Force   123

Chapter 7   Analysis of Findings Across Cases   153

Chapter 8   Task Forces as Agents of Policy Innovations- Analysis and Conclusions   165

Index   177
About the Author   179

Foreword

By Judith A. Winston

Former Executive Director of President William Clinton's, "One America in the 21st Century: Initiative on Race."

Washington, D.C.

Our nation's history is replete with efforts to reduce and ultimately eliminate the racial discrimination, tensions, and conflicts that have hindered our ability to realize fully the promise of America's Constitution and our democracy. From a resolute individual like Rosa Parks in 1955 refusing to give up her seat on the bus and the ensuing involvement of dedicated black workers in Montgomery, Alabama to the appointment in 1967 by President Lyndon Baines Johnson of the National Commission on Civil Disorders (the "Kerner Commission"), efforts small and large have attempted to mobilize the resources necessary to deal effectively with race relations. More recently, in 1997, President William Jefferson Clinton launched his Presidential Initiative on Race: One America in the Twenty-First Century to identify and begin to eliminate the racial inequities evident in communities throughout the United States. He did so at a time when there was relative prosperity in the nation. No major racial crisis or event sparked the decision to pursue the Race Initiative. The seven-person Advisory Board and the staff working on the President's Initiative on Race had the opportunity to observe directly the challenges that accompany an effort to engage the nation in a constructive dialogue on race and the development of policies aimed at eliminating the racial disparities produced by a long history of racial discrimination and negative stereotyping. Among the many lessons that we learned over the course of the President's Initiative on Race is the importance of local community engagement in improving race relations. There is no question that policy initiatives at the federal level need to be complemented by action at the state and local levels to meet the multi-faceted problems of racial conflict in America.

In this timely book, Richard Middleton, IV makes an important contribution to this effort by providing an analytical framework for understanding the critical elements that local communities have utilized to improve race relations. Utilizing his expertise as a social scientist, he describes in a straightforward manner the critical factors and circumstances that have affected mayoral use of race relations task forces as agents of race-based policy innovations in three cities. His analysis assists us in understanding what may motivate community leaders to engage in constructive problem-solving or what may impede them in seeking significant improvement in race relations.

Race continues to be an issue that divides communities. Recent events such as the perceived injustice in the charges and prosecutions against the "Jena 6" in Louisiana have dramatically demonstrated the need to do more at the local level to reduce racial tensions and conflict. With the publication of this study, city leaders and communities across the country will have important new resource for understanding better the ingredients necessary for a constructive response to racial dissention through the creation of task forces and similar entities. We should hope and anticipate that Richard Middleton, IV will build upon this study to illuminate further the combination of circumstances, leadership qualities, organizational configurations, and community support that are likely to produce positive results in reducing and eventually eliminating racial tensions and conflicts in communities across the country.

Acknowledgments

This book would not have been possible without the support and guidance of several important individuals. I am indeed grateful for the assistance of Dr. Minion K.C. Morrison, who was my Ph.D. dissertation supervisor. Dr. Morrison went beyond the call of duty in helping this process come to fruition. He was always ready, willing, and able to help me. Dr. Morrison made the entire research endeavor more rigorous, methodical, effective, yet enjoyable. Dr. Morrison always provided thoughtful insights, comments, and words of wisdom. His knowledge of the literature and key actors in the field was incomparable. Just as impressive as Dr. Morrison's scholarly knowledge on my research topic was the commitment he displayed in reading my work in a timely fashion. At all times I felt as though my research was a top priority for Dr. Morrison

I would also like to extend my gratitude to Dr. Richard J. Hardy and Dr. Paul Wallace. Dr. Hardy showed a commitment to help me develop this research topic. Dr. Hardy and Dr. Wallace always displayed total support for me in all my academic endeavors and proved to be invaluable assets for the development of my graduate experience.

I must extend thanks to Dr. Lael Keiser, a true scholar. Dr. Keiser impressed me with how thoroughly she read each chapter of this book. She always provided very appropriate comments and insights regarding my research. Having been a student of Dr. Keiser, I developed a strong respect for her research skills. I strive to follow in her footsteps and build as strong of a research program as she has.

There are a number of other individuals who I would be remiss not to mention. These individuals include: Dr. Robert Weems, Mr. William Whitcomb, Mrs. Marva Wortorson, Dr. Michael Smith, Mr. Michael Bates, Ms. Cassandra Butler, and Mr. Bruce Hanebrink. Finally, I would like to thank Dr. John Petrocik, Chair, Department of Political Science, University of Missouri-Columbia, for convincing me to seek the guidance of Dr. K.C. Morrison as my Ph.D. dissertation supervisor.

Chapter One: Introduction

This book is an analysis of mayoral use of race relations task forces as agents of race-based policy innovations in three municipalities. The central research question in this study is what explains the variation in the influence of race relations task forces on race-based public policy adoption by local level governmental and nongovernmental policymakers. With race relations continuing to assert itself as a pressing problem at the national, state, and local levels, it is important to investigate the efficacy of many of the tools communities use to address racial tensions. In this book, a case-study analysis of three communities that have invoked the use of race relations task forces is done. From analysis of these cases, major questions and contentions are addressed in an effort to make generalizations about the utility of municipal task forces as a whole. Most importantly, the case-study analysis provides the basis for tackling the major research question posed here: Whether mayoral race relations task forces are agents of race-based policy innovation and why or why not? Past research on the topic of policy innovation has traditionally approached investigating innovation by either looking at policy adoption by public bureaucracies as their unit of focus (Berry and Berry, 1990; Gray, 1973; Mohr, 1969; Welch and Thompson, 1980) or, using the influence of bureaucratic agents to explain agency policy adoption (Grupp and Richards, 1975; Walker,

1969). Race relations task forces present a new and interesting approach towards analyzing agents of policy innovation.

Task forces, generally speaking, are collections of citizens whose purpose is to assess a given issue, contemplate remedies, and produce policy recommendations directed towards addressing the problem at hand. Task forces are aggregations of individuals that assess fairly well defined issues and go about doing so by relying on a division of labor. Not all task forces come together on a whim. Many are created because of some event(s) that has a dramatic affect on the environment of governmental and nongovernmental organizations. These events often have the ability to induce marked changes in continuous, stable organizational environmental conditions. Such factors can be referred to as *environmen-*

tal shocks. Examples of environmental shocks can range from riots, high crime rates, and mass murders, to high filing rates of EOC complaints of racial discrimination in promotion and hiring in the workplace or alleged voter fraud and discrimination following a major election.

Shocks to an organization's environment can create a period of organizational instability, change, and innovation—or what can be called *punctuated equilibria* (Eldredge, 1985; Eldredge and Gould, 1972; Goertz and Diehl, 1995). Punctuated equilibria are temporary periods of instability sandwiched between periods of organizational stability.

Task forces have distinctive characteristics that differentiate them from other governmental bureaucracies. They are sometimes community based, but quite often are created by governmental bodies. In instances such as the latter, task forces can be thought of as government organized nongovernmental organizations or GONGOs (Nyang'oro, 1993). Task forces such as these are *not* permanent governmental institutions. Once they have fulfilled their assigned responsibilities, they disband. In addition, they are aggregations of individuals who are usually non-state actors. With regards to their life span, task forces come together for a *temporary* span of time to complete single or multiple tasks. It is important to understand the distinct characteristics of task forces as studied here so task forces and commissions are not confused with governmental bureaucracies that are also sometimes called commissions (e.g., Texas State Health and Human Services Commission). The latter are distinct in that they are permanent government commissions that are always sanctioned by local ordinance, state law or state constitution.

Task forces are collections of individuals who are typically non-elected officials, but who hold some level of qualification (knowledge of the subject, educational training, etc.) to serve on the force. It may not always be the case that all individuals on task forces are highly knowledgeable and/or have a background of expertise to serve on a particular task force. It could be the case that the individual is very interested in serving on the task force to fulfill a sense of civic duty, get involved in politics, or gain public exposure. In most cases, however, the appointing executive or assemblies seek to select members who, because of some special criteria, are thought to be adept at serving on the task force.

Because task force members are not popularly elected to serve on particular task forces, coupled with the fact that task forces generally disband fairly quickly, it is virtually impossible to hold task forces accountable for the recommendations they produce. In addition, task force members do not get a chance to reevaluate and reformulate their recommendations unless they reconvene. Because of these characteristics, task forces should not be as successful as traditional public bureaucracies in influencing policy adoption in other governmental and nongovernmental institutions. As such, it is important to investigate whether task forces are actually successful in influencing governmental and nongovernmental actors to adopt policies based upon task force recommendations.

In recent years, a growing number of American municipalities have invoked one particular type of task force to address a variety of local problems—mayoral task forces. Mayoral task forces have been formed to study water management, waste treatment, land usage and many other issues. Typically, mayors design these task forces to include local citizens and civic leaders, many who are considered experts on the subject being studied. Once formed, these task forces typically study the assigned problem, consider possible alternative solutions, and make recommendations. Typically, these recommendations are presented to the mayor and sometimes other city actors, such as the city council. They are, however, typically aimed at governmental as well as nongovernmental actors. These policymakers, of course, are free to heed or ignore the recommendations of the appointed task force.

A type of mayoral task force that has begun to attract greater attention is the race relations task force. The most notable of these task forces is the Chicago Commission on Race Relations (Tuttle, 1997). This force, in studying 5 days of rioting in Chicago that ultimately took the lives of 15 whites, 23 blacks, and saw 291 wounded and maimed, is one of the earliest task forces to have ever studied race relations and issued recommendations based upon its findings. More recently, President William Clinton's Initiative on Race staff, in a report titled "Pathways to One America in the 21st Century," cited over 120 local level public and private sector groups that have implemented race dialogues of some kind (Pathways to One America in the 21st Century 1997). As such, efforts have been made throughout history at the local levels to grapple with the problems of race relations.

Most attention on race relations task forces, however, has been on those at the *national* level. The most notable examples are the Kerner Commission Report of 1968 and President Clinton's "Initiative on Race." The Kerner Commission was called by President Lyndon B. Johnson following racial tensions in the mid-1960s and reported that increasingly America is becoming divided into two nations—one black and one white. President Clinton's recent race commission was called for the purpose of creating a national dialogue on racial issues. Understandably, there has been a great deal written about these national race relations task forces (Harris and Wilkins, 1988; Siegel, 1969; White, 1988; Wicker, 1968) but relatively scant attention has been paid to race relations task forces at the local level.

Given the growing popularity of mayoral race relations task forces, a number of important questions must be asked. Specifically, what role do mayoral race relations task forces play in influencing local governmental and nongovernmental institutions to adopt polices based upon task force recommendations? Do these task forces actually make recommendations, and if they do, what type of recommendations do they make? Are the recommendations produced by task forces merely symbolic or do they actually translate into meaningful policies that legitimize the creation of such forces? On the one hand, if such governmental task forces serve as nothing more than symbolic tools utilized by elected officials, what utility do they hold for communities? Or could it be the case that task forces lead public, as well as non-public sector officials, to actually heed task force advice and incorporate task force recommendations into their own policies? If task forces are successful in influencing policy adoption by other actors, then under what conditions are task force recommendations most likely to be adopted or ignored?

The purpose of this book is to investigate the variation in the impact of race relations task forces using organizational innovation as a framework. In doing so, the book explains the nature of the problem regarding race relations, constructs a theoretical framework that identifies variables that are important in explaining the variation in the impact of race relations task forces, outlines specific questions and contentions to be addressed, and develops a plan of analysis than can be utilized to address the questions raised. The central argument of this book is that *local level governmental, business, and civic policymakers will adopt more task force recommendations in cases where an environmental shock(s) is present in their organizational environment than will policymakers in instances where there is no environmental shock present in their organization's environment.*

A Brief History of the Use of Task Forces

History has provided examples of city, state, and federal government efforts towards utilizing experts to manage societal problems that arise as a result of industrialization and urbanization and to diminish the impact of the spoils system associated with the Jacksonian Democrats. This was evidenced by the wave of governmental reform that took place during the Progressive Era. Federal executive level commissions were one small part of the Progressive Era's governmental reform movement. For example, on June 1, 1905, Theodore Roosevelt created the five-member Keep Commission (chaired by Charles Keep, Assistant Secretary of the Treasury) whose purpose was to look into the government's salary policy and purchasing practices (Arnold, 1986). The general goal of Roosevelt in creating the commission was to increase executive level managerial control on government spending.

Peri Arnold (1986) found that Roosevelt's creation of the commission ushered in a new era in which the executive began taking on a mostly congressional-centered tradition of reform. In addition, it signaled an unprecedented blow to Congress' dominance over administration. The Keep Commission issued reports on eleven different areas, ranging from management of records to the economics of mailing envelopes. According to Arnold, the only recommendations that went above such "mundane specificity" were those that called for a central purchasing agency and a central statistical agency (Arnold, 1986).

Subsequent to Roosevelt's administration, yet another executive level commission was created—this time, in the Taft Administration. The Commission on Economy and Efficiency was an offspring of Roosevelt's earlier attempt to investigate how to curb administrative spending and reduce budgetary deficits. President Taft created the Commission on Economy and Efficiency in March of 1911 in an attempt to expand his overall inquiry into agency spending practices (Arnold, 1986). Frederick Cleveland headed the commission and its membership was dominated by individuals whose views towards government reform had been influenced by the municipal reform movement and the beginnings of public administration as an academic field. Cleveland, a product of the New York Bureau of Municipal Research (which claimed to be a collection of "efficiency experts"), headed the Commission on Economy and Efficiency (Arnold, 1986). Other members included William Willoughby, assistant director of the U.S. Census Bureau and scholar of local administration in Puerto Rico, and Merritt Chance, Post Office auditor. Also members of the commission were Frank Goodnow, Walter Warwick and Harvey Chase. Goodnow, Warwick, and Chase were professor of administrative law, an auditor, and an engineer and auditor, respectively. As a unit, the commission membership was heavily biased towards support of the government reform movement. Given that local level task forces have often been modeled after federal level counterparts, the analysis of the general structure, membership composition, and outputs of federal executive level commissions provides a good source for analysis of local level mayoral task forces.

Legislative level commissions, such as the Hoover Commission (also referred to as the Commission on Organization of the Executive Branch of Government), have not typically followed the same institutional structure of executive level commission. As opposed to the Taft administration commission, the Hoover Commission was created within a statutory framework that attempted to create a broadly representative commission insulated from partisanship. This commission, which Ferrel Heady calls a "mixed commission" divided appointment power three-ways (Heady, 1949). Of the twelve total members, each appointing officer was guided to make selections in such a way that only six members would come from "official life" and six who were "private citizens" at the time of appointment (Heady, 1949). The implications of this, as Heady notes, were threefold: 1) divisions along party lines did not occur, 2) partisanship was not an important factor in the reception given to the Commissions recommendations, and 3) the Commission's bipartisan nature lent weight to its recommendations (Heady, 1949).

The goals of the Hoover Commission were much the same as those of the Commission on Economy and Efficiency. Congress instructed the Hoover Commission to "investigate the existing organization and methods of all executive agencies in order to determine what changes were necessary to accomplish the purposes set forth" in the enabling legislation (Heady, 1949). The statute that created the Commission declared that the policy of Congress was "to promote economy, efficiency, and improved service in the transaction of the public business in all the agencies of the executive branch . . ." and it listed "limitation of expenditures, elimination of duplication and overlapping, consolidation of functions of a similar nature, and abolition of functions" as among the means to reaching the overall objective (Heady, 1949). Quite clearly, the Hoover Commission, unlike the Commission on Economy and Efficiency was given a broad grant of power in addition to very specific issues to address. The Commission saw itself as having such a broad grant of power that it took the discretion to define its purpose as being "clearly directed to explore the boundaries of governmental functions in the light of their cost, their usefulness, their limitations, and their curtailment or elimination" (Heady, 1949).

The Commission on Economy and Efficiency went about its work by using a system of subcommittees-each of which focused on one detailed issue. In addition, there were committees to negotiate differences between the commission itself and the agencies, as well as a commission of consulting experts who served as external advisers. Arnold notes that President Taft maintained a close relationship with the commission. Because the commission was an arm of the president, it found itself isolated from other executive level actors as well as Congress. Taft's commission, however, was met with opposition by actors within the executive branch (including the Dept. of Treasury) as well as Congress—who saw the agency as a threat to their oversight of the administrative apparatus of government (Arnold, 1986).

The Hoover Commission, like the Commission on Economy and Efficiency, decided to utilize a method that relied upon a division of labor for intense investigation of detailed issues. Heady argues this method became known as the "task force" method of operation (Heady, 1949). Instead of opting for a large staff to undertake all necessary investigations, the Hoover Commission resorted to assigning specific major problems selected for examination to a special study group "recruited for the particular investigation and retained only until its assignment could be completed." This system was characterized as one that called for, 1) careful planning of project assignments to avoid omission or duplications, 2) adequate guidance to the task forces in the conduct of their investigations, 3) close coordination of the work of related task forces, and 4) a schedule for the completion of task force reports (Heady, 1949).

With regard to the Commission on Economy and Efficiency, it produced recommendations that were made through presidential messages to Congress in 1912. Arnold notes that very few of the recommendations made were actually implemented. One accomplishment of note was the Classification Act of 1923, which was influenced by the recommendations of the Commission on Economy and Efficiency. In addition, the Appropriations Act of 1912, which specified the distribution of all government publications were to be centralized at the Government Printing Office, was enacted as a result of the recommendations of the Commission. In the long run, however, very few of the Commissions recommendations were heeded (Arnold, 1986). Why? Perhaps, as Arnold notes, Congress was not ready, nor willing, to give up much of its budgetary and managerial power over government agencies to the executive branch. One of the most noteworthy results of the work of the Commission, however, could be seen in the subsequent adoption of such commissions at the state level. Arnold notes that by 1915, thirteen state-level reorganization-planning commissions made policy recommendations (Arnold, 1986).

Arguably, the use of task forces at the local levels has largely been patterned after those at the national level. State and local level commissions were modeled after those implemented during the Progressive era's governmental reform movement. Scholars have written literature about the move by governors and mayors towards selecting apolitical experts to help states and cities confront the challenges of urbanization, industrialization and the overall increase of demands on local governments (Ebner and Tobin 1977; Flack, 1914; Hays, 1974; Lubove, 1967; Waters, 1916). Other than relying on knowledge of experts, most of these commissions took the form of permanent changes to the structure of state and local level governments—not temporary task groups. C. C. Waters has identified that four of thirteen economy and efficiency commissions established by 1915 had been established on a permanent basis—with one (New York department of efficiency and economy) later abolished by law (Waters, 1916). At the local levels, many cities adopted commission forms of government in favor of other types, such as an alderman form. These permanent institutional changes were not commissions in the sense as those analyzed here—those that are referred to as task forces.

More recent national level commissions include the Warren Commission of 1963. This commission was created by President Lyndon Johnson to investigate the murder of President John F. Kennedy's reputed assassin, Lee Harvey Oswald. Since this time, a plethora of task forces and commissions have sprouted as a result of elected and appointed officials' desire to address some social problem. As mentioned earlier, the seminal task force on race relations has come to be the Kerner Commission. The Kerner Commission, created by President Lyndon Johnson in 1968, has been heralded as the nation's first comprehensive examination of racial issues in the United States. The report looks into the causes of many urban riots and finds, "White racism is essentially responsible for the explosive mixture that has been accumulating in our cities since the end of World War II." In addition, the report argued for a massive redistribution of income to remedy problems rooted in social inequities. The commission's report has also been cited as the United States government's first official document that says racism exists and is a problem (United States, 1968).

Some thirty years later, President William Clinton began an "Initiative on Race" in order to provide a guiding light for conducting dialogues on race at local levels. This commission included several civic organizations, including Hope in the Cities, National Conference for Communities and Justice, and National Days of Dialogue. President Clinton's initiative did not provide much in the way of substantive statements on the current state of race relations in the United States. It did, however, serve to remind America's society that it was important to continue to discuss how people felt about racial issues and how interpersonal relations could be strengthened through mutual understanding.

Race Relations as a Focus of Study

While many gains have been made toward the elimination of the remnants of Jim Crow laws and de facto segregation, there remains social strife among races of people. The Los Angeles Riots in April of 1992, the O.J. Simpson trial in 1995, and the Texas dragging death of James Byrd, Jr. by white supremacists in

February of 1999, serve to remind us how quickly racial issues can divide our society (Ong, 1993; Schmalleger, 1996; Temple-Raston, 2002). State and local governments have increasingly found it more important to implement laws and policies that serve to address, circumvent, and remedy conflicts rooted in racial disharmony. One method by which local governments have begun to initiate the creation of such policies is through studying the nature of race relations.

What is race relations and why study race relations? The term "race relations" is a misnomer, according to Stephen Steinberg, professor of urban studies at Queens College. Steinberg questions the use of the term race relations because it applies "such benign language to such a malignant problem" (Steinberg, 2001). "It is rather like diagnosing a melanoma as a skin rash, and prescribing a topical salve. Putting the wrong name on a problem is worse than having no name at all," argues Steinberg (Steinberg, 2001). Steinberg favors replacing the term "race relations" with "racial oppression" as it conveys a greater since of the magnitude of the problem. While debating whether the term race relations adequately captures the degree of intensity of racial tensions in a community may largely be of concern for scholars of political agendas and instability (e.g., Baumgartner and Jones, 1993), Steinberg's argument serves to illuminate the importance of studying race relations.

Throughout the history of the United States, blacks have consistently lagged behind white Americans in virtually every measure of socioeconomic status (Barker, Jones, and Tate, 1999). While blacks have become better off in recent decades, the gap between black and white well-being has remained largely the same. According to many scholars, the gap between blacks and white may even be getting larger (Barker et al., 1999). Evidence abound demonstrates that whites feel the overall economic status of blacks has largely improved and, consequently, further government policies towards promoting black equality are no longer needed. Conversely, blacks feel additional affirmative steps need to be taken by not only governmental, but nongovernmental actors as well, towards bringing blacks up to a more level economic playing field as whites (Barker et al., 1999). These diametric viewpoints between the black and white communities clearly demonstrate a need for further dialogue about the nature of race relations and how to address such issues.

The examination of mayoral race relations task forces provides an opportunity to address a number of important questions. Specifically, what role do mayoral task forces play in influencing the adoption of public policies in local communities? Generally speaking, mayors create task forces in an effort to have its members investigate some past, immediate, or prospective social problem and produce policy recommendations that address those issues identified as the possible root of the problem. In addition, mayors may seek to gain electoral support from their constituents who are concerned about the issue. Given that these task forces aim to increase the quality of life by resolving community problems, local civic, governmental, and private sector organizations should be keen on the idea of adopting policies as recommended by task forces. As such, one should expect to find mayoral task forces to have a significant impact on shaping local level public policies. If local civic, governmental, and private sector organizations do adopt task force policy recommendations, under what conditions are they most likely to do so? Under what conditions are they most likely not to do so? These are the key issues that must be investigated.

Say, for example, a mayoral task force on neighborhood crime concludes high crime rates in a particular part of the city is caused by lax police patrols. This task force could recommend, among other things, police patrols during prime criminal activity times, adoption of neighborhood watch programs, and implementation of civic programs to teach individuals how to reduce the likelihood they will become the victim of a crime. In reaction to the high rates of crime in the city, local level governmental, civic, and private sector organizations might adopt these recommended policies that are aimed at curtailing the problem. It could be the case the task force, through its influence alone, leads these actors to adopt such policies. Or, it could be the case that local governmental and nongovernmental actors adopt such policies because of their own inclination and motivation. This book seeks to investigate these contentions using race relations as a focus of study.

Is it safe to assume that mayoral task forces will have a significant impact on the creation of local level public policies? Or, could it be the case that mayoral task forces do not lead to the adoption of policies designed to remedy an identified problem? Perhaps mayoral task forces only have symbolic value. Maybe there are factors that would not lead local government, civic, and private sector organizations to adopt policies as recommended by task forces. While task forces are often created because of some past, immediate, or future community crisis, it could be the case that a task force is developed when there is a general period of community stability. It could be the case that a task force is created to make sure that the status quo is maintained even when there are no indications a change is likely to occur.

A state, for example, may want to take the lead in ensuring its ambient air quality standards remain the same in locations identified as having better than average air quality. The state could create a task force on air quality—even when there is no past, immediate, or future indication of threats to the location's quality of air. It may be the case that the state is genuinely interested in maintaining ambient air quality in as many portions of its borders as possible. At the least, the public officials in the state would be viewed as a proactive leaders that do not sit around and wait for a sign of a problem before they take action. In such a case, however, what would be the impetus for local governmental and nongovernmental organizations to adopt policies recommended by the state air quality task force? Why would these actors exhaust any time, effort, or money in adopting such policies when there is no smog in their backyards? In such cases, the creation of the task force may serve as a mere symbol of a proactive government.

Research Approach

This book is a case study of three mayoral race relations task forces. The research approach is based on survey and interviews, as well as an analysis of municipal level data collected from each of the three case cities. From analysis of these data, generalizations are made about mayoral race relations task forces. The findings in each case study are then used to increase our understanding of mayoral task forces in general. In this book, I conduct an analysis of the number of local governmental and nongovernmental entities that adopt policy innovations aimed at addressing race relations problems as identified by the task force in each respective community. According to the literature on policy innovation, policies adopted—that is ideas, practices, or objects adopted—as new by an individual or aggregation of individuals are viewed as innovations (Rogers, 1962). The key is not whether the idea is new as measured by the interval in time since its first use or its invention; rather, it is whether the person or persons adopting the idea see it as new. In this book, the concepts of policy innovation and policy adoption are used interchageabley. Rather than defining these terms in light of the perception of the person adopting the idea and whether they see it as new, policy innovation (likewise, policy adoption) is conceptualized here as the organizational incorporation of problem-solving approaches that depart from traditional organizational policy regarding the same issue. By defining innovation in this manner, the muddiness in acurately measuring perceptions can be overcome.

With respect to local governments, the units of analysis are those policies adopted by divisions of municipal government that have been specifically identified in the task force recommendations. Similarly, the units of analysis for nongovernmental organizations are the policies adopted as specified in the task force recommendations. Policies not listed in the task force recommendations but are considered by the organizations to be innovative approaches to dealing with race relations are also examined. This book broadly categorizes the major policy areas into several major divisions. These divisions are drawn based upon assessing the major issue areas in the final reports of each race relations task force. These policy areas include: 1) commerce, 2) employment, 3) housing, 4) media, 5) religion, 6) community service and recreation, and 7) government. The actors selected to be surveyed and interviewed are identified through analysis of the task forces' final recommendations. In each final report, specific governmental and nongovernment organizations are identified and given recommended courses of action to address race relations in their respective communities.

Theoretical Framework

To explore the above issues, this work utilizes theory emanating from the literature on organizational innovation. The frameworks suggested by scholars who write in this tradition, such as Lawrence Mohr, are appropriate for use here because they explore the determinants of innovations in public agencies, e. g., the "degree to which they adopt and emphasize programs that depart from traditional concerns" (Mohr, 1969). According to Mohr, the concept of innovation is defined as "the successful introduction into an applied situation of means or ends that are new to that situation" (Mohr, 1969). Quite frequently, there is a tendency by political scientists to equate innovation with adoption of policies (Berry and Berry, 1990; Mohr, 1969). Innovation is suggested by Mohr to be a function of three major factors: 1) the motivation to innovate, 2) the strength of obstacles against innovation, and 3) the availability of resources for overcoming such obstacles.

In this book, the examination of determinants of policy adoption is extended from Mohr's analysis of public agencies to include local level civic, and nongovernmental organizations. While much of the past research on the topic has focused on governmental entities, it is important to include nongovernmental actors into the foray as well. The reasoning behind doing so is because one of the aims of bureaucracies, such as task forces, is to also influence policy adoption by nongovernmental actors. Therefore, it is important to investigate what role task forces play in motivating such actors to adopt policies based upon task force recommendations.

Theory on organizational innovation is an appropriate foundation because it allows for inclusion of task force influence as an explanatory variable for local governmental policy adoption. Past research on innovation does not look into the influence task forces have in leading governmental and nongovernmental actors to adopt policies (Grupp and Richards, 1975; Walker, 1969) look at the influence elected and appointed officials have on policy adoption by other state agencies). In most cases, the research only analyzes the role factors, such as fiscal health, electoral motivations, demographic characteristics, etc., have on state policy adoption. Investigating the influence task forces have on policy adoption through their production of recommendations is an exercise that has not been explored.

Organization of the Book

This book contains eight chapters. Chapter Two develops the framework guiding the exploration of mayoral race relations task forces throughout the book. This chapter establishes the conditions under which variation in the impact of mayoral race relations task forces on innovation in organizations can be explained. Chapter Three discusses the methodology used to analyze the major contentions. Chapter Three also discusses the background of each of the cases selected for investigation and the justification for the selection of these cases. Chapters Four through Six include an in-depth analysis of each case. These chapters follow the general pattern of discussing the case background, the dynamics of the work done by the task force, the recommendations produced by the task force and the influence the task force has on policy adoption by local level governmental, civic, and private sector organizations. Chapter Seven includes a discussion of the general findings across each case. This chapter analyzes the effectiveness of each task force in a comparison/contrast fashion. In doing so, Chapter Seven presents arguments about the effectiveness of task forces in meeting their desired goals. Lastly, Chapter Eight offers an overview of the findings in the book and discusses what the findings suggest for our understanding of the role of task forces in the governing process.

Bibliography

Arnold, P. E. (1986). *Making the Managerial Presidency.* Princeton, NJ: Princeton University Press.

Barker, L. J., Jones, M., and Tate, K. (1999). *African Americans and the American Political System.* Upper Saddle River, NJ: Prentice Hall, Inc.

Baumgartner, F. R., and Jones, B. D. (1993). *Agendas and Instability in American Politics.* Chicago: University of Chicago Press.

Berry, F. S., and Berry, W. D. (1990). State Lottery Adoptions as Policy Innovations: An Event History Analysis. *American Political Science Review, 84*(2), 395-415.

Ebner, M. H., and Tobin, E., M. (1977). *The Age of Urban Reform.* Port Washington, NY: Kennikat Press.

Eldredge, N. (1985). *Unfinished Synthesis: Biological Hierarchies and Modern Evolutionary Thought.* New York: Oxford University Press.

Eldredge, N., and Gould, S. (1972). Punctuated Equilibria: An Alternative to Phyletic Gradualism. In T. Schopf (Ed.), *Models in Paleobiology.* San Francisco: Freeman, Cooper.

Flack, H. E. (1914). Efficiency and Economy in State Governments. *American Political Science Review, 8*(1), 63-64.

Goertz, G., and Diehl, P. F. (1995). The Initiation and Termination of Enduring Rivalries: The Impact of Political Shocks. *American Journal of Political Science, 39*(1), 30-52.

Gray, V. (1973). Innovation in the States: A Diffusion Study. *American Political Science Review, 67*(4), 1174-1185.

Grupp, F. W., Jr., and Richards, A. R. (1975). Variations in Elite Perceptions of American States as Referents for Public Policy Making. *American Political Science Review, 69*(3), 850-858.

Harris, F. R., and Wilkins, R. W. (Eds.). (1988). *Quiet Riots: Race and Poverty in the United States.* New York: Pantheon Books.

Hays, S. P. (1974). The Changing Political Structure of the City in Industrial America. *Journal of Urban History, 1*(1), 6-38.

Heady, F. (1949). The Operation of a Mixed Commission. *American Political Science Review, 43*(5), 940-952.

Lubove, R. (1967). The Urbanization Process: A Historical Approach. *Journal of the Institute of American Planners, 33*(1), 33-39.

Mohr, L. B. (1969). Determinants of Innovation in Organizations. *American Political Science Review, 63*(1), 111-126.

Nyang'oro, J. E. (1993). *The Receding Role of the State and the Emerging Role of NGOs in African Development.* Paper presented at the All Africa Conference of Churches/Research and Development Consultancy Service.

Ong, P. (1993). *Losses in the Los Angeles Civil Unrest, April 29-May 1, 1992: Lists of the Damaged Properties and Korean Merchants and the L.A. Riot Rebellion.* Los Angeles: UCLA Center for Pacific Rim Studies.

Rogers, E. M. (1962). *Diffusion of Innovations.* New York: Free Press.

Schmalleger, F. M. (1996). *Trial of the Century: People of the State of California vs. Orenthal James Simpson.* Upper Saddle River, NJ: Prentice Hall.

Siegel, I. H. (1969). *The Kerner Commission Report and Economic Policy.* Kalamazoo, MI: W.E. Upjohn Institute for Employment Research.

Steinberg, S. (2001). Why the Term 'Race Relations' is a Misnomer. *Chronicle of Higher Education.*

Temple-Raston, D. (2002). *A Death in Texas: A Story of Race, Murder, and a Small Town's Struggle for Redemption*. New York: Henry Holt and Company.

Tuttle, W. M., Jr. (1997). *Race Riot: Chicago in the Red Summer of 1919.*

United States, Kerner Commission. (1968). *Report of the National Advisory Commission on Civil Disorders*. New York: Bantam Books.

Walker, J. L. (1969). The Diffusion of Innovations Among the American States. *American Political Science Review, 63*(3), 880-899.

Waters, C. C. (1916). Economy and Efficiency Commissions. *American Political Science Review, 10*(1), 96-97.

Welch, S., and Thompson, K. (1980). The Impact of Federal Incentives on State Policy Innovation. *American Journal of Political Science, 24*(4), 715-729.

White, V. D. (1988). *The Kerner Commission Report as it Relates to Newspaper Coverage of Blacks in a Small City with Competing Newspaper*. University of Missouri-Columbia.

Wicker, T. (1968). Special Introduction by Tom Wicker of the New York Times. In United States, Kerner Commission (Ed.), *Report of the National Advisory Commission on Civil Disorder*. New York: Bantam Books.

Chapter Two: Factors Affecting Race-Based Policy Innovations

To explain the variation of the impact of mayoral task forces on race-based policy innovation in communities, I use a number of factors (variables). Building on the seminal work of Lawrence Mohr, as well as a review of other pertinent literature, I use five main variables to explain the variance in race-based policy innovation. The five key variables used in this book to explain the variation in the impact of mayoral task force on policy innovation in local communities are (1) presence of an environmental shock, (2) the credibility of task force recommendations, (3) task force influence, (4) level of racial threat, and (5) political culture. To expand upon each of the major variables listed, I conduct further analysis in the next section in the form of a literature review.

This book builds upon the fundamental assumption that governmental and nongovernmental actors can be influenced by task forces to adopt various policies. If these institutions can indeed be persuaded to embrace a variety of policies, then it is important to investigate what factors may contribute to their doing so. Tackling the question, under what conditions are local level governmental, civic, and private sector organizations most likely to be influenced to adopt certain policies and how they are likely to be influenced, necessitates a discussion of the literature on policy innovation. This line of research is an outgrowth of a number of key studies that have investigated state level policy adoption patterns (Gray, 1973; Grupp and Richards, 1975; Mohr, 1969; Walker, 1969). Each of these strands of research builds upon the fundamental assumption that policy innovation is a function of a myriad of factors—social, political, and/or economic. Where the literature departs in agreement, however, is on which factor(s), (social, political, and/or economic) explains the *most* variance in state policy adoption. Often, the literature leads to confusion over where to draw the distinction between what is economic, what is political, and what is social. As a consequence, there is much muddiness in the research's ability to differentiate between otherwise similar concepts.

Many of the advances made in the policy innovation literature in political science are attributable to the seminal work of Lawrence B. Mohr. In his "Determinants of Innovation in Organizations," Mohr investigates what factors influence ninety-three state level health agencies to adopt non-traditional programs. Mohr argues innovation in organizations, generally speaking, can be linked to "size, wealth, environment, ideology, motivation, competence, professionalism, non-professionalism, decentralization, opinion leadership, and still other variables" (Mohr, 1969). In his study, Mohr finds organization size is the variable most useful in explaining why some health agencies are more likely to adopt non-traditional programs versus others. However, Mohr also concedes size can predict innovativeness only in as much as it "implies the presence of motivation, obstacles, and resources" (Mohr, 1969).

Mohr's thesis becomes problematic, however, once his key variables are operationalized. While Mohr leads one to believe he is identifying the key explanations for organizational policy adoption, he actually develops a model laden with collinearity. In other words, Mohr's motivation to innovate, strength of obstacles against innovation, and the availability of resources for overcoming such obstacles, *are all contingent upon and affected by social, political and economic factors* (Berry and Berry discover this, though they do not explicitly mention it, when they hypothesize both economic and political conditions can be expected to affect the motivation of state political officials to adopt a lottery) (Berry and Berry, 1990). In essence, Mohr develops a model that argues innovation is a function of the nothing more than the interaction of social, political, and economic factors—all of his schemes fall largely under these three labels. Consequently, it becomes more prudent to use a single concept that incorporates these disparate categories.

Five Key Factors to Explain Race-Based Policy Innovations in Cities

Presence of an Environmental Shock

In this book, I examine race-based policy innovation made by nongovernmental and governmental organizations. As such, I find it important to analyze relevant literature on innovation in both of these types of institutions. With regards to innovation in nongovernmental organizations, I find that political science research produces only a little in the way of consistent findings on innovation in nongovernmental organizations (Lynn Jr., 1997). However, there is substantial literature outside the discipline of political science that explores innovation in nongovernmental organizations.

The literature on policy adoption in nongovernmental organizations, according to Laurence Lynn, Jr., departs from two general approaches 1) the didactic literature, which concerns itself with prescription and is often based upon practice and experience, and 2) the literature that uses methods of social science to explain innovation in organizations. The former argues innovation is a result of market-oriented goals. Companies innovate in an effort to remain competitive, retain customer loyalty, and stay ahead of the technology curve (Peters and Waterman, 1982). The latter, which I am most concerned with, devotes attention to the external and internal environment of the organization in an effort to explain innovation. This line of literature views external stimuli as the most important factors that contribute to innovation in nongovernmental organizations.

In an analysis of innovation in organizations, James G. March and Herbert A. Simon argue that the rate of innovation in an organization is "likely to increase when changes in the environment make the existing organizational procedures unsatisfactory" . . . "the innovation process is not itself programmed" (March and Simon, 1958). March and Simon go on to note the innovation process in nongovernmental organizations might also be triggered by self-imposed goals that necessitate change and are accompanied by incentives to change. Nevertheless, they argue organizational practices are likely to change in coincidence with changes in factors external to the organization. The status quo is interrupted in such organizations and innovations take place during the process towards recouping a level of stability.

As a challenge to the heuristic-like, multistage models of innovation developed in the business literature on innovation, Roger D. Schroeder develops an explanation of how innovation evolves, shapes, and is shaped, by the organization. According to Schroeder, "innovation is stimulated by shocks" . . . [things such as] "new leadership, product failure, a budget crisis, and an impeding loss of market share" . . . "either internal or external to the organization" (Schroeder, Van de Ven, Scudder, and Polly, 1989). Along the lines of Schroeder's argument, James Q. Wilson notes innovations depend on "the chance appearance of a change-oriented personality" . . . "an agency that wishes to implement an innovation over the opposition of some of its members often needs to concentrate power in the hands of the boss sufficient to permit him or her to ignore (or even dismiss) opponents" (Wilson, 1989). Such a change in personnel structure can be viewed as an internal shock to the organization.

Utility of the Literature on Innovation in Nongovernmental Organizations for Studying City Politics

There are distinct advantages of the literature on innovation in nongovernmental organizations. The social science approach to explaining innovation in nongovernmental organizations provides evidence that internal and external shocks influence the organization. Factors, such as budget shortfalls, creation of new technology, or even leadership, can play a role in whether or not nongovernmental institutions innovate. This line of research provides useful insight into innovation in nongovernmental organizations that can be incorporated into a larger discussion of innovation as is done in this book. This literature also shares similar tenets with much of the political science literature on policy innovation in governmental organizations. While the innovation literature rooted in assumptions fundamental to the nongovernmental sector do not always carry over to the political science literature on innovation, it still contributes significantly to our understanding of innovation in governmental institutions.

As discussed earlier, many scholars of innovation have already noted the ability of shocks in the environment of a nongovernmental organization to lead to dramatic changes. So why have leading scholars of policy innovation in political science not already picked up on the connection between the literature on international conflict and private sector innovation organization with that of innovation in public organizations? Clearly, as discussed in the next section, political scientists have done a broad assessment of the agents policy change in public organizations. However, this literature tends to diffuse, so to speak, into a broad array of concepts. As such, I advocate that the use of a more manageable term can better bring together literature that is seemingly otherwise disparate.

Utility of the Literature on Innovation in Governmental Organizations for Studying City Politics

Frances Stokes Berry and William D. Berry, two of the leading scholars in the political science policy innovation literature, have done extensive analysis of the factors influencing innovation. These scholars have investigated state lottery adoptions as policy innovations, as well as tax innovation in the states (Berry and Berry, 1990, 1992). In their early findings, Berry and Berry argue that factors leading to policy innovation can be divided into two categories: internal and external. Three internal factors (social, political and economic), as well as external factors (regional diffusion), are thought to be useful in explaining what prompts states to adopt policies—specifically, lotteries (Berry and Berry, 1990). However, in their analysis of tax innovation in the states, Berry and Berry find a strict distinction between political and economic variables is not productive to explain tax innovation.

Instead of arguing that there is a firm distinction between economic and political factors, Berry and Berry hold that the ability to explain tax innovation in the states is greatest when political and economic conditions "converge to create a good political opportunity for adoption" (Berry and Berry, 1992). In other words, Berry and Berry discover factors, which otherwise seem to have distinctively political and economic features, actually prove to have spurious effects (statistically speaking). In particular, a large amount of time until the next election, existence of a fiscal crisis, and the presence of a neighboring state that previously or recently adopted a tax are statistically significant in predicting increases the likelihood a given state will adopt a tax. In addition, Berry and Berry find these effects have a multiplicative value. When all three factors are multiplied, the probability of tax innovation becomes even higher.

Much empirical evidence supports these aforementioned approaches to policy adoption in public sector organizations. However, the utility of the particular models in these investigations vary in their degree of strength. In support of the literature that argues the importance of diffusion, as well as social, economic, and political factors, scholars have found the likelihood of a state adopting a new program is affected by a number of variables. Among the findings include: 1) if other states have already adopted the idea (Berry and Berry, 1990; Gray, 1973; Grupp and Richards, 1975; Walker, 1969) 2) the fiscal health of the state (Berry and Berry, 1990) 3) the attachment of federal incentives to specific policies (Welch and Thompson, 1980) 4) the influence of policy entrepreneurs and elite perceptions of states as referents (Grupp and Richards, 1975; Minstrom, 1997) and 5) whether the environment to which an organization belongs has norms favoring change (Rogers, 1962). Conceptually, each of these approaches relies on the use of factors either internal or external, or both, to the environment of governmental organizations to explain policy adoption.

These approaches, however, are not without their limitations. One shortcoming is its lack of clarity in discerning what factors are actually external and internal to governmental and nongovernmental organizations. Herein lies the rationale behind integrating the concept of environmental shock into the political science literature on policy innovation. The political science innovation literature demonstrates separation of economic, social, and political variables is problematic. Strict delineation does not always prove as useful in predictive value, or as conceptually feasible as typically thought. While the predictive value of these concepts is not challenged here, this book argues instead of separating these concepts, the literature on policy innovation in governmental and nongovernmental organizations could use a more general concept that combines the various factors influencing innovation. In adopting such a concept, more parsimonious theories about policy innovation can be developed.

Because of the conceptual limitations regarding external and internal factors influencing innovation in organizations, there is a need for a more general concept that fuses disparate ideas. This book does this by using a concept already familiar to political science. As argued here, regional diffusion, as well as social, political and economic determinants of policy adoption, as concepts, can simply be viewed as *environmental shocks* (Baumgartner and Jones, 1993; Goertz and Diehl, 1995). *Environmental shocks*, as defined here, are events that have the ability to induce dramatic changes in continuous, stable environmental conditions and create a period of organizational instability, change, and punctuated equilibria—or innovation.

Many scholars argue it is difficult to disrupt stability in an organization, and any changes in organizational policies are usually only incremental. (Simon, 1977; Wilson, 1989). However, such an argument is not useful to explain the occurrence of innovation. Innovation, in itself, is an act that leads to policy decisions that are counter to the status quo in an organization and non-incremental in nature. It demonstrates a marked departure from the traditional way of approaching an issue. When an organization innovates, the stability of that organization is likely to have been threatened or is under threat. Environmental shocks are those forces that have the ability to induce such dramatic changes, such as innovations, (which can be thought of as punctuated equilibria) in an otherwise stable environment.

Gary Goertz and Paul Diehl are two scholars who study the impact of political shocks on the political process. In their analysis of interstate rivalries, Goertz and Diehl argue that breaking the stability of continuous patterns of behavior among political actors requires "a dramatic change in the environment of [these] relationships" (Geortz and Diehl, 1995). Such a dramatic change can be initiated by a political shock that "fundamentally alters the processes, relationships, and expectations that drive . . . interactions" (Geortz and Diehl, 1995). In the case of the U.S.-Soviet relations, Geortz and Diehl argue few scholars thought the Cold War would end in the foreseeable future—a reflection of incremental thinking in political science. However, the culmination of the Cold War serves as a shock that altered not only the U.S.-Soviet feud, but also many of the problems in the Third World provoked by the U.S.-Soviet rivalry.

A small number of political science scholars note the effects of environmental shocks on disrupting the stability in organizations. Aaron Wildavsky, in a study of organizational behavior, discovers incremental behavior is normal in bureaucracies. However, he notes agencies sometimes undergo dramatic changes as a result of shocks, such as changes in the organizations leadership structure. (Wildavsky, 1975). Bruce Bueno de Mesquita, in his analysis of international conflict patterns, concludes a large shock, (specifically, positive expected utility) may be a necessary precursor to break the stability of international conflict relations (Bueno de Mesquita, 1980). Baumgartner and Jones find there are patterns of stability in agenda access and agenda setting in government that are disrupted by rapid, unpredictable change (Baumgartner and Jones, 1993). Literature outside of political science, most notably the biological theory of punctuated equilibria, argues evolution occurs after major disruptions in the geological and climatic environment. After such periods of punctuated equilibria, stability returns (Eldredge, 1985; Eldredge and Gould, 1972).

Using environmental shock as a concept to explain organizational innovation also involves understanding environmental shocks may be either exogenous or endogenous to an organization. Discerning whether a shock is internal or external to an organization's environment, however, necessitates examining the context of the situation. A shock could be external or internal—depending upon the researcher's level of analysis (e.g., the level of analysis could be the organization or the broader governmental structure). As such, investigation of environmental shocks is sometimes muddy. Understanding the differences in the level of analysis across various strands of literature, however, facilitate a grasping of these variations.

Empirical investigation of environmental shocks also requires searching for dramatic changes in continuous, stable environmental conditions of an organization. Such changes serve as a key factor to explain the occurrence of periods of punctuated equilibria—which, in this book, are characterized by changes in how organizations look upon and allocate resources to their clientele (innovations).

The Credibility of Task Force Recommendations

The new institutionalist approach would predict institutions to act strategically when confronting other institutions. As such, in cases where multiple principals each have control over selection of agents, each set of selecting principals will try to offset the political strength of the others by nominating committee and task force members that hold political philosophies different from those of the other nominating principals. The implications of this on the number of policymakers who adopt task recommendations should be considerable. In cases where a task force is independently staffed and under the auspices solely of the mayor, task forces should be partisan in their membership composition. As such, the recommendations they produce should carry less credibility. This should decrease the likelihood of the adoption of their recommendations by local level officials. The thinking behind this contention is that governmental and nongovernmental actors should view the policy recommendations produced by task forces in such instances as being nothing more than the recommendations of the mayor and task force members. The recommendations should be viewed as the product of the self-interests and motivations of a small, select group of individuals.

In cases where a task force is staffed jointly by the mayor and city council (perhaps as well as other governmental officials), task forces should be more bipartisan in their membership composition. The implications of this are that task force recommendations should carry more credibility and be more likely to be adopted by local officials. Governmental and nongovernmental actors should view the policy recommendations produced by task forces in these cases as being the product of competing interests. The recommendations should be seen as being less driven by the personal agendas of like-minded individuals, but instead, the policy concerns of a broader sect of the city's government. The bicameral process by which the nomination and confirmation of task force members takes place gives the staffing of the task force the credibility typically associated with a system of checks and balances.

How Task Force Recommendations are Useful to Policymakers

What use do task force recommendations have for governmental and nongovernmental organizations during periods of organization instability? Task force recommendations developed by task forces serve as a body of information that can be used by governmental and nongovernmental actors during periods of organizational stress. For instance, if there are disruptions caused by some exogenous shock to the environment of governmental and nongovernmental organizations, it directly affects the stability of that organization. Such shocks bring about a sense of urgency that the efficiency of the organization is being threatened. Stability and routine are important in government agencies and there is a natural tendency for them to avoid actions that might "set a controversial precedent" (Wilson, 1989). Consequently, governmental and nongovernmental actors should adopt task force recommendations because of the need to quickly bring stability back to their environment. Because task force recommendations are a readily available body of research based information, which is otherwise costly and time-consuming information to acquire, governmental and nongovernmental actors should be influenced to adopt such policies. These are contentions, however, that must be examined.

The Influence of Task Force Expertise

If policymakers view task force recommendations as useful for their organizations, then arguably task forces carry some level of influence over why these actors adopt the recommendations. Political science literature on bureaucratic influence, although it does not typically contemplate the relationship between bureaucratic behavior and nongovernmental actors, is a useful point of departure for understanding how task forces might influence policy adoption by governmental as well as nongovernmental actors. Bureaucratic influence on the policy process is well documented in political science (Meier, 1993; Perrow, 1986; Rourke, 1984; Woll, 1963). The literature on the role of the bureaucracy in the policy making process is, in part, a departure from the bureaucratic influence tradition in political science (and to a lesser degree, principal-agent models, which recognize that bureaucrats attempt to influence the behavior of elected officials). Scholars who write in the tradition of the bureaucratic influence line of literature believe agency behavior can significantly influence the institutional behavior of elected officials, but not vice versa (Eisner, 1991; Eisner and Meier, 1990; Khademian, 1992; Rourke, 1984).

Bureaucratic influence scholars also argue that not only does the bureaucracy enjoy a level of independence from political principals but that agencies influence the behavior of political principals as well. According to George Krause, the bureaucratic influence line of literature attempts to exhibit how agencies influence the behavior of political institutions by using measures, such as budgetary signals agencies receive from elected institutions, that demonstrate empirical changes in the preferences of political principals (Krause, 1999).

Recent scholarship on policy innovation in governmental organizations does a better job of conceptualizing factors that can be used to explain how bureaucrats can influence policy adoption. One scholar who lays such a foundation is Virginia Gray. In her analysis of state policy adoption in the areas of education, welfare, and civil rights, Gray argues political and economic variables explain the most variance in which states are the first to adopt laws in these three policy areas (Gray, 1973). She finds the most innovative states are both wealthier and more competitive than sister states at the time they adopt specific laws (Gray, 1973). In addition, policy innovation spreads, or *diffuses*, from one state to another. Consequently, states are key reference points for other states when contemplating the adoption of new policies. Implicit in Gray's analysis is a finding that the policy decisions of state bureaucrats serve as a reference point for bureaucrats in other states.

In their analysis of state level policy adoption, Fred Grupp and Alan Richards rely on what they view as a solely political explanation to the spread of policy innovation. Their regional diffusion approach argues that states are influenced by the recommendations of policy elites about the effectiveness of policy innovations in nearby states. As a result of these elite perceptions, policy makers in innovating states tend to emulate other state's policies when confronted with local problems (Grupp and Richards, 1975). Grupp and Richards' work brings to light the importance of the contributions made by elected and appointed officials in the formation of public policy in the states. Their inclusion of elected and appointed officials in their analysis is an approach largely untapped in the policy innovation literature. The investigation of the role of elected and appointed officials who serve on various boards, commissions, task forces, non-profit organizations, etc., is an endeavor worthy of undertaking. Such a research focus can illuminate just what role these individuals play in policy innovation.

One scholar who argues the importance of elected and appointed officials as sources of diffusion of policy innovation is Jack Walker. In a study of diffusion of innovations among the American states, Walker finds there are specialized communication networks of "federal and local officials, journalists, academic experts, and administrative consultants . . . " that are ". . . sources of information and policy cues" (Walker, 1969). Such actors, in convening at conferences, publishing newsletters, etc., bring together "officials from all over the country and facilitate the exchange of ideas and knowledge among them, thus increasing the officials' awareness of the latest developments in their field" (Walker, 1969).

The importance of task force members in the policy process can be thought of in a similar manner as Walker and Grupp, and Richards', view of the influence of elected and appointed officials on innovation. Task forces members can indeed be sources of information and policy cues due to the specialized knowledge they gain in studying specific policy issues. Clearly, there exists information asymmetry in the relationship between task force members and governmental and nongovernmental actors. Task force members, through their work on in-depth analysis of a pressing issue, have more knowledge about the problem at hand and practical solutions than do local governmental and nongovernmental actors. Consequently, they are in a position to issue insight and perhaps even warnings that the consequences of not taking the prescribed course of action could be continued disruption in the organization's stability.

If it can be accepted that task force members play a similar role as elected and appointed officials, then they also be expected to become a part of a network of advocates and information sources on policy innovation. Consequently, the perceptions and recommendations of task force members, in many ways, become elite perceptions. These individuals typically know if task forces have been utilized in neighboring or demographically similar cities to study problems such as those under investigation by their own task force. In addition, task force members are likely to look to the effectiveness, or lack there of, of the policy recommendations developed by other similar task forces. In summation, task force members become experts on how to solve the problem.

The utility of including task force influence into this analysis stems from the policy innovation literature's general oversight of the role that bureaucrats play in influencing policy adoption by governmental and nongovernmental institutions. Interestingly enough, policy innovation scholars have not paid much attention to the role of bureaucrats in the policy innovation process. One of the fundamental assumptions in the policy innovation literature, as well as this book, is that governmental and nongovernmental institutions *can* be influenced by a myriad of factors to adopt various policies. This book adds to the literature on policy innovation by including the influence of task forces to the list of variables that can be used to explain innovation. If we could not assume governmental and nongovernmental institutions can be influenced to adopt certain policies, then there would be no use in discussing whether task forces are actually agents of policy innovation. In addition, it is important to isolate the influence of task forces as a variable to discover if its explanatory power is greatest when used by itself or in conjunction with some other set of variables.

Level of Racial Threat in the City

Another factor that merits discussion here is the possible role that race plays in influencing innovation. The subject matter of focus in this book is not only innovation, but race relations as well. The literature on policy innovation alludes to the possibility policies geared towards certain types of issues may produce certain types of outcomes. (see also Lowi, 1964). If this is the case, then we might expect to find racial demographics playing a very important role in the decisions governmental and nongovernmental actors make about adopting policies geared towards racial issues. Consequently, an analysis of the literature on race as it applies to policy decisions is useful.

A plethora of political scientists have come to argue race plays a major role in policy decisions (Alvarez and Brehm, 1997; Burnham, 1974; Carmines and Stimson, 1989; Fording, 1997; Giles and Hertz, 1994; Key, 1949; Lieske, 1993; Meier, Stewart Jr., and England, 1989). In V. O. Key's groundbreaking work, *Southern Politics*, Key notes "individuals make choices among alternatives that are often shaped by their context" (Key, 1949). State governments often behave differently in situations where the number of blacks is proportionately higher than in contexts where the numbers are lower (Key, 1949). Specifically, Key's "racial threat hypothesis" holds large black populations are often seen as a threat to whites and lead to distinct political attitudes and behaviors among whites. Most notably, Key found that whites living in communities with large black populations were most likely to support candidates and policies favoring segregation (Key, 1949).

Other scholars have found evidence supporting Key's argument of the role of racial context on policy choices. Michael Giles has demonstrated racial threats, or large percentages of blacks in specific districts, affected voting behavior in the 1990 Louisiana Senatorial race in which David Duke was a candidate. Large black populations also were seen as influencing the change in party identification over time—from Democrat to Republican—in Louisiana parishes (Giles and Buckner, 1993; Giles and Hertz, 1994). Likewise, James Glaser found racial context has "a strong and consistent effect on racial-political attitudes" (Glaser, 1994). In his study, Glaser concludes racial threats are real, specifically in the shape of group conflict. Such environmental factors have the ability to influence political stances on racial policies (Glaser, 1994).

The politics of race can be argued to have potentially different effects on communities. Locales vary in the size of their minority populations and can be expected to face race relations problems that are unique or similar in magnitude as other cities. Rodney Hero notes that racial diversity leads to a dilemma that is present in *all* of the states, not just those with large minority populations (Hero, 1998). Hero calls these phenomena a "politics of heterogeneity" (Hero, 1998).

Other scholars go on to argue that the degree to which race plays a role in policy adoption is a direct function of the size of the minority populations in communities. Specifically, theories of racial threat argue that as the level of black concentration increases, white resistance to race sensitive policies becomes greater. Michael Giles and Kaenan Hertz, in "Racial Threat and Partisan Identification," find evidence supporting this racial threat hypothesis (Giles and Hertz, 1994). These scholars investigate how as the Democratic Party in the South begins to depend more on black voters, it experiences a decline in white adherents. As the number of blacks who identify with the Democratic Party, and the policies it espouses, increases, white feel more threatened and subsequently abandoned the part in favor of the opposition—the Republican Party. The political impact of racial demographics of policy adoption is an important factor that must be assessed in this discussion on race relations task forces. The racial threat factor is used in this book to discover if in contexts where the threat posed by a minority group is higher than in other contexts, policymakers adopt fewer race-based innovations.

⑤ *The Political Culture of the City*

The political science literature on political culture is highly influenced by the work of scholars such as Gabriel Almond and Sidney Verba (1963), Daniel Elazar (Elazar, 1984; Elazar, Gray, and Spano, 1999), and Lucian Pye and Sidney Verba (Pye and Verba, 1965; Verba and Pye, 1978). Of particular utility is Elazar's thesis that the politics of a state or community are affected by its culture—be it moralistic, individualistic, or traditionalistic. This framework serves as an often-cited foundation for research on race and political culture. Elazar argues that the political processes and policy outcomes of a state and local community's governing, social, and corporate institutions are the results of dominant cultural values. Those values, in turn, are argued to be the product of the dominant religious and racial groups of that geographic area.

Elazar argues that there are three main types of political cultures and that all states/communities have at least one of those types of cultures as the predominant culture. According to Elazar, the individualistic political culture is characterized by emphasis being placed on private concerns. It places paramount importance on limited community intervention, whether governmental or nongovernmental, into the private activities of citizens. Political actors, in cases where norms are high, are expected to provide high quality government services. In cases where the norms are lower, political actors are expected to serve themselves and those who directly support them. Ties to political parties are viewed to be strong due to public feeling that parties are the vehicles to maintaining a network of loyalty and obligation of politicians to their constituents. Politics is also viewed as an arena for professionals and having little room for amateurs (Elazar et al., 1999).

In the moralistic political culture, according to Elazar, both the general public and political actors conceive of politics as a public activity grounded the forwarding of the public interest (Elazar et al., 1999). In addition, individualism is checked, so to speak, by a commitment to using nongovernmental (but governmental if necessary) power to intervene into areas typically considered private activities. Government should do so when it is necessary to do so for the public good or the well being of the community. In the moralistic culture, government is also considered a positive actor that holds a responsibility to promote the general welfare of the community. As such, political actors are expected to act on behalf of the community and not for the benefit of themselves. Political party affiliations are often abandoned on in favor of focusing on the merits on the political actor themselves. In addition, the political arena is not viewed as merely a showplace for charismatic career politicians. Instead, amateurs are seen as prospective political actors that have the ability to serve in government leadership positions as well as the experienced politicians (Elazar et al, 1999).

The traditionalistic political culture, according to Elazar, is characterized by its likeness to the moralistic culture in that it views the role of government as an actor with a positive role in the community. However, in the traditionalistic culture, the role of government is more prohibitive in that its role is to secure the continued maintenance of the existing social order. To do so, government operates to limit meaningful political power to a small and self-perpetuating group of actors typically drawn from an established elite. This group of individuals often accedes to power because of their family ties or social position. The political arena has no room for those outside of the established clique nor does it tolerate amateurs. Such individuals are not expected to be even minimally active in politics. Elazar notes that in many cases, they are not even expected to vote. Political leaders are expected to seek personal gain through politics as well as maintain the status quo of the social order. Changes in the existing political and social structure typically do not come to fruition unless leaders in such cultures are strongly pressed by outside influences (Elazar et al., 1999).

Elazar's conception of political culture is used as a point of departure for the study of the role of culture in influencing how policy decisions are made. A number of scholars have built upon Elazar's formulation of political culture in policy innovation research and expanded upon the various methods of measuring political culture (Aiken and Alford, 1970; Canon and Baum 1981; Johnson 1976). Of interest here is how the literature treats political culture within the context of race-based policy outputs. A search, however, reveals there is scant literature that uses political culture to explain policy innovation at the local levels oriented in racial issues. Perhaps part of the reason behind this is because when using political culture to explain race-based policymaking, the differences between culture and race is difficult to delineate. This could be due to the fact that racial threat and political culture tend to be measured quite similarly—based upon racial concentration.

Hero and Tolbert (1996) argue that political culture, in many ways, may actually be a mere surrogate for racial diversity. Hero and Tolbert argue that much of state/local level politics is the result of racial diversity and political culture may mask or even act as a proxy for racial diversity. They provide empirical evidence that Elazar's (1984) political culture categories for the states highly match their diversity typologies with a small number of important departures from their general patterns (specifically, California, Michigan and New York are classified differently. Hero and Tolbert attribute this to the fact that they take into consideration large minority populations (e.g., blacks and Latinos) while Elazar does not). According to these scholars, the states they call homogenous states (having few minorities and few white ethnics) tend to be moralistic. The states they call heterogeneous states (having large white ethnic populations and significant minority populations) tend to be individualistic, the states they call bifurcated states (large minority populations and large white non- ethnic populations) tend to be traditionalistic (Hero and Tolbert 1996). The concern of Hero and Tolbert is that political culture may indeed play a role in the political processes in the states, but to attribute so much to culture is a misspecification because culture itself is heavily shaped by racial and ethnic diversity.

The utility of the Hero and Tolbert analysis for this book is twofold. First, it allows for discovery of whether racial threat and political culture could be surrogates for one another. Clearly, Hero and Tolbert's formulation of racial/ethnic diversity is centered largely upon the levels of racial concentration in a given geographic area. This is also the case with the racial threat hypothesis. Secondly, their analysis allows for extrapolation of the key differences between explanations grounded more on racial context (such as Hero and Tolbert's diversity categories) and those that have underpinnings oriented more towards factors such as political and social structures (such as Elazar's notion of political culture).

In this book, I use Elazar's formulation of political culture as an important factor to explain the variance in race-based policy innovations. I argue that the context in which political decisions are made is indeed important and cannot be overlooked. Although Elazar's formulation of political culture is measured at the state-level, data exists by which measurement of political culture at the local level can be done. Typically, scholars utilize data such as immigration patterns, religious identification, and political participation rates to measure political culture. Because data such as these are not available across all three cases (particularly for Columbia), I rely largely on political ideology to measure political culture. As such, I cannot measure political culture in the more conventional manner. It could be the case that what I measure is more in line with being political ideology. Nevertheless, I use pre-existing analysis of the political cultures of each of my three cases done by leading scholars who study the politics in each of those three cases. From these analyses, I conclude that Madison illustrates a moralistic culture, Columbia a traditionalistic culture, and Kansas City an individualistic political culture.

My expectations of the role of political culture on race-based innovations are taken largely from the body of literature on political culture and innovation (Aiken and Alford 1970; Cannon and Baum 1981; Johnson 1976). This literature finds that cities with majorities that hold public-centered values are more innovative with respect to polices benefiting the community as a whole than cities dominated by groups with private-centered values. For theoretical purposes, I contend that policy innovations geared towards addressing race relations in a community are policies that benefit the community as a whole. I make this assumption despite the fact that some may consider race-based policy innovations as beneficial only to minorities due to such policies often being redistributive in nature. However, I contend that in communities where racial problems exist, the community as a whole typically does not benefit from the conflict. Consequently, race-based innovations are benefit the community by bringing stability—even if such policies are redistributive. For comparison purposes in my argument on culture, I contend that moralistic cultures are the most public-centered, traditionalistic cultures the median, and individualistic cultures the most private-centered.

The previous discussion is the foundation for the construction of a research design that can be used to analyze the major contentions presented in this book. The next chapter is a discussion of the research methodology guiding this study. In this book, I use a case study approach in order to conduct my analysis. Specifically, the cases I examine are mayoral race relations task forces in three cities: Columbia, Missouri; Kansas City, Missouri; and Madison, Wisconsin. Surveys and interviews are used to generate a body of data for contentions analysis. Chapter Three also includes a brief overview of each of these cases and discusses why they are appropriate to use in this investigation.

Bibliography

Aiken, M., and Alford, R. R. (1970). Community Structure and Innovation: The Case of Public Housing. *American Political Science Review, 64*(3), 843-864.
Almond, G., and Verba, S. (1963). *The Civic Culture; Political Attitudes and Democracy in Five Nations.* Princeton, NJ: Princeton University Press.
Alvarez, R. M., and Brehm, J. (1997). Are Americans Ambivalent Towards Racial Policies? *American Journal of Political Science, 41*(2), 345-374.
Baumgartner, F. R., and Jones, B. D. (1993). *Agendas and Instability in American Politics.* Chicago: University of Chicago Press.
Berry, F. S., and Berry, W. D. (1990). State Lottery Adoptions as Policy Innovations: An Event History Analysis. *American Political Science Review, 84*(2), 395-415.
———. (1992). Tax Innovation in the States: Capitalizing on Political Opportunity." *American Journal of Political Science, 36*(3), 715-742.
Bueno De Mesquita, B. (1980). An Expected Utility Theory of International Conflict. *American Political Science Review, 74*(4), 917-931.
Burnham, W. D. (1974). The United States: The Politics of Hetereogeneity. In R. Rose (Ed.), *Electoral behavior: A Comparative Handbook* (pp. 653-726). New York: Free Press.
Canon, B. C., and Baum, L. (1981). Patterns of Adoption of Tort Law Innovations: An Application of Diffusion Theory to Judicial Doctrines. *American Political Science Review, 75*(4), 975-987.
Carmines, E. G., and Stinson, J. A. (1989). *Issue Evolution: Race and the Transformation of American Politics.* Princeton, NJ: Princeton University Press.
Eisner, M. A. (1991). *Antitrust and the Triumphs of Economics: Institutions, Expertise, and Political Change.* Chapel Hill, NC: University of North Carolina Press.
Eisner, M. A., and Meier, K. J. (1990). Presidential Control versus Bureaucratic Power: Explaining the Reagan Revolution in Antitrust. *American Journal of Political Science, 34*(1), 269-287.
Elazar, D. J. (1984). *American Federalism: A View from the States.* New York: Crowell.
Elazar, D. J., Gray, V., and Spano, W. (1999). *Minnesota Politics and Government (Politics and Governments of the American States).* Lincoln, NE: University of Nebraska Press.
Eldredge, N. (1985). *Unfinished Synthesis: Biological Hierarchies and Modern Evolutionary Thought.* New York: Oxford University Press.
Eldredge, N., and Gould, S. (1972). Punctuated Equilibria: An Alternative to Phyletic Gradualism. In T. Schopf (Ed.), *Models in Paleobiology.* San Francisco: Freeman, Cooper.
Fording, R. (1997). The Conditional Effect of Violence as a Political Tactic: Mass Insurgency, Welfare Generosity, and Electoral Context in the American States. *American Journal of Political Science, 41*(1), 1-29.
Giles, M. W., and Buckner, M. A. (1993). David Duke and Black Threat: An Old Hypothesis Revisited. *The Journal of Politics, 55*(3), 702-713.
Giles, M. W., and Hertz, K. (1994). Racial Threat and Partisan Identification. *American Political Science Review, 88*(2), 317-326.
Glaser, J. M. (1994). Back to the Black Belt: Racial Environment and White Racial Attitudes in the South. *The Journal of Politics, 56*(1), 21-41.
Goertz, G., and Diehl, P. F. (1995). The Initiation and Termination of Enduring Rivalries: The Impact of Political Shocks. *American Journal of Political Science, 39*(1), 30-52.

Gray, V. (1973). Innovation in the States: A Diffusion Study. *American Political Science Review, 67*(4), 1174-1185.

Grupp, F. W., Jr., and Richards, A. R. (1975). Variations in Elite Perceptions of American States as Referents for Public Policy Making. *American Political Science Review, 69*(3), 850-858.

Hero, R. (1998). *Face of Inequality: Social Diversity in American Politics.* New York: Oxford University Press.

Hero, R., and Tolbert, C. J. (1996). A Racial/Ethic Diversity Interpretation of Politics and Policy in the States of the U.S. *American Journal of Political Science, 40*(3), 851-871.

Johnson, C. A. (1976). Political Culture in American States: Elazar's Formulation Examined. *American Journal of Political Science, 20*(3), 491-509.

Key, V. O. (1949). *Southern Politics in State and Nation.* New York: A. A. Knopf.

Khademian, A. M. (1992). *The SEC and Capital Market Regulation: The Politics of Expertise.* Pittsburgh, PA: University of Pittsburgh Press.

Krause, G. A. (1999). *A Two-Way Street: The Institutional Dynamics of the Modern Administrative State.* Pittsburg, PA: University of Pittsburgh Press.

Lieske, J. (1993). Regional Subcultures of the United States. *The Journal of Politics, 55*(4), 888-913.

Lowi, T., J. (1964). American Business, Public Policy, Case Studies and Political Theory. *World Politics, 16,* 677-715.

Lynn Jr., L. (1997). Innovation and the Public Interest: Insights From the Private Sector. In A. A. Altshuler and R. D. Behn (Eds.), *Innovation in American Government.* Washington, D.C.: Brookings Institution Press.

March, J. G., and Simon, H. (1958). *Organizations.* New York: Wiley.

Meier, K. J. (1993). *Politics and the Bureaucracy: Policymaking in the Fourth Branch of Government.* Pacific Grove, CA: Brooks/Cole Publishing Company.

Meier, K. J., Stewart Jr., J., and England, R. (1989). *Race, Class, and Education.* Madison: University of Wisconsin.

Minstrom, M. (1997). Policy Entrepreneurs and the Diffusion of Innovation. *American Journal of Political Science, 41*(3), 738-770.

Mohr, L. B. (1969). Determinants of Innovation in Organizations. *American Political Science Review, 63*(1), 111-126.

Perrow, C. (1986). *Complex Organizations: A Critical Essay.* New York: Random House.

Peters, T. J., and Waterman, R. H. (1982). *In Search of Excellence: Lessons from America's Best-Run Companies.* New York: Harper and Row.

Rogers, E. M. (1962). *Diffusion of Innovations.* New York: Free Press.

Rourke, F. E. (1984). *Bureaucracy, Politics, and Public Policy.* Boston: Little, Brown.

Schroeder, R. D., Van de Ven, A. H., Scudder, G. D., and Polly, D. (1989). The Development of Innovation Ideas. In A. H. Van de Ven, H. L. Angle and M. Scott Poole (Eds.), *Research on the Management of Innovation: The Minnesota Studies.* Chicago: Ballinger Pub.

Simon, H. (1977). *Models of Discovery.* Boston: D. Riedel.

Walker, J. L. (1969). The Diffusion of Innovations Among the American States. *American Political Science Review, 63*(3), 880-899.

Welch, S., and Thompson, K. (1980). The Impact of Federal Incentives on State Policy Innovation. *American Journal of Political Science, 24*(4), 715-729.

Wildavsky, A. B. (1975). *Budgeting: A Comparative Theory of Budgetary Processes.* Boston: Little, Brown.

Wilson, J. Q. (1989). *Bureaucracy: What Government Agencies Do and Why They Do It.* New York: Basic Books.

Woll, P. (1963). *American Bureaucracy.* New York: Norton.

Chapter Three: Research Approach

This chapter details the methodological procedures employed in conducting this research. The chapter contains five major sections. In section one, the epistemological basis for the use of a case study approach is explained. This is followed by a discussion of how the cases in this book are selected and a justification for the selection of these cases. The third section involves a discussion of the data collection methods I use. Section four lays out the research variables and contentions. Finally, in section five, the data analysis techniques I employ are explained.

This book is an exploratory study conducted through the use of a case study approach with multiple—cases. The case study approach is classified as a qualitative approach in social science research. The qualitative approach has its origins in the counter—movement to the positivism tradition in the late Nineteenth Century (Creswell, 1994; Smith, 1983). The qualitative method has significant advantages in social science research. One, it enables the researcher to probe deeply into specific social events and human behavior from the perspective of the unit being analyzed. It is mainly investigative in nature and involves the researcher analyzing social phenomenon by contrasting, comparing, and classifying the object of study (Miles and Huberman, 1984). The underlying assumption of a qualitative approach is that the researcher makes sense out of their experiences, and in the process, create their own reality (Locke, Spirduso, and Silverman, 1987).

Epistemological Basis for the use of a Case Study Approach

The foundational basis for case study approaches emanates from a body of literature on qualitative research and inquiry (Holstein and Gubrium, 1997; King, Keohane, and Verba, 1994; Lincoln and Guba, 1985; Merriam, 1988; Ragin and Becker, 1992; Van Evera, 1997; Wolcott, 1994; Yin, 1994). Although case-study approaches exist where quantitative data is used, the qualitative approach typically relies on either simple exploratory types of analysis without the use of quantitative data or employs the use of both. One of the major critiques of the case study approach is that it lacks rigor. Scholars have noted that many case study researchers have done poor work by allowing their personal views to influence their findings (Yin, 1994). While this is often one of the major limitations of a case study approach, it is not unique to this school of research (Rosenthal, 1966; Sudman and Bradburn, 1982). Safeguards must be built into the research design, as is done here, to minimize any researcher biases.

Another criticism of the case study method is that it suffers from a lack of external validity (Merriam, 1988). One of the critiques of such an approach is that it produces little in the way for the possibility of generalizing. Scholars, such as S. B. Merriam, note that "part of the difficulty lies in thinking of generalizability in the same way as do investigator using experimental or correlational designs (Merriam, 1988)." Counter to the claims regarding lack of ability to generalize, case studies are generalizable to theoretical propositions (Yin, 1994). Simply put, case studies rely on analytical generalizations and can be designed to allow for the enhancement of assumptions of a body of similar cases. Merriam argues that the method to increase external validity in conducting case studies, the researcher should: (1) Provide a detailed description so that anyone interested in transferability has a base of information appropriate to the judgment, (2) Establish the typical or model category of the case; that is, describing how typical the case is compared with others in similar context so that users can make comparisons with their own situations; and (3) Conduct a cross—case analysis (Merriam, 1988).

In the analysis of each case, detailed information of the cases under investigation is provided in an effort to meet these prescriptions. Additionally, the use of multi-case, cross-case analysis, the sampling method used, surveys and interviews, and procedures for coding and analyzing data enhance the generalizability of the findings.

Rationale for Using a Case Study Approach

The case study approach is the best strategy for tackling questions and contentions set out in this book. R. K. Yin notes that such an approach has advantages when questions of "how" and "why" are the focus of a study that examines a contemporary set of events over which the researcher has little or no control (Yin, 1994). Research on local level task forces is at its nascent stages and is virtually non-existent. In addition, there exists no research on how these entities are used to influence policy adoption in the communities that create them. For these reasons, it is essential that a body of knowledge be developed from which subsequent studies can follow. A case study approach is the best method towards achieving this goal.

The goal of this study is to foster an understanding of the efficacy of task forces, specifically mayoral race relations task forces, as agents of policy adoption in local communities. Because the literature on this topic is scant, a case study approach is best suited to facilitate the generation of data and analysis of community experiences with task forces and their context. The case study approach is the best strategy towards doing this because "case studies stress the holistic examination of a phenomenon, and they seek to avoid the separation of components from the larger context to which these matters may be related (Jorgensen, 1989)."

Selection of the Cases

This research uses a case study approach to address relevant questions and generate contentions. Specifically, analysis of three mayoral race relations task forces is done. The method for selecting cases is a purposive sampling method (Singleton, Straits, and Miller Straits, 1993). A purposive sampling method is one in which the investigator relies on his or her own expert judgment to select the cases that are representative or typical of the population. This selection method is chosen for two reasons. First, the lack of literature on task forces necessitates that I examine the cases of mayoral race relations task forces that exist, examine their characteristics, and build a framework that describes the general features of mayoral race relations task forces. This facilitates using my expert judgment to select cases typical of the larger body of mayoral race relations task forces. Secondly, this type of sampling mechanism allows for selection of cases from which generalizations can be made about similar types of task forces.

In identifying cases for selection, I chose municipalities that had recently used race relations task forces and a span of time had lapsed whereby the work of the task forces had a chance to take effect. In this book, three cases were selected for analysis: Kansas City, Missouri; Columbia, Missouri; and Madison, Wisconsin. Each of these cities had created mayoral race relations task forces in the past five years. A large enough amount of time had passed in each case such that it allowed for sufficient investigation of the purported influence by each task force over policy adoption in the respective communities. Secondly, these cases were selected because of the nature of the thesis posed here. It was necessary to select at least one case where a task force was created as the stated result of some event (what I call an "environmental shock") and one case where a task force was created as a result of no evident shock. A deliberate decision was also made to include one case in which there was some speculation as to whether or not the task force was created as the result of some environmental shock in the community. The reason for this was to further enhance the ability to detect important sources of variance in the cases. Each of the aforementioned cases adequately fits the criteria set out here and can therefore be justified as warranting selection.

A Brief Background of the Cases

Mayor's Task Force on Race Relations
Kansas City, Missouri

The city of Kansas City is the second largest city in the state of Missouri with a population of 435,141 (United States Census Bureau, 1990). Kansas City is a relatively mixed racial city in that it is 29% African American (black and African American are used interchangeably throughout to refer to the same racial group). The vast majority of Kansas Citians live in urban areas and work inside their county residence. About 51% of the residents of the city have at least a high school diploma and about 32% have at least some college education. However, far more whites (168,527 or 58% of whites) than blacks (50,185 or 39%) are at least high school graduates. An even larger disparity exists between the number of whites who have at least a bachelor's degree (53,933 or 19% of white Kansas Citians) and blacks that hold at least the same (7,319 or 6% of black Kansas Citians). As such, there exists a huge gap between the levels of education attainment by race in Kansas City (United States Census Bureau, 1990).

The majority of Kansas Citians work in retail trade, finance, health services, and other related professional services. A large number of these workers (43,053) work in administrative support positions, including clerical work. Another 30,385 persons work in managerial and professional specialty occupations. The per capita income for Kansas City in 1989 was $13,799. However, the per capita income for whites was much higher than that for blacks-$16,367 for whites and a paltry $8,487 for blacks (United States Census Bureau, 1990). These numbers with regards to the black and white gap in Kansas City mirror the national trends in cities of a similar size.

As these figures illustrate, the city of Kansas City has serious problems of economic and social disparities between blacks and whites. By all implications, these differences have been the impetus for long and deeply rooted racial tensions in the city. Consequently, the need for creating a race relations task force in Kansas City can be understood and justified.

Mayor Emanuel Cleaver II created the Kansas City Mayor's Task Force on Race Relations in February of 1996. In defining the issue of race relations as it pertains to Kansas City, Mayor Cleaver stated, "Race relations, I believe, are stagnant . . . and if they are not improving, then they are worsening. There has not been an honest dialogue on race in this country for the last several decades (Mayor's Task Force on Race Relations, 1996)." Mayor Cleaver noted that his perception of the status of race relations in Kansas City led him to ultimately create the Kansas City task force. Although the mayor did not cite any particular events with racial undertones, there had been a number of confrontations and violent incidents involving the local police and residents of the city that posed a challenge for him in his hopes to build racial harmony in the community.

Despite facing potential obstacles, Mayor Cleaver created the task force and gave the city's local chapter of the Urban League the responsibility to oversee the task force. This task force was charged to, 1) determine the status of race relations in the community, 2) determine where the community needed to go, and 3) look at a variety of aspects of life in Kansas City through the lens of race relations, studying business, housing, law enforcement, media, religion, and more (Mayor's Task Force on Race Relations, 1996). Membership on the Kansas City task force included over 300 participants. The structure included two general co-chairs, vice chairs, cluster chairs and co-chairs, and cluster members.

Mayor's Columbia Race Relations Task Force
Columbia, Missouri

The city of Columbia, which is located approximately at the halfway point between Kansas City and St. Louis on U. S. Interstate 70, is the largest city in Boone County, Missouri. With a population of 69,101 (United States Census Bureau, 1990), Columbia is not a very racially diverse city. Approximately 85% of the city's population is white and 9.8% are black. Columbia is an urban area that is largely surrounded by small farm towns. Although a metropolitan area, it does not have the same level of urban development as Kansas City or Madison.

With regards to educational attainment, about 45% of the residents of Columbia have at least a high school diploma and about 35% have at least some college education. However, far more whites (27,069 or 46% of whites in Columbia) than blacks (2,292 or 34% of blacks in Columbia) are at least high school graduates. The disparity between the number of whites who hold at least a bachelor's degree (14083 or 24% of white Columbians) and blacks that have at least a bachelor's degree (625 or 9% of black Columbians) is rather large. Although overall there exists a huge gap in the levels of educational achievement by race in the city of Columbia, these differences are not as magnified as they are in Kansas City (United States Census Bureau, 1990).

The vast majority of Columbians work in educational services, health services, and retail trade. As a matter of fact, these three sectors together combine for about 58% of the industry where Columbians are employed. A large number of these workers work in educational services (7066) and health services (6293)—which only makes sense considering Columbia is mainly a college town (United States Census Bureau, 1990). The city is home to the University of Missouri (with an approximate enrollment of 23,000 students), Columbia College and Stephens College.

The per capita income for Columbia in is approximately $12,452. However, the per capita income for whites was much higher than that for blacks--$13,355 for whites but only $6,933 for blacks (United States Census Bureau, 1990). This is a large disparity, but not as big of a disparity that exists in the case of Kansas City. Nevertheless, Columbia's economic stratifications by race have similar political consequences for race relations in the community. As such, the need for a race relations task force in Columbia is warranted.

Mayor Darwin Hindman created the Columbia, Mayor's Columbia Race Relations Task Force in January of 1996. Towards defining the issue of race relations in Columbia, Mayor Hindman argued, "Race relations has been a national problem for years. Solutions have defied the best efforts of people in government and the nongovernmental sector alike. The Mayor's Race Relations Task Force will not be able to solve the race relations problem in Columbia, but I think that people may be surprised at the contribution it will make (Mayor's Columbia Race Relations Task Force, 1996)." The task force was primarily charged with determining the history and current status of race relations in Columbia (Mayor's Columbia Race Relations Task Force, 1996). The Columbia Mayor's Race Relations Task Force consists of 30 appointees. The structure of the task force includes two co-chairs and 28 members divided among nine subcommittees.

Mayor's Task Force on Race Relations
Madison, Wisconsin

Madison is the capital and one of the largest cities of the state of Wisconsin. Long noted as being a liberal town, the city of Madison is a city uniquely built on an isthmus and is surrounded by 15,429 acres of lakes. With a population of 191,262 (United States Census Bureau, 1990), Madison is the least racially diverse city of the three cases. Approximately 90% of the city's population is white, 4% are black and 4% Asian. Madison, by appearance, is a very picturesque city. The metropolitan area boasts being the home to more restaurants per capita than any other city in the United States. In addition, the city offers boating, beaches, botanical gardens, and over 200 city parks. To say the least, Madison is a nature lover's kind of town.

With regards to educational attainment, about 53% of the residents of Madison have at least a high school diploma and about 40% have at least some college education. By comparison, Madisonians have a higher level of educational attainment than those in both Columbia and Kansas City. As with the cases of Kansas City and Columbia, more white Madisonians (95,676 or 55% of whites in Madison) than blacks (3090 or 39% of blacks in Madison) are at least high school graduates. The number of whites that hold at least a bachelor's degree (43,820 or 25% of white Madisonians) is higher than the number of blacks that have at least a bachelor's degree (943 or 12% of black Madisonians) (United States Census Bureau, 1990). As with the other two cases studied here, there exists a large gap between the levels of education achievement by race in the city of Madison.

The vast majority of Madison residents work in educational services, health services, and retail trade. As with Columbia, these three sectors together combine for a large percentage of the total industries where local residents are employed—about 43% of all industry. A large number of these workers work in educational services (18,894) and health services (11,294). This is understandable considering that Madison, like Columbia, is a college town. The city of Madison is home to the University of Wisconsin (with an approximate enrollment of 41,000 students), and the small, private Edgewood College.

The per capita income for Madison is $15,143—making Madison the most affluent city out of the three cases (at least in terms of per capita income)(United States Census Bureau, 1990). However, Madison holds the distinction of having the largest disparity in per capita income between whites and blacks of all three cases. The per capita income for whites in Madison is much higher than that for blacks--$15,901 for whites and only $7,610 for blacks. These figures illustrate that Madison, although many consider it to be a liberal town, has significant polarizations between blacks and whites socially and economically. Again, as with the other two cases, these differences in Madison have serious implications on the nature of race relations in the community.

In March of 1998, Madison Mayor Sue Bauman, created a Task Force on Race Relations that was approved by the city's Common Council. Mayor Bauman argued that she was creating the task force, "to ensure that all Madison residents are able to share, to the greatest extent possible, in the things that cause us to be highly acclaimed (Task Force on Race Relations, 1998)." The race relations problems in Madison, however, went much deeper than the mayor's definition alluded. The city of Madison was having its image of a liberal college town tarnished by these events. In an effort to meet her goal, Mayor Bauman created a task force and gave it two charges:

1. Review the findings and recommendations of the EOC Ad Hoc Committee on Alcohol Licensing and Traffic Stops of African Americans, and to develop a plan for implementing appropriate recommendations, including immediate, as well as long term steps.
2. Develop a plan for community activities including forums that result in a strategic plan for respecting diversity and undoing racism.

In essence, Mayor Bauman gave the task force study three main duties: 1) to study the process of alcohol licensing in Madison, 2) to investigate whether there was any racial profiling in the traffic stops of African Americans, and 3) to study the findings of the two smaller committees and incorporating their findings into an overall plan to improve race relations in Madison. As a result of the special nature of this task force, the policy recommendations produced by the Madison task force also include three additional policy areas not present in the other two cases: a) alcohol licensing review, b) traffic stops, and c) study circles.

The Madison, Task Force on Race Relations consists of 22 members. Interestingly, two of the members are Mayor Susan Bauman (ex officio) and city alderman Ken Golden. This case presents the unique opportunity to analyze how the presence of the mayor and another elected official on the task force influences the policy outputs of that task force. The overall structure of the task force includes one chair, 15 task force members, and 6 staff team members.

Data Collection Methods

In analyzing each case, this book utilizes data garnered from three main sources: 1) interviews of the mayors and other local community leaders in each of the three case cities, 2) surveys and interviews of task force members, and 3) surveys and interviews of local governmental and nongovernmental actors. While this process is not pure "triangulation," it does touch the surface of combining dissimilar sources of data to study the same unit (Merriam, 1988). Because "flaws of one method are often the strengths of another, and by combing methods, observers can achieve the best of each, while overcoming their unique deficiencies (Denzin, 1970)." In addition, to the aforementioned data sources, data from the final reports of each task force is used as a secondary source. Each task force has produced a final report that includes a list of task force members, the organizational structure of the task force, the key issues debated, and the policy recommendations that were produced.

The two main sources of data to measure policy innovation in this book are surveys and interviews. Task force final reports are used as a secondary source towards facilitation of data generation. The task force final reports are used primarily to garner information concerning each task force's respective findings and recommendations regarding race relations in their respective communities. From this, survey and interview questions are created. The surveys and interviews are used to generate data regarding the factors affecting innovation as well as policy innovation itself. Of most interest in the data generated by the surveys and interviews is whether various governmental and nongovernmental actors have adopted any of the policy recommendations produced by these task forces.

Task Force Final Reports

Analysis of the final reports produced by each respective task force was the first step towards creation of the surveys and interviews. Upon completion of their work, each task force produced a final report. In the case of Kansas City, the task force produced an "interim" final report—the implications of which are discussed in Chapter Six on Kansas City. The final reports in the cases of Madison, and Columbia, were obtained through the office of the mayor. In the case of Kansas City, the task force's final report was obtained through the city's local Urban League chapter. Each city's task force produced a final report that included, among other items, a) a statement by the city's mayor regarding the purpose and goals of the task force, b) a table of contents, c) an overview statement by the task force's chairs/co-chairs of the findings of the task force upon the culmination of its work, d) acknowledgements, e) task force members, and f) the findings and recommendations of the task force. In the case of Madison and Columbia, the findings and recommendations of each task force were divided by the respective committees' findings and reports. In the case of Kansas City, the findings and recommendations were summarized in whole.

The portion of the task force final reports of most concern in this book was the findings and recommendations. This body of data was most salient to this book because it was the foundation of the focus of analysis upon which the entire investigation was conducted. The findings and recommendations, in essence, were the prescriptions that I hoped to find that local governmental and nongovernmental actors adopted. From analyzing whether local actors indeed adopted such policies or whether they did not, the major research endeavor—to explain the variation in adoption of task force recommended policies by local governmental and nongovernmental actors—could be achieved.

Participant Selection

To produce data that measure race-based policy innovation, I selected participants who were governmental and nongovernmental actors living in metropolitan areas of the communities under study. Governmental and nongovernmental actors ranged across a broad spectrum in ethnicity, political philosophy, and age. To produce data towards measuring many of the more secondary questions I developed, I selected participants who were task force members in each of the three respective cases. These actors also ranged across a broad spectrum in ethnicity, political philosophy, and age.

Usually, a researcher attempts to produce a sample large enough to which estimates about the population can be made. However, in scientific research it is often hard to know the approximate size of a population. Some scholars (Snedecor and Cochran, 1989) note that ultimately an element of arbitrariness may be in the answer finally given. In this book, the extremely large size of the population of governmental and nongovernmental actors, as well as the frequent inability to clearly identify actors in that population, makes it difficult to utilize traditional statistical approaches towards selecting a sample size. It is possible, however, to more clearly articulate the population sizes of each task force. For Madison, the population size is 15, Columbia, 30, and Kansas City, approximately 300.

Given that I was able to identify the population size of the task forces, I turned to the other universe of actors that I was studying in this book—local level governmental, civic, and business policymakers. In order to facilitate an appropriate sample selection method for the local level policymakers, I reduced the population in each category of governmental and nongovernmental actors across all cases to a population of 45 (nine policy categories multiplied by 5). In each case, I oversampled by 10 to increase the likelihood I would receive a higher number of responses.

To create a sampling method for the task force members, I decided to use a 50% confidence interval. As such, for Madison I selected seven participants (50% of 14), and for Columbia I selected 15 participants to survey (50% of 30). Because the population in the Kansas City case was much larger, I decided to select a smaller, more manageable number of participants to survey. I found that although the Kansas City task force had over 300 participants, it generally relied on 20 cluster chairs and co-chairs for the production of its reports. As such, in keeping with the 50% confidence interval for all three cases, I selected 10 participants to survey from the Kansas City task force.

With respect to a random aspect in the selection of participants, this book identifies a sub-set of actors (as identified in the task force final reports) and selects participants accordingly. For governmental actors, those actors selected for participation are department heads and upper-level staff due to their power to make policy decisions in their respective areas. With nongovernmental actors, a random sample of these actors was selected in each case. Further explanation of this selection process is given in the next section.

Surveys were mailed to each participant and included a cover sheet explaining the nature of the project as well as a disclosure statement regarding the confidential nature of their participation. Each packet accompanied material to facilitate the return of the surveys. In some cases, participants were contacted by electronic mail and chose to return their surveys through this medium. A small number of other members opted to complete the surveys through the medium of a phone interview. A spreadsheet of all actors selected for survey was kept. Upon mailing the surveys, I recorded that date on which the surveys were disseminated on a spreadsheet. Likewise, when surveys were returned, I recorded the date of return on the same spreadsheet.

Surveys

This book's major source of data generation is through the use of surveys. A number of survey questions are used to construct a measure of innovation as well as a number of the factors used to explain policy innovation. In this section, explanation is given on how the survey questions are developed and utilized to facilitate data generation. The focus of analysis for race-based policy innovation is the number of local governmental and nongovernmental actors that have adopted policies as a consequence of those policies being recommended by the task forces in that particular community. The policy can be either the precise policy recommended by the task force or some derivation thereof. The key, however, is to determine if the specific policy or policies adopted are directly attributable to the task force in each respective community having recommended that policy be adopted.

I used the following procedures to develop survey questions that would facilitate the generation of data to measure race-based policy innovation. First, I created a listing of each task force's findings and recommendations categorized by policy area. Each finding(s) were listed sequentially with its respective recommendation(s) in each task force's final report. Once I compiled a complete listing of the findings and recommendations made by each task force, I then reviewed the findings and recommendations to identify exactly whom the task forces were recommending adopt the specific policies.

For example, the Kansas City task force found that a number of problems exist with housing discrimination in the city of Kansas City. Among their recommendations was the following: *All these activities to ensure fair housing will require a monitoring organization that goes beyond the activities of the existing Human Rights Commission. The Task Force urges that the Kansas City Civil Rights Consortium undertake this responsibility.* In most instances, as with these recommendations, each task force identified specific governmental and/or nongovernmental actors to whom their recommendations were aimed. With this recommendation it was easy to discern that the Kansas City Civil Rights Consortium was the unit of focus. The Kansas City task force clearly stated that the Kansas City Civil Rights Consortium should adopt policies within its department aimed at ensuring all the activities recommended by the task force, under housing policy concerns, are carried out.

In some cases, it was not as easy to discern to whom the task forces were directing their policy recommendations. It was sometimes the case the task force would make a recommendation, but would not identify a specific governmental or nongovernmental actor who they felt should adopt that recommendation. For example, with regards to the Columbia task force, the following finding was made: *Some real estate agents who buy into the stereotypes associating black residents with crime purposely direct new residents seeking homes away from "black" neighborhoods.* The corresponding recommendations to this finding were as follows: *1) All real estate agencies that serve the City of Columbia should engage current and new employees in annual diversity training workshops to diminish the prejudiced assumptions that influence a real estate agent's assistance to a client. Projections or assumptions about the kind of people who live in a particular neighborhood where the buyer may want to purchase a home ventures into discriminatory and prejudicial activity that an agent should not initiate, 2) Efforts should be taken to diversify neighborhoods by race, culture and economic status, 3) Citizens should be apprised of the fact that complaints about discriminatory practices in real estate can be referred to the Missouri Commission on Human Rights and specialty boards such as the Missouri Real Estate Commission.*

One of the recommendations to this specific finding called for identification and survey of a set of actors of a population too large to analyze here. Throughout this book, when such instances were the case, a small sample of randomly selected actors (3-4) was drawn. With regards to this particular recommendation, a random sample of real estate agencies that serve the city of Columbia was selected for survey. These actors were selected through conducting a search for real estate agents in the city of Columbia listed in the city's yellow pages directory listed on the World Wide Web.

Another of the recommendations to the aforementioned finding did not clearly state or imply a particular actor or set of actors who should adopt this policy. In such cases, no attempt was made to identify any specific actor(s) for survey purposes. However, this book recognized such instances for a later discussion on the ambiguity of task force recommendations. With regards to other recommendations where it was not clearly identifiable who should adopt the recommended policy, but where it was implicit to whom the policies were directed, special attention was paid to the policy recommendation. In such cases I determined what governmental/nongovernmental unit to whom that particular recommendation was addressed. With regards to recommendations such as these, a number of plausible actors could have been identified as implicitly addressed in the recommendation. However, the key was to discern which actors were most closely attached to the policy recommendation as a result of their delegated perfunctory duties in their line of work. In this case, it just so happened that the two major actors in the City of Columbia who were engaged in a line of work that would have attached them to such policy concerns was clearly stated in the recommendation—the Missouri Commission on Human Rights and the Missouri Real Estate Commission. The method used in this book to determine which actors were most closely attached to otherwise ambiguous policy recommendations was examination of the structure of each city's government. From this, I identified each of the city's boards and commissions. Finally, I analyzed the various boards' and commissions' mission statements. The mission statements were key to determining what governmental unit was most closely attached to a specific policy concern.

Once this analysis was conducted across all policy concerns of the three cases, then a complete list of actors to be surveyed was compiled along with their contact information. To identify the key individual to be surveyed, I examined the personnel structure of the various governmental and nongovernmental units. In each case, I identified the person(s) who are in a position to directly adopt the recommended policies is done. With regards to governmental actors, these individuals included board and commission directors and top-level staff, city councilmen, county aldermen, city managers, police chiefs, commerce and economic development directors and other top ranking public officials. Concerning nongovernmental actors, these individuals included newspaper and radio editors, business proprietors, ministers of churches, lending agents, and real estate agents, as well as other civic leaders. The names and contact information for these individuals was gathered through the use of (a) the city's governmental home page on the World Wide Web, and (b) the city's yellow pages listed on the World Wide Web.

The aforementioned process also helped facilitate creation of the specific survey(s) each actor received. In this book, not all actors receive identical surveys. The reason for this was illuminated by the earlier discussion of the task force findings and recommendations. Each survey, in essence, was a survey concerning the findings and recommendations of each of the major policy concerns. For example, from compiling the findings and recommendations of the Kansas City task force on the issue of housing, a unique survey is created which lists the findings and recommendations of the task force with regards only to housing. The same was done for each of the major policy concern areas. Only those actors to whom the recommendations were addressed in that specific policy concern area were surveyed regarding their adoption of those particular policies. In cases where a governmental or nongovernmental actor was mentioned or implied across more than one policy concern area, those actors receive multiple unique surveys.

Each survey contains specific questions designed to measure policy innovation. To measure whether or not the targeted governmental and nongovernmental actors have adopted policies recommended by the task forces, the following was asked in each survey:

Listed below are some of the pertinent findings and recommendations produced by the task force that are aimed at your department/office (some may not apply to your department/office—in such cases, please ignore those particular ones). Please read each of the findings and the corresponding recommendations.

For each of the listed recommendations, will you please state whether or not your office/department has adopted that specific recommendation, or some form thereof, as part of your department's/office's official policy.

Adequate space was provided for each actor being surveyed to elaborate on whether or not any of the policies recommended (or some form thereof) by the task force had been adopted.

Minus the listing of the policy findings and recommendations according to policy concern areas, each survey for the respective case is the same. These additional questions facilitate the measurement of the key factors. The first set of questions in the survey are general information questions which include the following: 1) your name, 2) your place of employment, 3) your official capacity and title at your place of employment, 4) how would you characterize your own personal political stance (e.g., liberal, Republican, moderate Democrat, nonpartisan, etc., and 5) please tell me about the number and type of constituents your department/office serves. These questions are asked to garner general information about the actor who is being surveyed. The fourth question, concerning political stance of the surveyed, is asked in order to help explain how political philosophy might explain some of the variance in who adopts recommended task force policies. A further discussion of this is done later in this section. Also, question number five, concerning the number and type of constituents the actor's department/office serves, is asked in an effort to illuminate how constituency size and type might also help explain some of the variance in who adopts recommended task force policies. This question, however, is not asked in an effort to measure any major factors used in this book. Rather, it may serve to shed on light on possible alternative explanations to explaining some of the variation in policy adoption.

Research Approach

Environmental Shock

First, to measure the variable concerning the presence of an environmental shock, two methods are employed. First, researcher identification of whether a shock is present to at least the internal environment of the community and to the external environments of the local level policymakers organizations is stated. This is done through prior knowledge of the impetus behind the creation of each task force. In each task force's final report, in the forward written by each city's mayor, there is mention of the impetus behind the creation of the task force. In the case of Madison, for example, Mayor Susan Bauman created her city's task force as a result of many African Americans in the community beginning to complain that the share of traffic citations given in the city to African Americans was disproportionately higher than the percentage of blacks that lived in Madison. In addition, many owners of black managed establishments in Madison were having their liquor licenses revoked. These proprietors claimed that the point system used to cite violations of local ordinances by such establishments was based upon ambiguous rules. Madison, consequently, serves as a case because it demonstrates a condition of the implementation of a task force where an environmental shock exists. These shocks could have an effect upon the internal environment of local level organizations. There could be actors in Madison upon whom blacks begin to call for changes in the manner in which they treat blacks versus non-blacks. Whether any actors feel the reverberations of these shocks will be examined.

It is important to discuss what constitutes an environmental shock. Not all events that occur in a community can be considered a shock. To discern if an event is an actual environmental shock is like asking if a tree falls in the woods, does it make a sound; vis-à-vis is an event a shock if it is not identified as such? Answering this question by analyzing the literature proves fruitless because the literature does not identify how to recognize an environmental shock. As such, in this book I argue that a shock does not become an actual environmental shock until the leaders in a community's governing and business institutions (e.g., mayor, city council, CEOs of companies, etc.) recognize them as shocks. The events that are identified by these individuals as having an effect on the community then become factors that can lead to period of punctuated equilibrium, or more precisely, policy innovation. While other secondary level actors may identify events that have the potential to become environmental shocks, the recognition of the potential shocks by actors that are in a direct position to make policy decisions are paramount because only they have the ability to make substantive policy changes.

The case of Kansas City represents an instance of a task force created where no tangible environmental shock, of any sort, existed. The case of Columbia, on the other hand, illustrates a case where a potential environmental shock exists, but is not recognized by the city's mayor as being a significant factor. Neither mayor in these two cities acknowledges any specific conflict, threat, or other external or internal cause behind their creation of the task force. In both cases, each mayor claims their own personal belief that race relations are "stagnant" in their respective communities is cited as the rationale behind the creation of the task force. In Kansas City, there is no tangible catalyst that can be identified as the impetus behind each mayor creating the task force. In Columbia, however, there are a number of events that can be cited as a reason why its mayor would create his task force. As a result, these two cases are important to study because they contrast the case of Madison—where an environmental shock does exist.

The second source to determine the presence of an environmental shock in the survey is to ask whether or not there is a possible cause behind the creation of the task force that has gone unidentified by the mayor in each case. In all three cases, task force members are asked what factors they believe prompted their city's mayor to create that task force. This question is asked to uncover if a possible environmental shock might actually exist but has gone unidentified by the task force members and/or the mayor. This question also facilitates discovery of whether or not the mayor in each case may be trying to downplay the instability in the community created by the environmental shock. The mayor may do this in order to convince his constituents that there are no problems in the community and his administration is running an effective office. In addition, the mayor could be forwarding some hidden agenda. Questioning the task force members regarding this issue, interviewing the mayors in each case as well as examining their campaign speeches, statements and state of the city addresses, is used to reveal any allegations of other agendas in the use of the race relations task force by the mayor.

Once identification of the actual existence of an environmental shock is done, the next major step is to determine if the actor(s) actually see the shock as a threat to their organizational environment. For example, it could be the case in Madison, that the Madison-Dane County school board will not adopt any task force policy recommendations because, 1) they do not see the complaints regarding traffic stops and alcohol licensing as personally affecting their department, and 2) they do not see race relations, on a whole, as directly affecting the stability of their organization. To measure whether actors feel directly affected by the environmental shock, this book asks the following questions to all surveyed except the task force members:

How has your department/organization been directly affected by race relations problem in [city x], and, How would you assess the state of race relations in [city x]?

Collectively, these three cases are good cases for analyzing the first major argument regarding task force influence on policy innovation. Each case exhibits the presence of or lack of an environmental shock. To measure the presence of an environmental shock, I created two categories—a simple "yes"/ "no" dichotomy. The case of Madison fell under the "yes" category and Kansas City and Columbia the "no" category.

Credibility of Task Force Recommendations

An important factor that can contribute to variance in policy adoption across cases is the credibility of task force recommendations. This can stem directly from who makes the recommendations—a partisan or bipartisan task force. The implications of this on the number of policies adopted by governmental and nongovernmental actors should be considerable. In cases where a task force is partisan in its membership composition, task force recommendations should carry less credibility. Due to the low credibility of task force recommendations, local level actors should adopt fewer task force recommendations. The rationale behind this contention is that governmental and nongovernmental actors should view the policy recommendations produced by task forces as being the goals of the mayor and task force members—not prescriptions untainted by political agendas. Task force recommendations should be viewed as the product of the self-interests and motivations of a very small, select group of individuals.

Conversely, in cases where a task force is bipartisan in nature, task force recommendations should carry more credibility. This higher level of credibility should lead to more local level officials adopting the recommendations produced by the task force. The thinking behind this contention is that governmental and nongovernmental actors should view the policy recommendations produced by task forces in these cases as being the product of competing interests and having been debated in a dialogue of that leads to more objectivity. The recommendations should also be seen as being less driven by the personal agendas of a group of like-minded individuals, but instead, the policy concerns of a broader sect of the city's population.

Recalling the earlier discussion on the Hoover Commission, Heady, in an empirical analysis, finds that partisanship of a task force serves as an important factor in the reception given to task force recommendations. If governmental and nongovernmental actors question the partisan nature of the task force in these cases, it may result in their ignoring the recommendations made task force members. On the other hand, Heady finds that if a task force has a bipartisan nature, it may lend weight to its recommendations (Heady, 1949).

Recalling the earlier discussion on the introductory questions to the surveys, question number four is used to garner data on the political stance of the task force members. Interviews with the mayors in each of the three cases are used to gather data on the political stance of the mayors. The political philosophies of these actors are surveyed in order to determine whether the task forces are partisan or bipartisan in their membership composition. The assumption is made that task forces that are more bipartisan produce recommendations that are more credible than those produced by task forces that are more partisan in nature.

For the purpose of secondary assessment of bureaucratic discretion and political control theories as applied to policy adoption in each of the three cases, I also asked task force members to elaborate on the amount of discretion they had while serving on the task force. To generate data to measure this, I asked task force members the following questions:

What type of input did [Mayor of city X] have in the Task Force's (especially, your own committee's) regular deliberations, brainstorming, discussions, hearings, etc.?

Likewise, what type of input did the City Council and other city government officials have in the Task Force's (especially, your own committee's) regular deliberations, brainstorming, discussions, hearings, etc.?

What type of input did [Mayor of city X] have in the Task Force's (especially, your own committee's) creation of final recommendations?

*In your response, please elaborate on the amount of discretion you as an individual, and your committee as a whole, had in creation of final recommendations

Likewise, what type of input did the City Council and other city government officials have in the Task Force's (especially, your own committee's) creation of final recommendations?

*In your response, please elaborate on the amount of discretion you as an individual, and your committee as a whole, had in creation of final recommendations

To measure this variable, I concerned myself the partisan nature of the task force. I took the responses of those surveyed pertaining to questions regarding their personal political identification and compiled a complete listing of all responses. I assessed the overall variance in the political identifications of the task force members to determine whether or not the task force could have been considered partisan or bipartisan. As such, I created categories based upon the degree of partisanship of the task forces. The case of Madison illustrated the most bipartisan task force, the Columbia task force the median of the three cases, and the Kansas City task force the least bipartisan of the three. As the degree of bipartisanship increased, I concluded that the task force's recommendations were more credible.

Task Force Influence

The importance of the credibility of who makes policy recommendations and how this can influence local level officials to adopt those policies is documented in the literature (Walker, 1969). The fact that policy recommendations are made by elected and appointed officials is noted to be an important factor in whether those policies actually diffuse (Walker, 1969). Walker argues there are specialized communication networks of "federal and local officials, journalists, academic experts, and administrative consultants . . . " that are " . . . sources of information and policy cues (Walker, 1969)." The influence of task force members on policy adoption can be thought of in a similar as the influence of elected and appointed officials on the same. Task forces members serve as sources of information and policy advice due to the specialized knowledge they bring to the table in studying issues such as race relations. In addition, task force members should gain more credibility and influence due to the knowledge they acquire in studying race relations as they affect each respective community. In each of the three cases, the perceptions and recommendations of task force members can be thought of as expert-based prescriptions. If governmental and nongovernmental actors know that these prescriptions are expert-based, they should be more likely to adopt their recommendations.

As argued previously, task force recommendations serve as a body of information for governmental and nongovernmental actors to feed upon. Disruptions caused by some exogenous shock to the environment of these institutions may directly affect the stability of the organization. Such shocks can bring about a sense of fear that ability of the organization to function effectively is being threatened. Stability and routine are important in government agencies and there is a natural tendency for them to avoid actions that might "set a controversial precedent (Wilson, 1989)." Consequently, governmental and nongovernmental actors should adopt task force recommendations because of the need to quickly bring stability back to their environment. Because task force recommendations are a readily available body of research based information, which is otherwise costly and time-consuming information to acquire, governmental and nongovernmental actors should be influenced to adopt such policies.

To measure if task forces are indeed source of policy innovation, governmental and nongovernmental actors are asked a number of questions. These questions allow for discovery of whether policies adopted were the result of the influence of the task force recommending them, or for alternative reasons—such as self-motivation of organizational department heads, personal benefit to the organization, etc. It would seem that using the number of policies adopted by those surveyed would be the most conventional method towards measuring the influence of the task force on policy innovation. However, because influence is such a broad concept, it can be measured in a number of ways. In this book, influence is defined as raising one to an awareness of an issue and motivating one to take action to address that issue. The key to measuring influence is in the responses by those actors being surveyed. We look for these individuals to mention things along the lines of the following: The task force impressed me with the hard work they did, the number of experts they had on the task force, and motivated me to adopt these policies to take action to address race relations in [city X].

To measure this variable, the following questions are asked:

If your department/office HAS adopted such a policy, or some form thereof, will you please elaborate on the impetus behind doing so?

If your department/office HAS not adopted such a policy, or some form thereof, will you please elaborate on why it has not done so (e.g., do not feel the organization is personally affected by race problems in Kansas City, the recommendation would not benefit the department, suspicious of the political motivations of the task force members, etc.)?

What do you know about the [City of Kansas City's] race relations task force and the recommendations produced by the task force?

To measure task force influence, I took the responses of those surveyed to questions pertaining to questions regarding the influence the task force had on their adoption of recommended policies. I created two categories – "Task Force Influenced" and "Task Force did not Influence." Responses that indicate strong, lukewarm, or even marginal influence by the task force were included in the first category, "task force influenced." Responses that the task force did not influence policy adoption fell into the category "task force did not influence." In cases where no indication was given, responses were coded as "no response given."

Racial Threat

The literature on public policy, as discussed earlier, notes that policies geared towards certain types of issues often produce certain types of outcomes (Lowi, 1964). If this is the case, then perhaps racial demographics play an important role in the decisions governmental and nongovernmental actors make about adopting policies geared towards racial issues. A number of scholars argue race plays a major role in policy decisions (Alvarez and Brehm, 1997; Bobo, 1983; Burnham, 1974; Carmines and Stinson, 1989; Fording, 1997; Giles and Hertz, 1994; Key, 1949; Lieske, 1993; Massey and Denton, 1993; Schuman, Steeh, and Bobo, 1988). Most notably, V. O. Key argues that, "individuals make choices among alternatives that are often shaped by their context (Key, 1949)." Local governments often behave differently in situations where the number of blacks is proportionately higher than in contexts where the numbers are lower (Key, 1949). This "racial threat hypothesis" holds that large black populations are often seen as a threat to whites and lead to distinct political attitudes and behaviors among whites. In his study, Key found that whites living in communities with large black populations were most likely to support candidates and policies unfavorable to improving the social and economic status of blacks (Key, 1949).

Other scholars have also found that in contexts where the threat posed by a minority group is higher, the dominant group's response is more hostile than in contexts where the threat is low. Michael Giles and Kaenan Hertz, in "Racial Threat and Partisan Identification," find evidence supporting this racial threat hypothesis (Giles and Hertz, 1994). These scholars investigate how as the Democratic Party in the South begins to depend more on black voters, it experiences a decline in white adherents. Using voter registration data from parishes in Louisiana from 1975-1990, they find higher black concentrations are associated with declines in the percentage of white registered voters who are Democrats and an increase in the percentage that are Republicans. In addition, they find that the threat posed by blacks is concentrated mostly to those parishes with low median incomes. In those parishes with higher median incomes, the level of black concentration appears to be unrelated to white Republican voter registration.

Not all studies, however, have found evidence supporting the racial threat hypothesis. Although Donald Kinder and Tali Mendelberg, in "Cracks in American Apartheid: The Political Impact of Prejudice among Desegregated Whites," argue that the level of concentration of blacks should play an impact on the attitudes held by whites (Kinder and Mendelberg, 1995), their empirical analysis does not support their contention. These scholars argue that public views on racial policy seemingly shapes what the national government actually does in terms of adoption of race sensitive policies. Kinder and Mendelberg analyze data measuring attitudes of whites on policies where the racial dimension is clear and where the racial dimension is implicit. They find that where whites are racially isolated, (where there are low levels of black concentrations) the political potency of prejudice increases. This finding is counter to the racial proximity hypothesis articulated by V. O. Key. Kinder and Mendelberg, acknowledging surprise with their findings, argue that proximity threats should be associated with everyday commerce and exchange between whites and blacks—not necessarily that proximity leads to threats. While proximity may or may not lead to threats, it does, according to Kinder and Mendelberg, offer to whites the opportunity to become acquainted with the black community.

Although Kinder and Mendelberg find evidence counter to what is predicted by the racial threat hypothesis, a wealth of literature still supports the contention that higher levels of black concentrations lead to more hostility by whites towards policies sensitive to blacks. Scholars, such as Rodney Hero, even go on to argue that the degree to which race plays a role in policy adoption is a direct function of the size of the minority populations in communities (Hero, 1998). Hero calls this a politics of heterogeneity. Richard Fording's study (1997) on the size of the black community does indeed affect the degree to which race plays a role in policy adoption. He finds that whites, in contexts where the size of the black population is large, are more resistant to adopting policies sensitive to African Americans. Fording provides empirical evidence that in cases where the size of the black population, in the form of electorate power, is large, black insurgency against white resistance on AFDC growth is effective. In contexts where the size of the black population in terms of electorate power is small, having a tolerant white electorate is a precondition to a successful black uprising against AFDC growth (Fording, 1997).

Key's "racial threat" theory and Hero's "politics of heterogeneity" concept are useful underpinnings towards argument building regarding the affect size of the black population in a city has on policy adoption. These frameworks lead to a prediction that the larger the black population becomes in a given locale, the less likely governmental and nongovernmental policy makers are to adopt policies aimed improving the social, economic, and political position of blacks. Likewise, as the level of concentration of blacks becomes lower in a given area, the more likely governmental and nongovernmental policy makers are to adopt policies favorable towards improving the social, economic, and political status of blacks.

In this book, the three cases are majority white cities with varying sizes of black populations. Because of the variance in the size of their black populations as a percentage of the total population, these cases allow for argument analysis regarding the role racial demographics play in policy innovation. In the case of Kansas City, the total percentage of the city's population that is black is 29.6 %. Madison, on the other hand, has a much smaller percentage of blacks as its total population—only 4.2%. Lastly, the total percentage of the city of Columbia's population that is black is 9.9% (United States Census Bureau, 1990).

These demographic figures have important implications for argument building. Because each case illustrates an example of a city where the overall structure of governmental and nongovernmental policy makers is made up of whites and there is also a presence of black population, the racial threat hypothesis can be used. Specifically, one would expect to find that in Kansas City, governmental and nongovernmental policy makers should be the least likely to adopt policies favorable towards improving race relations. The case where one would expect to find the highest likelihood of policies adopted by white policy makers that are amenable to improving race relations and the social status of blacks should be Madison. To analyze these contentions, the racial demographics of each city are analyzed in the context of the number of actors who actually adopt task force recommended policies. In this book, I expect to find that policy makers in Kansas City are less likely than those in Columbia and Madison, and those in Columbia, less likely than those in Madison, to adopt policies recommended by the task forces in each respective city.

To measure this variable, I utilized 1990 Census Bureau data of the total percentage of the population that was black in each of the three cities. Racial threat was measured by the percentage of blacks as a total of the city's total population as compared to the percentage of whites as a total of the city's population. I concluded that the higher the percentage of the total population that was black, there was a higher level of racial threat. These percentages were used in a comparison format to examine across cases to determine if race indeed had any explanatory power for predicting policy innovation.

Political Culture

As noted in Chapter Two, the political science literature on political culture is highly influenced by the seminal work of Daniel Elazar (1984; Elazar, Gray, and Spano, 1999). Elazar argues that the politics of a state or community are affected by its culture. The political processes and policy outcomes of a state and local community's governing, social, and corporate institutions are the results of dominant cultural values. Those values, in turn, are argued to be the product of the dominant religious and racial groups of that geographic area (Elazar et al., 1999).

Elazar argues that there are three main types of political cultures—individualistic, moralistic, and traditionalistic. According to Elazar, the individualistic political culture is characterized by emphasis being placed on private concerns. It places paramount importance on limited community intervention, whether governmental or nongovernmental, into the private activities of citizens. In the moralistic political culture, both the general public and political actors conceive of politics as a public activity grounded in a notion of the public good and devoted to the forwarding of the public interest. Individualism takes a back seat to the commitment towards using nongovernmental (but governmental if necessary) power to intervene into areas typically considered private activities. The traditionalistic political culture, finally, is characterized by its likeness to the moralistic culture in that it views the role of government as an actor with a positive role in the community. However, in the traditionalistic culture, the role of government is more prohibitive in that its role is to secure the continued maintenance of the existing social order. To do so, government operates to limit meaningful political power to a small and self-perpetuating group of actors typically drawn from an established elite (Elazar et al., 1999).

In this book, I use Elazar's formulation of political culture as a variable that can explain the variance in race-based policy innovations. I use pre-existing analyses of the political cultures of each of my three cases done by leading scholars who study the politics in each of those three cases. I find that Madison illustrates a moralistic culture, Columbia a traditionalistic culture, and Kansas City an individualistic political culture. With regards to my expectations of the role of political culture on race-based innovations, they are taken largely from the body of literature that analyzes the role of political culture on innovation (Aiken and Alford, 1970; Canon and Baum, 1981; Johnson, 1976). This literature finds that cities with majorities that hold public-centered values are more innovative with respect to polices benefiting the community as a whole than cities dominated by groups with private-centered values. For theoretical purposes, I contend that policy innovations geared towards addressing race relations in a community are policies that benefit the community as a whole. For comparison purposes in my argument on culture, I contend that moralistic cultures are the most public-centered, traditionalistic cultures the median, and individualistic cultures the most private-centered.

To measure political culture, I used pre-existing analyses of the political cultures of each of my three cases done by leading scholars who study the politics in each of those three communities. I found that Madison illustrated a moralistic culture, Columbia a traditionalistic culture, and Kansas City an individualistic political culture. I noted that the literature on culture and community based innovation finds that cities with majorities that hold public-centered values were more innovative with respect to polices benefiting the community as a whole than cities dominated by groups with private-centered values. For comparison purposes in my argument on culture, I contended that moralistic cultures were the most public-centered, traditionalistic cultures the median, and individualistic cultures the most private-centered.

Interviews

Two types of interviews were employed: open-ended structured interviews and informal interviews. In each case, interviews were conducted with one person at a time. As with those surveyed, each person interviewed was assured of the confidentiality of the information they provided and that their anonymity would be protected. Of those interviewed, only two individuals expressed a problem in disclosing their identities. An application for permission to conduct the interviews (as well as surveys) in this book was filed with the appropriate Institutional Research Board (IRB) and subsequently granted. As with the survey participants, interviewees were debriefed on the IRB policies regarding their participation and disclosure of their identification.

Primary Interviewees

The first major task in identifying interviewees was to determine who would be interviewed. The overriding criteria on whom to select to interview was the knowledge each individual could offer to the research and his/her potential to contribute to the development of an understanding of the use of task forces for policy advocacy. Based on this thinking, I decided to conduct interviews with the mayors who created and staffed each of the respective task forces. These interviews were conducted to facilitate testing many of the contentions set forth throughout this book.

Interview Questions

Through the use of open-ended, structured interviews, respondents were allowed to address issues that I raised. I pre-prepared a series of questions to which answers were sought. During the interview process, I was an active listener, and probed respondents to clarify or expand their responses. In only one case, Kansas City, was I not able to conduct an interview. The nature of the interviews dealt mainly with six major questions, which included the following: 1) What was your impetus behind creating the task force, 2) What was your thinking in selecting individuals to serve on the task force (in terms of social, political, and economic backgrounds of prospective task force members), 3) What is your personal view about the nature race relations in your city, 4) What is your personal political stance, generally speaking, 5) What do you hope to accomplish the task force, and 6) What have you learned from the city's experience with the implementation of this task force.

Secondary Interviewees

In addition to interviewing the mayors of each of the three cities, interviews with two local level civic leaders in Kansas City were also conducted. In particular, interviews with the Director of the Kansas City Harmony and the Kansas City Urban League were done. Through the use of informal interviews, these respondents were allowed to address issues raised by the researcher. The development of data from these surveys was facilitated by allowing the interviewees to elaborate on their understandings, experiences, and feelings about the efficacy of the task force in Kansas City. I had not prepared before hand a series of specific questions to which answers were sought. However, I asked a number of questions that led the interviewees to elucidate on the influence the task force has had on policy adoption in Kansas City. During this interview process, I was an active listener, and probed respondents to clarify or expand their responses.

Interviews with these two individuals were done for two reasons. The first of these reasons stemmed from of the unique context of Kansas City's experience with its race relations task force. The Kansas City task force, under the direction of the local Urban League chapter, was argued to have not been as proactive as desired in fulfilling their delegated responsibilities to oversee the implementation of the task force. Consequently, this lack of ardor lead to another local level entity, the Kansas City Harmony, taking control of the responsibilities delegated to the task force and the Urban League. These interviews were conducted to shed light on the political battles present in the case of Kansas City.

Data Processing and Analysis Techniques

Analysis for this study comes from a research method that emulates Czudnowski's cross-systemic and cross-level analysis with common levels of integration (Czudnowski and Eulau, 1976). For analysis purposes, each case is first analyzed separately while using each of the variables. Many scholars advocate that the first job in conducting case studies should be description (Merriam, 1988; Yin, 1994). According to Patton, rigor in qualitative analysis depends on "presenting solid descriptive data to enable independent readers to make their own interpretations (Patton, 1990)." This task is accomplished in an analysis of each case presented in Chapters Four, Five, and Six. These chapters are followed by a cross-case analysis, Chapter Seven, used to integrate data, find commonalities across cases, to identify unique characteristics of each case, and to develop categories, typologies, and theories that help interpret the data.

Preliminary Analysis

The major method of recording data used during the data collection phase was to review the surveys completed by participants. Upon receipt of each survey, the document was logged in on a spreadsheet. This spreadsheet listed the name of the person to whom the survey was sent, the date the survey was sent, and the return date. Surveys were perused to make sure the participant addressed each question. During this phase, more emphasis was placed on collecting data than on the actual analysis of data and writing of text. In collecting data during the interview phase, the researcher took notes during the interviews, briefly reviewed the documents upon completion of the interviews, and logged the interviews on to a spreadsheet for accuracy of the date and time of the interview

Intensive Data Analysis

The intensive data analysis phase relied upon two primary sources: (i) the data produced from questions generated during the conceptual portion of the book and, (ii) the conceptual and theoretical insights gained during the analysis of literature. During this analysis, the data were organized separately by case, summarized into a spreadsheet, and then analyzed. The analysis of data is presented in the chapters corresponding to each case.

In conducting the analysis, the data was organized according to the variables used. I turned to the initial discussion of these variables to ensure the original contentions set forth were actually addressed. As discussed earlier, multiple factors (variables) were used. These key variables, once again, included the following: environmental shock, partisan nature of the task force, task force influence, and racial threat. The variable of focus here was the number of actors who adopted race-based innovative policies.

To measure the number of actors who adopted race-based innovative policies, I recorded the responses to the survey questions designed to measure this variable. These questions were discussed previously in this chapter. I summarized the responses as falling into one of following corresponding categories: (i) actor reports that none of the task force recommended policies were adopted, and (ii) actor reports that task force recommended policies were adopted. For category (i), I recorded the data point as a zero if the respondent indicated that none of the task force recommendations were adopted. For the second category, (ii), I recorded the data point as a one if the respondent indicated that at least one of the task force recommendations had been adopted. From this, I summarized the totals for each of the two categories across all cases. This allowed for measurement of the number of actors who adopted race-based innovative policies.

The data for this variable was continuous level data, and ranged from zero up to the total number of actors who participated in the study.

The next three chapters involve an analysis of the three cases selected for examination; Chapter Four, Madison; Chapter Five, Columbia, and Chapter Six, Kansas City. In each chapter, the data garnered from the surveys of task force members, governmental and nongovernmental policy makers, and interviews of local officials, is assessed and placed in the context of a discussion that illuminates the findings from analyzing each of the major contentions. In addition, a number of other research questions are brought forth and tackled as they arise through the process of data analysis.

Bibliography

Aiken, M., and Alford, R. R. (1970). Community Structure and Innovation: The Case of Public Housing. *American Political Science Review, 64*(3), 843-864.
Alvarez, R. M., and Brehm, J. (1997). Are Americans Ambivalent Towards Racial Policies? *American Journal of Political Science, 41*(2), 345-374.
Bobo, L. (1983). White Opposition to Busing: Symbolic Racism or Realistic Group Conflict? *Journal of Personality and Social Psychology, 45*, 1196-1210.
Burnham, W. D. (1974). The United States: The Politics of Hetereogeneity. In R. Rose (Ed.), *Electoral behavior: A Comparative Handbook* (pp. 653-726). New York: Free Press.
Canon, B. C., and Baum, L. (1981). Patterns of Adoption of Tort Law Innovations: An Application of Diffusion Theory to Judicial Doctrines. *American Political Science Review, 75*(4), 975-987.
Carmines, E. G., and Stinson, J. A. (1989). *Issue Evolution: Race and the Transformation of American Politics*. Princeton, NJ: Princeton University Press.
Creswell, J. W. (1994). *Research Design: Qualitative and Quantitative Approaches*. Thousand Oaks, CA: SAGE Publications.
Czudnowski, M. M., and Eulau, H. (Eds.). (1976). *Elite Recruitment in Democratic Polities: Comparative Studies Across Nations*. New York: SAGE Publications.
Denzin, N. K. (1970). *The Research Act: A Theoretical Introduction to Sociological Methods*. Chicago: Aldine.
Elazar, D. J. (1984). *American Federalism: A View from the States*. New York: Crowell.
Elazar, D. J., Gray, V., and Spano, W. (1999). *Minnesota Politics and Government (Politics and Governments of the American States)*. Lincoln, NE: University of Nebraska Press.
Fording, R. (1997). The Conditional Effect of Violence as a Political Tactic: Mass Insurgency, Welfare Generosity, and Electoral Context in the American States. *American Journal of Political Science, 41*(1), 1-29.
Giles, M. W., and Hertz, K. (1994). Racial Threat and Partisan Identification. *American Political Science Review, 88*(2), 317-326.
Heady, F. (1949). The Operation of a Mixed Commission. *American Political Science Review, 43*(5), 940-952.
Hero, R. (1998). *Face of Inequality: Social Diversity in American Politics*. New York: Oxford University Press.
Holstein, J. A., and Gubrium, J. F. (1997). *The New Language of Qualitative Method*. New York: Oxford University Press.
Johnson, C. A. (1976). Political Culture in American States: Elazar's Formulation Examined. *American Journal of Political Science, 20*(3), 491-509.
Jorgensen, D. (1989). *Participatory Observation: A Methodology for Human Studies*. Newbury Park, CA: SAGE Publications.
Key, V. O. (1949). *Southern Politics in State and Nation*. New York: A. A. Knopf.
Kinder, D. R., and Mendelberg, T. (1995). Cracks in American Apartheid: The Political Impact of Prejudice Among Desegregated Whites. *The Journal of Politics, 57*(2), 402-424.
King, G., Keohane, R. O., and Verba, S. (1994). *Designing Social Inquiry: Scientific Inference in Qualitative Research*. Princeton, NJ: Princeton University Press.
Lieske, J. (1993). Regional Subcultures of the United States. *The Journal of Politics, 55*(4), 888-913.

Lincoln, Y., and Guba, E. G. (1985). *Naturalistic Inquiry*. Newbury Park, CA: SAGE Publications.
Locke, L. F., Spirduso, W. W., and Silverman, S. J. (1987). *Proposals that Work: A Guide for Planning Books and Grant Proposals* (2nd ed.). Newbury Park, CA: SAGE Publications.
Lowi, T. J. (1964). American Business, Public Policy, Case Studies and Political Theory. *World Politics, 16*, 677-715.
Massey, D. S., and Denton, N. A. (1993). *American Apartheid: Segregation and the Making of the Underclass*. Cambridge, MA: Harvard University Press.
Mayor's Columbia Race Relations Task Force. (1996). *Report to the Mayor*. City of Columbia, MO.
Mayor's Task Force on Race Relations. (1996). *Interim Report to the Mayor*. Kansas City, MO: City of Kansas City (MO).
Merriam, S. B. (1988). *Case Study Research in Education: A Qualitative Approach*. San Francisco: Jossey-Bass Publishers.
Miles, M. B., and Huberman, A. M. (1984). *Qualitative Data Analysis: A Sourcebook of New Methods*. Newbury Park, CA: SAGE Publications.
Patton, M. Q. (1990). *Qualitative Evaluation and Research Methods* (2nd ed.). Newbury Park, CA: SAGE Publications.
Ragin, C. C., and Becker, H. S. (1992). *What is a Case?: Exploring the Foundations of Social Inquiry*. New York: Cambridge University Press.
Rosenthal, E. (1966). *Experimenter Effects in Behavioral Research*. New York: Appleton-Century-Croft.
Schuman, H., Steeh, C., and Bobo, L. (1988). *Racial Attitudes in America: Trends and Interpretations*. Cambridge, MA: Harvard University Press.
Singleton, R. A., Straits, B. C., and Miller Straits, M. (1993). *Approaches to Social Research* (2nd ed.). New York: Oxford University Press.
Smith, J. K. (1983). Quantitative versus Qualitative Research: An Attempt to Clarify the Issue. *Educational Researcher*, 6-13.
Snedecor, G., and Cochran, W. (1989). *Statistical Methods* (8th ed.). Ames, IA: Iowa State University Press.
Sudman, S., and Bradburn, N. M. (1982). *Asking Questions: A Practical Guide to Questionnaire Design*. San Francisco: Jossey-Bass.
Task Force on Race Relations, Alcohol License Review Commission Workgroup. (1998). *Final Report*. Madison, WI: City of Madison.
United States Census Bureau. (1990). *Census Data*.
Van Evera, S. (1997). *Guide to Methods for Students of Political Science*. Ithaca, NY: Cornell University Press.
Walker, J. L. (1969). The Diffusion of Innovations Among the American States. *American Political Science Review, 63*(3), 880-899.
Wilson, J. Q. (1989). *Bureaucracy: What Government Agencies Do and Why They Do It*. New York: Basic Books.
Wolcott, H. F. (1994). *Transforming Qualitative Data: Description, Analysis, and Interpretation*. Thousand Oaks, CA: SAGE Publications.
Yin, R. K. (1994). *Case Study Research: Design and Methods* (2nd ed.). Newbury Park, CA: SAGE Publications.

Chapter Four: Madison, Wisconsin Mayor's Race Relations Task Force

This chapter is a case-study analysis of the city of Madison's Mayor's Race Relations Task Force. In this chapter, I give a brief background of the city and the impetus behind the community's creation of its race relations task force. In doing so, special attention is paid to the major environmental shocks that serve as a catalyst for innovation by city officials and nongovernmental actors. The context of the discussion includes elaboration on the findings from the data generated by surveys and interviews. I also discuss findings specific to the major questions and contentions presented in this book. In this chapter, I argue that three main factors can best explain why local level policymakers in Madison adopt more task force recommendations versus those in Columbia and Kansas City: (1) the political culture of Madison, (2) the presence of an environmental shock, and (3) political control over the implementation of task force recommendations.

City Background: Madison, Wisconsin

The city of Madison is the seat of state government in Wisconsin. With a population around 200,000, Madison boasts being the home of the University of Wisconsin, and having a small town charm yet a range of cultural and recreational activities usually found in much larger cities. The city is frequently cited for numerous prestigious awards, among them, America's #1 Most-Wired city, #1 Healthiest City for Women, and Runner-up for top retirement site in the United States (City of Madison, 2001). One of the more celebrated claims made by Madisonians is that the city is a liberal town. In many respects, the politics of Madison are centered on upholding this image and promoting such ideals as part of the city's culture. Because of this, the city is particularly susceptible to adopting new policies to address racial tensions in an effort to protect its reputation.

For most of its history, Madison has been a predominately white town. According the 1990 U. S. Census, Madison is 90% white, 4% black, and 4% Asian. In having this type of relatively homogenous population, Madison has not had the same type of historical identification with racial issues nor experienced the level of racial confrontations as other cities of comparable size (e.g., Shreveport, Louisiana, Savannah, Georgia, or Charleston, South Carolina). These racial demographics, by and large, have enabled Madison to promote itself as a community of racial tolerance and harmony. The recent growth in the nonwhite communities in Madison (16% of the total community), however, has begun to put a strain on the city's once stable nature of race (United States Census Bureau, 1990).

The political culture of Madison has been characterized in two main ways. First, scholars of Madison politics have noted that the Democratic Party has dominated the political landscape for years (Nichols, 2001). Consequently, many political analysts and academicians have called Madison a town of liberals (Buhle, 1990; Epstein, 1958). In support of this acclamation, many Madisonians have noted that their city is home to one of the first local level Equal Opportunity Ordinances and the first lesbian congresswoman (survey response). Harder evidence has also supported the notion that Madison is a strongly pro-Democratic Party city. An analysis of presidential election voting patterns in Dane County since 1980 reveals that locals have been staunch supporters of Democrats in each of these elections. Even in 1984, when Walter Mondale won only 10 counties in the entire state of Wisconsin, Madison supported him for the presidency by more than 50% of the vote.

In addition its characterization as a liberal town, the political culture of Madison has also been said to espouse progressive ideals (Nichols, 2001). Evidence has supported this claim also as Madisonians have supported third and fourth party candidates for local electoral offices. Analysts of Madison politics have noted that the over the past seven years, the Progressive Dane Party, an affiliate of the New Party, has become a formidable opponent in city politics. This party has typically been even more left-leaning than even the Democratic Party. Madison's inclination towards support of multi-party systems is partly due the history of influence exerted in Wisconsin politics by former governor Robert La Follette. There has been a substantial literature written on La Follette and how he was a key leader in the progressive movement in Wisconsin (Johnson, 1964; Krieger, 1993; Marguiles, 1968; Miller, 1982; Unger, 2000). Historians and scholars have argued that La Follette attempted to make Wisconsin the setting for an experiment in social democracy (Blake, 1998).

While at first glance, these characteristics of the political scene in Madison may seem to support the notion that the city is indeed a town of liberals and progressives, the concept of liberalism and progressivism (as I will demonstrate later in this chapter) must be placed in the broader context of the social, political, and economic demographics of Madison. As one survey participant noted, "it is easy to be liberal in a lily white environment" (survey response). In this book, I find that culture does indeed play a major role in the politics of innovation in the case of Madison. The politics of Madison are connected to the city's political culture—its progressivism (which can be characterized by the Progressive Dane party's support of policies such as tax justice, local sovereignty, better social services, democratic economic development, living wages, etc.) and its liberalism (Nichols, 2001). From its historical roots to modern day politics, citizens in Madison have been avid participants in politics, voicing their opinions on a myriad of issues—such as "public schools, land-use questions and historic preservation (Campbell and Martell, 1999)."

In this book, I argue that Madison espouses a liberal moralistic political culture—one that views communal good of paramount importance to self-interested, wealth oriented goals (Blake, 1998; Elazar, Gray, and Spano, 1999). The culture of Madison is affected by the Democratic and Progressive philosophies prevalent in its social and governing institutions (Blake, 1998). The city is a leader in championing liberal policies on moral issues, such as race, gender, and sexual orientation, as well as social welfare programs. Unlike in many other moralistic political cultures, Madison leans towards the left end of the political spectrum on many politically sensitive issues (e.g., school prayer, sexual orientation discrimination, etc.). Many actors in Madison fight to promote the cause of those groups traditionally discriminated against by conservatives and even cold war-era liberals and Yellow Dog democrats (Blake, 1998). As such, policies sensitive towards minorities and the poor are much more likely to be adopted in Madison than in other conservative moralistic cultures.

To further set the context of a discussion of innovation in Madison, I find it necessary to briefly mention Daniel Elazar's conceptualization of moralistic political culture. According to Elazar, "(in) the moralistic political culture both the general public and the politicians conceive of politics as a public activity centered on some notion of the public good and properly devoted to the advancement of the public interest" (Elazar et al., 1999). Elazar goes on to note that:

> In the moralistic political culture, individualism is tempered by a general commitment to utilizing communal, preferably nongovernmental, but governmental if necessary, power to intervene into the sphere of private activities when it is considered necessary to do so for the public good or the well-being of the community. Accordingly, issues have an important place in the moralistic style of politics, functioning to set the tone for political concern. Government is considered a positive instrument with a responsibility to promote the general welfare (Elazar et al., 1999).

The city of Madison's status as a progressive and liberal town that espouses many of the principals of a moralistic culture is an important factor in why the city's governmental and nongovernmental institutions are likely to be more open to the adoption of policies that call for equitable treatment of all people regardless of race, gender, and sexual orientation. In having such a culture, policy makers in Madison are more likely to be receptive to governmental institutions intervening in the political and social fabric of the community. Because these institutions espouse many of the tenets of a moralistic political culture, then one of the ultimate goals of these institutions should be to promote the common good for the city. A finding that local level policy makers adopt recommendations towards improving race relations in the community is one way of demonstrating if Madison's leaders are indeed concerned about promotion of such goals.

Summary of the Context of Politics in Madison and Implications for Innovation

Despite its moralistic, liberal and progressive political culture, it is not enough to say that Madison's politics can be explained as the result of change-oriented leaders. The politics of innovation in Madison must also be understood as being deeply rooted in the city protecting and fostering an image, held internally and externally, that the community is in fact a liberal and forward thinking town, and that it has an environment of racial tolerance and harmony—even though this may not be the reality. Any events, or shocks, to Madison's environment can serve as a vehicle for innovation in this community. Consequently, disruptions to the city's environment (particularly the alleged racial profiling of African Americans in traffic stops and targeting of minority owned establishments that serve liquor in Madison) serve as catalysts that can lead to major changes in how local governmental and civic leaders approach the issue of race relations. Specifically, these events can cause Madisonians to be particularly more sensitive to the issue of race relations and to adopt policies aimed at improving upon their status.

The Impetus Behind the Madison Mayor's Race Relations Task Force

In the Spring of 1998, the city of Madison's Equal Opportunity Committee (EOC) issued a very controversial report regarding alcohol licensing and traffic stops of African Americans. The EOC had formed an ad hoc committee to study allegations of disparate treatment of blacks versus white with regards to both these issues. In a report, the EOC found that, with regards to alcohol licensing, there was a lack of explicit standards and criteria to be used in the exercise of discretion at critical states in the decision-making process as it related to disorderly violations and making such references to the city attorney's office for formal action. A lack of such standards, according to the ad hoc committee, created a situation where the process invited disparate impact in the exercise of judgment. Consequently, the ad hoc committee, as well as blacks in Madison, argued that these subjective standards were not neutral and reflected cultural bias against black owned establishments. Blacks in the community felt black owned business establishments were being targeted as well as receiving more punitive treatment as compared to white owned establishments.

With regards to traffic stops, the EOC ad hoc committee compiled a statistical data set that demonstrated there was a disparity between the incidence of African Americans in Madison's population and the percentage of citations given to them. Blacks in the community felt they were often stopped for no reason, other than the fact they were black, and not given an explanation by police officers as to why they were stopped. In addition, blacks felt police officers berated them and did not act in a professional manner when conducting these stops. These findings produced by the EOC ad hoc committee prompted a number of local governmental and civic leaders, mostly whites, to claim the committees findings were unfounded and racist.

The events following the report issued by the EOC ad hoc committee prompted Mayor Sue Bauman to develop the idea for a race relations task force. Whereas blacks were not backing down from their stance that police actions were racially motivated, a number of white Madison common council members and police department officials allegedly made racists statements concerning the EOC ad hoc committee and its report. At one point, the situation grew so contentious that high-ranking police officials offered to not enforce city ordinances if it meant they would not be viewed as racist. Tensions grew between blacks and whites in Madison as neither camp was willing to abandon their respective position on the issues. This situation was clearly one of Madison's most embarrassing moments in terms of its history and image as a city that could boast racial tolerance and harmony. Because of these shocks to Madison's environment, Mayor Bauman created the task force and gave it the responsibility to: (1) review the controversial findings issued by the EOC ad hoc committee and develop a plan for implementing *appropriate* (emphasis added) ones, including immediate and long-term implementation steps, and (2) develop a plan for community activities, including forums, which would result in a strategic plan for respecting diversity and undoing racism (Task Force on Race Relations, 1999).

In an interview with Mayor Bauman, the rationale behind her creation of the task force was illuminated. According to the mayor, her impetus behind creating the task force stemmed from "the report of the ad hoc committee alleging racial profiling in traffic stops in the city, questions about the committee's methodology (who they had or had not talked to in making conclusions), and the fact the committee's votes were split when the report reached the council (S. Bauman, Interview, March 22, 2001)." Mayor Bauman felt that the report made the EOC look bad, and rather than risking the credibility of the EOC, she decided that a task force should be created with a dual charge—to look at the

EOC ad hoc report and to look at the broader question of race in the community. By creating this task force, Mayor Bauman clearly hoped to apply a soothing balm, so to speak, to the wounds inflicted on the city's image, the relationships between actors in the community, and restore (what was thought to be) stable nature of race relations.

The Dynamics of the Madison Mayor's Race Relations Task Force

Mayor Bauman, along with the common council, sanctioned the task force in the Spring of 1998. They approved 13 members, along with a ceremonial position held by the mayor herself and a vice chair position for a city alderman. The task force that was created represented a cross-section of the city's population. From surveying task force members, I found that task force members included officials in higher education, the legal profession, officials from city boards, as well as local citizens engaged in grassroots activism. Task force participants reported that their political affiliations ranged from republican, moderate republican, progressive, liberal, independent, moderate democrat, to democrat. As such, the task force had a bipartisan membership composition. Task force members included men and women, some of which were black, white, Asian, and Latino. As evidenced by these surveys, Mayor Bauman was careful to craft a task force that was bi-partisan in nature (despite Madison being largely a town of liberals) and represented an ethnic cross-section of the city's population (despite the fact Madison is a mostly white town).

When nominating individuals to serve on the task force, Mayor Bauman reported that she had a large amount of discretion in selecting task force participants. According to the mayor, interest in participating on the task force was wide spread. The mayor solicited participation from the general public (she asked for recommendations of who might be interested in serving) and received names of individuals who were "not the usual suspects" (S. Bauman, Interview, March 22, 2001). While she did not totally want people she did not know, she was seeking a mix of people who had participated in past community task forces and then some who were new to the political process. The mayor indicated that she wanted "a cross section of the Madison community—people from different races and backgrounds" (S. Bauman, Interview, March 22, 2001).

Interestingly, Mayor Bauman did not feel that having to work in conjunction with the common council and the city manager to staff the task force (as required by local ordinance) had any ramifications on her ability to create an effective task force. The mayor felt as though the common council largely acquiesced to her judgment about who should serve on the task force and only participated in the process by performing their legal right and duty to confirm her nominations.

The contention was set forth in Chapter Three that task forces staffed under a dual-institutional construct would result in the selection of participants from a cross-section of social, political, and economic backgrounds. The reason for this was that both sets of political principals (the mayor and city council) would act strategically to ensure no one political principal could exert sole control over the task force. The prediction was made that this would be done through the means of staffing the task force with participants that represent diffuse viewpoints—especially from those of the nominating principal. As evidenced by the case of Madison, task forces staffed under a dual-institutional construct do not always result in both sets of political principals maneuvering for control over staffing of the force and can still result in the selection of members that represent a cross section of the population. According to Mayor Bauman, "the membership was largely determined by the mayor and the council agreed appointments should be done by the mayor. There was no discussion in terms of this person versus that person. The council input was just saying 'yes'" (S. Bauman, Interview, March 22, 2001).

What was interesting about this case was that although the mayor largely selected the task force's members, she did not use this power to exclusively nominate individuals whose political affiliations were most closely aligned with her own. Although this process was predicated on a system of checks and balances, and was in essence carried out through the discretion of a single institution, it still resulted in an outcome more consistent with a bi-cameral process.

This finding can perhaps be attributed to the type of political ideology espoused by many of the political leaders in the city of Madison. In Madison, common council members who are affiliated with the Progressive Danes hold a formidable position on the city council—holding 8 of 20 seats. Thus, political decisions, such as confirmation of task force nominees, are likely to be made in a manner reflecting progressive types of ideals. As the literature notes, in towns where moralistic and Progressive Party ideals are prevalent, political parties are considered "useful political devices but are not valued for their own sakes. Regular party ties can be abandoned with relative impunity for third parties, special local parties, or nonpartisan systems if such changes are believed helpful in gaining larger political goals" (Elazar et al., 1999). The process of confirming task force by nominees by the common council clearly demonstrated that selecting qualified participants was of paramount importance to choosing individuals based on political party ties.

In support of the position that political party ties are often relegated to a secondary status of importance in Madison politics, analysts note, "it is the individual that Madison voters tend to scrutinize, not his or her political affiliation" (Campbell and Martell, 1999). Consistent with this argument is the finding regarding Mayor Bauman's staffing of the task force. Clearly in Madison, the mayor, as evidence through her nomination process, places notions of party loyalties on the back burner in favor of selecting task force members who have a diverse set of political, social, and economic backgrounds.

So what effects, if any, would Mayor's Bauman discretion in staffing the task force have on the credibility of the task force's recommendations? Mayor Bauman reports that even if Madison city ordinances gave her the sole discretion to staff the task force's members, she doubts it would have much effect on the credibility of the task force recommendations produced. Perhaps the mayor's beliefs stem from the type of political context in which she governs. In cities with moralistic political cultures, such as Madison, there is considerably more amateur participation in politics. There is also much less of what Americans consider "corruption in government and less tolerance of those actions that are considered corrupt, so politics does not have the taint it so often bears in the individualistic environment" (Elazar et al., 1999). The mayor also notes that despite being required by local ordinance to have task forces sanctioned and all subsequent nominations confirmed by the common council, she could have used an executive order to create such a task force. However, "having the council say 'yes' we want this task force gave it a little more legitimacy. On the one hand, it made the task force broader based, and secondly, it gave assurance that the council would be there and support the recommendations (S. Bauman, Interview, March 22, 2001).

The evidence in this case points to the likelihood that when task forces are staffed under a dual-institutional construct, mayors do not necessarily seek council approval to give credibility to the selection process or the task force recommendations that are produced. Rather, mayors seek some assurance that the council will say, so to speak, we share your sentiment, we feel this is a worthy effort, we support you, and are in this with you all the way. As Mayor Bauman notes, she could have used an executive order to create the task force and pre-empt the council's power to otherwise vote down her nomination. But instead of doing so, the Mayor wants some level of assurance that the council agrees that creation of the force is necessary and they will support the recommendations it produces. The rationale for this could be that the mayor wants someone to share the blame should the task force fail to meet its goals.

The selection of task force participants by Mayor Bauman resulted in the creation of a task force whose members had a diverse range of reasons that motivated them to serve. In addition, task force participants came to the force with varied training that they felt made them particularly well suited to serve on the task force. A sample of task force participants was surveyed and asked to cite factors that motivated them to serve on the task force. Of the seven task force members sent surveys six responded (see Table 4:1). This represented a return rate of 85 percent. The task force members who responded provided insight into the general characteristics task force members bring with them to their job.

Among the motivating factors task force members cited for their participation on the task force included their personal attachment to race sensitive issues. One task force member noted that he was racially profiled and stopped by the Madison police department while walking in his own neighborhood. This member reported that he filed a complaint that was investigated and later ruled to be unfounded. Consequently, this member felt he was a part of the larger issue at hand. Another member reported that she wanted to simply meet people, pay her dues to the city, become involved in city politics, and help reveal what she felt was an underlying prejudice in the city. Yet another source said that he too wanted to do something good for the city, but also wanted to bring a fresh perspective to so many "liberal voices" (survey response). He also reported that he was motivated to serve to learn more about himself, as well as for more personal reasons.

As evidenced by the survey responses, task force participants bring to the job a myriad of reasons that motivate them to serve on the force. These factors ranged from personal attachment to the issue, civic-mindedness, social-awareness, the desire to meet people, and the interest in engaging in stimulating dialogue. The contention that task force participants have some type of special training or background that makes them particularly well suited to serve on such forces was presented in Chapter Three. Task force participants were asked to cite reasons they felt made them adept to serve on the Madison race relation's task force. One member reported she was particularly sensitive to and knowledgeable about the issue of race relations due to her skin color. This member felt that because of her skin color, both blacks and whites ostracized her—thus helping her understand the issue of racism from a non-white as well as non-black perspective. Other task force participants reported that they felt their formal training and academic background made them skilled to serve on the task force. A source reported that he had been involved in addressing race issues at the university level for 15 years. Another member cited her academic training—a degree in journalism and psychology with an emphasis in public relations.

Not all task force members, however, reported that they felt they had some type of special training that made them well suited to serve on the task force. In particular, two task force respondents reported that they felt they did not really have any special training. They did feel, however, they were both well read on the subject. One of these respondents noted that his only attachment to race issues, in fact, was that he had known many black leaders. In general, however, task force participants reported they did have (or at least they feel they have) some type of background or training that made them adept, but maybe not particularly a perfect match, to serve on the task force.

The data generally indicate that task force members feel that they have some type of special training or background that makes them suited to serve on such a task force. From assessing the backgrounds task force members cited as evidence of the suitability for serving on a race relations task force, I found that task forces have an eclectic mixture of individuals with varying degrees of backgrounds and trainings—some of which are more closely associated with experience and knowledge of race related issues than others. In having this type of diversity, the task force does not necessarily achieve the level of status typically associated with a blue-ribbon task force. Nevertheless, such task forces have a fair representation of individuals with backgrounds commensurate with the level of specialization necessary to effectively and efficiently study the issue at hand.

The contention that task forces were often created as the result of an environmental shock was presented in Chapter Three. In the case of Madison, it was argued disruptions to the city's environment served as a catalyst for innovation in this community. To analyze the contention that disruptions to the city's environment actually existed in this case, Mayor Bauman was asked to elaborate on her reasoning for creating the task force. It was found, from an interview with the mayor, that these environmental shocks (racial profiling in traffic stops and liquor licensing) did indeed lead the mayor to create the task force. However, I also wanted to know if there might have been any other agendas the mayor was promoting in creating this task force. To address this, I first asked task force participants to elaborate on why *they* felt the mayor created the task force. By and large, all respondents indicated that the mayor's reason for creating the task force was because the mayor and the city council, as well as many Madisonians, "were very reluctant to accept the findings of the EOC regarding alcohol licensing and traffic stops" (survey response).

Clearly, the creation of the race relations task force in Madison had much to do with the fact the mayor did not want the problem of racism to be exacerbated. However, two respondents indicated that the mayor might have had more personal agendas in creating the task force. According to one of these two task force members, it was the "mayor's self interest in being and remaining mayor" behind why the task force was created (survey response). This member felt that the task force was a media builder—it guaranteed a year or two of press coverage. For this member, the lack of provisioning of funding by the mayor showed "what she was really all about" (survey response). The other member argued, "there could be political reasons why the mayor created (the task force). Should could be trying to attract people from the minority community . . . to show signs of support for the community as a whole by dealing with race relations" (survey response).

The survey responses suggested that the Madison task force was largely created for the purposes of addressing a pressing community problem—specifically racial profiling in alcohol licensing and traffic stops. These shocks to the environment of Madison were the impetus behind creating the task force to study the city's race-related problems and recommend prescriptions as to how the city might once again retain its stable environment. However, the contention was also made in Chapter Three that mayors and city council members might create task forces for electoral motives. It was found that most task force members felt the mayor did not have any other agendas—such as electoral motives. One reason for this could be the trust in government officials typically found in cities with political cultures characteristic of Madison. In such cities, "politics is ideally a matter of concern and duty for every citizen. Government service is public service, placing moral obligations upon those who serve in government more demanding than those of the marketplace. Politics is not considered a legitimate realm for private economic enrichment and a politician is not expected to profit from political activity and in fact is held suspect if he does" (Elazar et al., 1999).

The allegation that task force members trusted the mayor's intentions because of their being the type of social capital likely to do so, however, did not dismiss the possibility that there were electoral motives. I wanted to utilize other means to discover if the mayor had other agendas in creating the task force. As such, I turned to an investigation of Mayor Bauman's campaign speeches and state of the city addresses. My analysis of these documents provided good indication.

The use of the task force as an electoral tool by Mayor Bauman began shortly after her bid to become the city's chief executive. In the April 1997 mayoral election, Sue Bauman became the city's first female mayor. Upon coming to office, one of the challenges she faced was the growing discontent in the community over alleged racial profiling in the community. The creation of the race relations task force in December of 1997 proved to be a device towards increasing her political standing among Madison residents. During her 1999 reelection bid, the mayor reiterated the city's success with the race relation's task force she created. She noted that the task forced had reviewed the findings of the ad hoc EOC reports and created a plan to "undo racism and celebrate diversity in [the] city" (Channel 3000.com News, 1999). The mayor took a strong stand on her view about race relations in Madison by saying "racism and economic discrimination have no place in Madison" (Channel 3000.com News, 1999).

Mayor Bauman won a large victory in the 1999 election. Her focus on the race relations task force proved to be resilient long after the culmination of its work in 1999. In her State of the City address, July 17, 2001, Mayor Bauman listed five policy areas in which she "tried to emphasize in [her] administration" (State of the City Address, July 17, 2001). Of those five policy areas, she spoke first and at length about the race relations task force. In her address, she noted that the city had received an Outstanding Achievement City Livability Award from the U. S. Conference of Mayors and Waste Management for its effort in addressing race relations (State of the City Address, July 17, 2001). Her focus on the race relations task force in various dialogues in which she engaged demonstrated that the task force was also a major campaign tool of hers.

Assessment of the Work of the Madison Mayor's Race Relations Task Force

In order to accomplish the first goal of reviewing the EOC ad hoc committee's findings, the task force created two working groups: the Traffic Stops Working Group and the Alcohol Licensing Review Committee (ALRC). The ALRC used as part of its method of investigation the services of the city's attorney's office, the police department, the EOC ad hoc committee, the Madison-Dane county tavern league and the staff of the mayor's office (Task Force on Race Relations, 1999). The group held open forums in which the

Table 4:1

Madison Mayor's Race Relations Task Force
Select Task Force Member's Profiles And Responses

- Gender

4 Male
2 Female

- Political Affiliation

3 Democrat/Progressive
1 Republican/Moderate Democrat
1 Moderate Republican
1 Independent

- Motivation to Serve on the Task Force

4 Civic Engagement
1 Attachment to the Issues
1 To Learn More About the Issues

- Expertise/Background

4 Academic and Professional Background
2 No special background/training

public could share their experiences with both the police department and the ALRC in relation to obtaining and retaining a liquor license. The ALRC found many of the EOC's earlier findings to be on target and others to be without merit. The committee ultimately made a number of recommendations for alcohol licensing, including random checks of all area businesses that served liquor. These prescriptions were aimed at promoting an environment of more equal treatment of all Madison area establishments that served liquor.

I discovered that the task force was also an electoral tool that the mayor hoped would improve and solidify her reputation among Madisonians. I found that through the medium of campaign speeches and state of the city addresses, the mayor used the task force heavily in discourse with the media and her constituents.

The traffic stops working group chose to use several different levels of investigation in order to complete its tasks. The group began by discussing with police personnel aspects related to patrols, traffic stops, questionings, complaints, resolutions, and actual occurrences between the police and citizens (Task Force on Race Relations, 1999). Second, the group reviewed the police statistical data set used by the EOC ad hoc committee. An emeritus professor from the University of Wisconsin-Madison's Criminal Justice program was brought in to assist the group in understanding the data. Third, the group reviewed tapes of public hearings held by the ad hoc committee. Finally, the working group reviewed a number of documents and communications from various city agencies and citizens regarding police stops (Task Force on Race Relations, 1999).

Although the data the group used to draw its conclusions was not accessible, the committee did summarize its major findings in its report. The traffic stops working group found there was a dissonance between policy procedure and what was expected of citizens. Residents of Madison were found to not understand police procedures and to have misunderstood what police were supposed to do in a given situation. The group also concluded that Madison policemen needed to do a better job of identifying themselves and why they were stopping citizens—especially in cases where no citation was given. With regards to racial profiling, the group concluded that the statistical data generated by the EOC demonstrated a disparity between the occurrence of African Americans given citations and the number of blacks in the community. Part of this finding was attributed to beefed-up patrols requested by blacks in particular neighborhoods affected by unusually higher crime rates. The task force produced a number of recommendations—among them, the creation of a brochure for citizens providing information of police procedures and what to do if were stopped by a police officer.

The two working groups completed their first task on October 20, 1998 and turned to its second responsibility on how to improve race relations in the city of Madison. To complete this goal, the task force first looked to the national Study Circles program introduced in President Clinton's "Initiative on Race" (as discussed in Chapter One). Secondly, the force delved into an earlier report that had been issued by the city's EOC ad hoc community on community, race, and ethnic relations in 1994. Third, the task force held focus groups with 15 community organizations and received public comment and input at every task force and working group meeting. The task force also held a public hearing in February of 1999 to solicit ideas and recommendations from the community-at-large. Upon completing their investigation of race relations in Madison, the task force concluded that *there were race relations problems in Madison and the Dane County area*. Among the recommendations the task force produced included a community-wide dialogue to improve race relations entitled, "study circles on race" (Task Force on Race Relations, 1999). The task force also made a number of recommendations concerning economic development, education, multicultural issues, home-ownership, and outreach and training.

The contention was presented in Chapter Three that mayors and city councils might try to exert control over the recommendations task forces produce. This prediction was based on principal-agent models. Such theories predict that political principals will try to control their agents (through staffing, offering incentives, etc.) and have them produce policy outputs in concert with their own personal agendas and philosophies. On the other hand, it was noted that theories of bureaucratic discretion predict that task force members, as bureaucrats, will retain a great deal of discretion and can not be influenced by political principals. To investigate these contentions, task force members were asked to describe and elaborate on the amount of discretion they had in completing the tasks charged to them as well as producing final recommendations.

In going about conducting their work, all Madison task force members reported that they retained complete discretion. One member reported that although a city council member sat on the task force and offered input into the recommendations, and despite the mayor also attending meetings, "we wrote what we felt was reasonable . . . we went much further than what the mayor expected or wanted" (survey response). In line with this finding, another source noted that the members had "complete discretion even though a city council member was present. He did not use his position to bully or influence" (survey response).

These findings suggest that task forces can and do retain a great deal of discretion in going about fulfilling their responsibilities. Even in cases where political principals are active participants on the task force, members are given a large amount of discretion to complete their jobs. One possible reason for this is that mayors and council members do not want to damage the credibility of the task forces recommendations by having its members reveal the final product was made under duress and coercion and is laden with political agendas. Additionally, mayors and council members may feel that task force members, due to their level of training and educational background, are better skilled to address the issue and make appropriate recommendations.

The task force members who participated in this study were asked to report their personal assessment of race relations in Madison before and after the implementation of the force. The responses demonstrated that members had different views on the task forces actual impact. Two members reported that the major impact of the task force was the creation of a dialogue. Another source reported that before the task force, "there was an atmosphere of mistrust and fear. Afterwards, there was more understanding and appreciation of diversity. The prejudice and bigotry still existed, but maybe more covertly" (survey response). One member's response in particular stood out. His comments served to support my underlying argument that the politics of innovation in Madison are part of its desire to protect its image. This member stated, "a lot of lip service was being paid to issues like diversity to sooth the liberal conscience. However, the institutions of the community—police, schools, employers, retail outlets—were slipping into the protect mode, which usually lead to the implementation of a host of discriminatory practices and policy as well" (survey response). After the task force finished its work, the member noted, the city incurred very high demand for participation in the study circles. "The study circles had a waiting list to join them, and there were more than the usual suspects joining. Even the police department implemented all of the recommendations" (survey response). In all, the task force members took with them from their experience a view that the task force had created awareness to the issue of race related problems in the city and created an impetus for innovation in the community.

Data Analysis of Task Force Recommendations Adopted

Five major contentions were presented in Chapter Three. The underlying thesis was that policymakers in cities where an environmental shock existed would adopt more task force recommendations that would policymakers in cities where there was no environmental shock. The case of Madison, as discussed in the previous sections, clearly illustrated an instance where environmental shocks existed. As such, I expected to find that local governmental and civic leaders adopted task force recommended policies due to the instability inflicted upon the city's environment. I was also interested to discover if these actors felt the environmental shock affected the internal or external portion of their environments.

To investigate these inquiries with regards to Madison, I surveyed a random sample of governmental and nongovernmental actors in the city of Madison. These surveys allowed for the generation of a body of data by which policy innovation could be measured. Potential survey participants were contacted initially on February 14, 2001. I made five different follow-ups, one a month, to encourage participation of all initially contacted. After a five-month period, I concluded my data collection. These efforts resulted in nine of 55 surveys being returned (return rate of 16%). The relatively low rate of return was attributed to the sensitive nature of the surveys. Many actors responded that they did not feel comfortable providing policy matters specific to their departments and organizations. Of the actors that did participate, eight were government and one non-governmental. The analysis of data generated by these surveys is presented in the next section (see Table 4:2).

Findings

The respondents in the data set were eight governmental actors that included officials in the city's Parks Division, Transit Division, Office of Community Services, City Attorney's office, Community Development Association Committee, the City EOC Committee, and the Madison Common Council. One nongovernmental actor also participated in the study. Of the nine actors who responded, eight reported that they did indeed adopt policies recommended by the Madison race relations task force. Many of these actors also reported that the environmental shock present in the city of Madison did have an impact on their organization—thus leading them to adopt task force recommended policies. When asked about the effects on the environmental shock on policy adoption in their organization, a number of responses included the following:

"We are affected because we do not receive many job applications from minorities . . . something is wrong . . . we are looking into it."

"Our office is closely tied to neighborhood and community based programs . . . we are often called in to mediate issues that have a race relations context."

"We receive complaints to our office."

"Minority bar owners claimed they were not made aware of their legal obligations . . . but we are not directly affected by race relations problems" (survey responses).

Not all policy makers responded that their organization was affected by the environmental shocks. One source gave no indication if the environmental shock had an effect on his organization, but noted that his organization had not adopted any task force recommended policies. This actor reported that no task force recommendations were adopted because "these [recommendations] do not affect my office" (survey response). However, this respondent's lack of policy adoption may have had something to do with his personal views about the task force. His responses indicated to me that he was displeased with some of the proceedings that occurred respective to the task force's policy making. He argued, "The mayor made some good appointments but some of the proceedings were ineffective . . . some city lawyers aligned themselves to my annoyance . . . . I disciplined them" (survey response). Perhaps this policymaker's attitude with respect to the task force discouraged him from adopting task force recommendations.

One policymaker reported that his office had adopted a number of task force policies as well as ignored others. Among the reasons he state that some policies recommended by the task force were not adopted was because they were "not within our jurisdiction . . . we believed there were higher more cost effective priorities related to integration and positive race relations" (survey response). In areas where policies were adopted, however, his department was very aggressive. Upon recommendation of the task force, this policy maker's office adopted two policies specifically recommended by the task force and four policies that were indirectly attributable to the force.

A source reported his office had not adopted any task force recommended policies. However, he also indicated that the environmental shock did impact his organization. The finding that his department did not adopt policies but felt affected by the shock went counter to my thesis. Upon further investigation, I discovered that this respondent had studied the task force's recommendation but concluded that adoption of them would be detrimental to his organization. This was an important discovery because it provided evidence that other mitigating factors, other than the presence of an environmental shock, might play in whether or not local level policy makers adopt task force recommendations.

The one non-governmental actor who responded reported that his organization had also adopted task force recommended policies. This actor, however, gave no indication as to whether he felt the organization was affected by the environmental shock. His personal views about race relations in Madison provided me some clue as to perhaps his predisposition to adopt policies sensitive to race relations. This actor reported that he was a Democrat and that he felt the city of Madison was "a contradiction . . . it is seen on the outside world as being liberal, but is one of the most conservative and racist small towns I have lived in" (survey response). This policy makers political party identification and personal views about the nature of race relations in Madison were consistent with that of an individual who would be inclined to adopt policies sensitive to race relations.

Additional Factors Assessed to Explain Policy Innovation

For assessment of other factors that could have had an impact on the policy adoption by these actors, I also measured a number of other variables— including personal political stance, constituency size, and personal view on the nature of race relations in Madison. Of the governmental and nongovernmental actors in the sample, each responded that their personal political stance was characterized as "liberal," "democrat," or "progressive" (survey responses). None of the actors indicated that they identified with the Republican Party or were anything other than liberal, democrat, or progressive. This included the two respondents who indicated that they had not adopted any of the task forces recommended policies. Consequently, I found that liberals, democrats, and progressives alike either adopted policies or did not adopt policies. I could not demonstrate that policy makers who are more right wing were more likely to not adopt task force recommended policies as hypothesized.

With regards to constituency size, the respondents who reported they had adopted policies indicated that their constituencies included a broad range of populations. The policymakers who responded noted that their constituencies ranged from the entire city to small more concentrated groups. This was also the case with policy makers who did not adopt recommendations. One of the two actors that indicated no recommended policies were adopted reported that her department's constituency size was around 40,000 riders a day. I found it surprising that her department did not adopt any task force recommendations given the large number of people her department served and the nature of its service. Arguably, many of this policymaker's clients should have been members of Madison's minority community. I would have expected that her department would have been particularly susceptible to adopting polices sensitive to race.

The other actor who indicated no task force policies were adopted reported his constituency size was "all city employees, agencies" (survey response). Again, this was the policy maker who held some personal displeasure with the politics surrounding the task force. Despite having such a large constituency, this respondent nevertheless ignored the task force recommendations. This finding gave further credence to my contention that personal displeasure with the politics of the task force likely led this actor to not adopt task force recommendations.

I was interested in discovering if policymaker's views on race relations in Madison might have had any relationship to whether or not they adopted task force recommendation. As argued earlier and demonstrated by the survey responses, most Madisonians did not acknowledge that the city has any serious problems with race relations. Most respondents in the case of Madison argued that race relations in their city were "pretty fair, not perfect, troubled but not a crisis, better than in most cities" (survey responses). Despite this rather benign view of race relations in Madison, each of these actors adopted task force recommendations. Consequently, I surmised that it was not requisite that these policymakers held some notion that race relations in Madison were in dire straights before they would adopt policies aimed at addressing racial issues.

Only three policymakers in this case indicated that they felt race relations in Madison were problematic. One of these policymakers argued that there were some "serious issues . . . the community power has always been white and people of color have face huge barriers" (survey response). The other two policymakers also felt that Madison was "a rather racist town" (survey response). Like the other policymaker's in this case, each of these actors adopted task force recommendations. In contrast, however, these actors held a much more pessimistic view of the nature of race relations in Madison. When assessed in the context of the entire pool of respondents, the data indicated that personal views of race relations in the community does not have a clear connection to whether or not policy makers adopted task force recommendations. There were

Table 4:2

Madison Mayor's Race Relations Task Force
Select Local Level Policymaker's Profiles And Responses

- Organization/Department among Respondents/Size of Constituencies

8 Governmental
1 Nongovernmental

4 >150,000
4 <50,000

- Profile of Respondents—Political Affiliation

1 No political ties
4 Liberal
3 Democrat
1 Progressive

- Profile of Respondents—Gender

4 Male
5 Female

those who felt race relations were problematic and adopted recommendations and those who felt race relations were relatively fine, yet they also adopted task force recommendations.

Findings on the Impact of an Environmental Shock and Other Factors in Policy Innovation

In the case of Madison, I found that most local level policymakers reported that they felt affected by the environmental shock present in the community—the external environment of their organizations. However, survey respondents also provided some indication that the disruptions affected the internal environment of their organizations as well. Many respondents noted that actual changes occurred in their organizations in terms of the level of supply and demand of services, requests, and complaints by African Americans after the shock was encountered. In the one case where a policy maker reported task force recommendations were not adopted despite his organization being affected by the environmental shock, the actor noted that the recommendations were at least contemplated. Only after it was determined that adopting the policy would be detrimental to the organization was the policy not adopted. As a result of these data, I tentatively concluded that environmental shocks do play an important role in leading policy makers to adopt policies. However, if these policies were thought to be detrimental to the organization, the shock was not enough in itself to lead the organization to adopt the recommended policies. In addition, if policies were viewed as not being applicable to a given organization (or outside that organization's jurisdiction) the presence of an environmental shock was not enough to lead to the adoption of task force recommended policies.

In Chapter Three, the contention was made that the credibility of task force recommendations would have an effect on the number of task force recommendations adopted by local level policymakers. This argument was based upon the expectation that task forces whose membership composition were partisan in nature would be viewed by local level actors as driven by partisan political agendas of task force members. Task forces recommendations would be seen as espousing the ideologies and philosophies of a group of like-minded individuals and not a broader section of the community. As such, partisan task forces produced non-credible recommendations. As a consequence of this, local officials would not have adopted task force recommendations. I also argued that task forces whose membership composition was bipartisan in nature would be less likely viewed by local level actors as driven by partisan political agendas of task force members. As such, bipartisan task forces were said to have produced credible recommendations. As a consequence of this, local officials would have adopted task force recommendations.

I argued in Chapter Three that greater bipartisanship in task force membership would induce policymakers to adopt more task force recommendations. As indicated earlier, local level governmental and nongovernmental actors in Madison did indeed adopted task force recommended policies. For measurement of this variable, the case of Madison illustrated a task force that was highly bipartisan in its membership composition. However, although it was found that the task force was largely bipartisan and local level policymakers adopted task force recommendations, the survey respondents provided no information that allowed for elaboration on the explanatory power of this variable. Local level officials gave no indication as to whether the partisan nature of the task force had any impact on whether or not they adopted task force recommended policies. This finding, at this early stage, was surprising. However, it may be the case that such a finding will be the norm across all three cases. As such, it order to make any conclusions regarding the explanatory power of this variable in explaining policy adoption by local level officials, this finding must be compared across all three cases.

In Chapter Three, I argued that there would be a relationship between the influence of task force members and the number of task force recommended policies adopted by local level governmental and nongovernmental actors. This contention was based upon the expectation that task forces served as policy experts and reference points for local level officials. I argued that as the level of influence of task force members increased, the number of local level officials who adopt task force recommendations would increase. In the case of Madison, survey respondents provided no indication that task force members were or were not influential in their adoption of policies. Task force members gave no response as to whether they adopted recommended policies as a result of the influence of task force members or whether they did so for other reasons. These findings led me to suspect that (although it cannot be stated with any certainty at this early stage of the analysis) task force members did not hold a level of influence that was strong enough such that policy makes would cite it as having been important factor in whether or not they adopted task force recommended policies. However, this finding regarding the relationship between task force influence and policy adoption by local level officials must be juxtaposed to the findings of the other cases before any conclusions can be drawn about this contention.

The role of the level of racial threat in the city and the number of local level governmental and nongovernmental actors who adopted task force recommended policies was presented in Chapter Three. I noted that theories on racial threat predicted policymakers would adopt more task force recommendations the lower the level of racial threat in that community. I expected to find that because the level of racial threat in the city of Madison was lower than in the other two cases, policymakers would adopt more task force recommendations than actors in the other two cities.

The finding that six of nine (66%) local level officials in Madison who responded said they adopted task force recommended policies was an important discovery. This early finding indicated that a low level of racial threat might have had a correlation to the number of actors who adopted task force recommendations. However, this finding must be placed in the context of a discussion of the findings across all cases before any conclusions can be drawn.

In Chapter Three, I argued that Elazar's formulation of political culture served as a key variable to explain the variance in race-based policy innovations. I noted that I used pre-existing analyses of the political cultures of each of my three cases done by scholars who study the politics in each of those three cases. In this chapter, I found that Madison illustrated a case of a community with a moralistic political culture. With regards to my expectations of the role of the political culture of Madison on race-based innovations, I expected to find that because Madison was a community with majorities who held public-centered values, it would be more innovative with respect to polices benefiting the community as a whole than cities dominated by groups with private-centered values. Again, the finding that six of nine (66%) local level officials in Madison who responded said they adopted task force recommended policies was an important discovery. However, as with the racial threat argument, this early finding on political culture and the number of actors who adopted task force recommendations must be placed in the context of a discussion of the findings across all cases before any conclusions can be drawn.

One additional factor that I did not predict would play a role in the number of actors who adopted task force recommendations was a mechanism of oversight built into the substantive portion of the task force's final report. The city of Madison officially adopted all of the task force's recommendations. This, however, did not mean that the local level governmental and nongovernmental policymakers themselves would officially adopt the recommendations into their respective organizations. So, after adoption of the task force final report and recommendations, the city of Madison went an additional step further to provide some level of assurance that policymakers would adopt the recommendations. As such, I found that oversight of the implementation of the task force recommendations by the city of Madison came to play an important role in the number of actors who adopted task force recommendations. As discussed in Chapter Two, I found that political influence, or political control, theories, predicted elected officials would enjoy a significant amount of control over their administrative agencies. Principal-agent models, I noted, posited that political principals were able to control bureaucratic agents by creating a structure of dependency. Despite being at a disadvantage in information on how the bureaucracy went about performing its tasks, principal-agent models predicted elected officials would use various incentives to control bureaucratic performance (Moe, 1984; Niskanen, 1971; Stein, 1990; Weingast, 1984; Wood, 1988).

In my analysis of the case of Madison, I found that budgeting and requiring reports were two techniques used by Mayor Bauman and the Common Council to gain a level of control over the policymaking decisions by local level governmental actors. To a lesser degree, the city also attempted to monitor the actions of nongovernmental actors in an effort to ensure they would adopt many of the task forces recommendations.

In order to control the policy adopting by local level actors, two important features were built into the city of Madison's race relations task force by the mayor and Common Council. First, with regards to reporting, the city made a "measuring outcomes recommendation" that called for substantive measurements to be created and used as a guideline by which oversight of the implementation of the recommendations could be done. The city then resolved that the Equal Opportunities Commission (EOC) was to take the responsibility for the overall monitoring of the Race Relations Task Force Report. Specifically, the EOC was given the job to "periodically report to the Council about progress and implementing the recommendations contained in the report . . .[these] reports from the EOC [were to] occur initially within one-hundred twenty (120) days of the adoption of the report and at six (6) month intervals thereafter until such time as monitoring this report [was] no longer relevant"(Madison Mayor's Race Relations Task Force Final Report).

To facilitate the EOC's monitoring of agencies and development of a report regarding the progress being made with implementation of the recommendations, the city of Madison required that each of the city agencies that were either named in the task force's final report, or staff commissions that were named in the final report, to "within ninety (90) days of adoption of this resolution, submit a work plan to the EOC describing the strategy they intend to use for deciding whether or not to move forward on the recommendations and, if approved, on how they intend to implement the recommendations assigned to them" (Madison Mayor's Race Relations Task Force Final Report). With regards to nongovernmental actors, the city gave the EOC the responsibility to "work with non-city entities to monitor the response of these entities to the recommendations" (Task Force on Race Relations, 1999). Finally, the city required the EOC to convey all information regarding the implementation of the task force recommendations to the Common Council.

Finally, the city required that funding for all of the adopted recommendations and any of the 19 additional proposals, that were ultimately approved, to be approved by a separate Common Council action in the form of a resolution or through the city budget. Consequently, the various agencies could not simply request money for the programs without the city first reviewing such requests and critiquing them. This gave the city of Madison the ability to make a determination if the use of funds by the various city agencies for programs said to be aimed at addressing the race relations task force recommendations were actually legitimate.

The requirement that all city agencies (most prominently, the EOC) and administrative heads give reports on the progress they were making in the implementation of the task force recommendations was an important tool used by the city of Madison to control the behavior of these political agents. In addition, the requirement that any funds to be used for implementation of the recommendations must be approved by the Common Council was another important feature of political control used by the city. Indeed, political science literature on controlling political agents finds that executives and legislatures design structure of control in order to ensure wanted policy outputs. In the case of Madison, the creation of the task force went beyond mere symbolism by the simple fact that the city formally adopted the task force's recommendations and required all city agencies to work towards demonstrating that the recommendations had been adopted in their respective departments through implementation.

Summary

The preliminary findings pointed to a number of different items. First, the findings revealed that where there was an environmental shock, local level policymakers adopted task force recommendations. Local level officials' indicated that the damage done to the city's reputation as a liberal town by an increase in racial tensions, led their departments to become more sensitive to the city's problems. This disruption to the city's image was said to have affected the external environment of these organizations.

Respondents in this case also indicated that the environmental shock discussed affected the internal and external environment of their organizations. These organizations saw increases in the number of complaints filed by blacks in Madison, and changes in the level of supply and demand for public services. Consequently, these actors felt a need to integrate innovative policies into their organizational structures. However, if these policies were thought to be detrimental to the organization, the shock was not enough in itself to lead the organization to adopt recommended policies. In addition, if policies were viewed as not being applicable to a given organization (or outside that organization's jurisdiction) the presence of an environmental shock was not enough to lead to the adoption of task force recommended policies.

The importance of political culture was examined. The politics of innovation in Madison were found to be connected to the city's political culture. I found that is was not enough to say that Madison's politics could be explained as the result of change-oriented, progressive-minded leaders. Rather, I found that the politics of innovation in Madison were to be understood as being deeply rooted in the city's desire to protect its image that it was a community of liberal and forward thinking people, and that it had an environment of racial harmony—even though this may not have been the reality.

Other factors that were taken into consideration did not seem to have any clear trends towards demonstrating explanatory value except for one—the policy makers personal view of race relations in Madison. Because there was no variance among the personal political affiliations reported by respondents, it was not possible to determine with any degree of confidence if this variable had any impact. With regards to constituency size, there was variance present, but there was no clear pattern of policy adoption as explained by the size of the policy maker's constituency. Lastly, the personal view about race relations in Madison that was held by the policymaker appeared to have some connection with policy adoption by these respondents. Of the six respondents who indicated task force recommendations were adopted, only one felt that race relations in Madison was "less than troubling (survey response)." This respondent did not feel race relations in Madison to be a pressing issue, yet his department adopted task force recommended policies. The respondent who indicated that she felt race relations in Madison were "troubled and challenged," indicated that the task force recommendations were considered but not adopted due to their lack of feasibility. These findings demonstrated that in cases where policy makers viewed race relations in Madison to be a serious matter and affecting their organization directly, their departments usually adopted task force recommendations. However, in cases where policy makers were forced to balance concerns of policy feasibility and their personal views on race relations, the evidence points to the likelihood that concerns of the potential effects of the policy on the organization trumped personal views on race relations.

In cases such as Madison, where the task force was bipartisan in its membership composition, it was argued that local level policymakers would more adopt task force recommendations. The case of Madison illustrated a task force that was bipartisan in its membership composition. Although it was found that local level actors adopted task force recommendations, survey respondents provided no information that allowed for discussion of the explanatory power of this variable. Task force members gave no indication as to whether the partisan nature of the task force had any impact on whether they adopted recommended policies. It was found that in order to make any conclusions regarding the importance of this variable in explaining policy adoption by local level officials, such findings had to be compared across all three cases.

The contention was made that where task forces members were influential, local level officials would adopt more task force recommendations. In the case of Madison, survey respondents provided no indication that the task force was or was not influential in their adoption of policies. Task force members gave no response as to whether they adopted recommended policies as a result of the influence of task force members or if they adopted such policies for other reasons. These findings suggested that, although it could not be stated with any certainty, task force members did not hold a level of influence in influencing whether policymakers adopted task force recommendations. In addition, it was stated that to make any conclusions regarding the importance of this variable in explaining policy adoption by local level officials, this finding had to be compared across all three cases.

The city of Madison was said to illustrate a case where the level of racial threat by blacks was very low. The city was found to be only 4% black—thus it had the lowest level of racial threat of my three cases. The finding that six of nine (66%) local level officials in Madison who participated in this study actually adopted task force recommended policies was an important discovery for measurement of policy innovation. This early finding indicated that a low level of racial threat may have been connected to the likelihood local governmental and nongovernmental actors adopted task force recommendations.

It was noted that to make any conclusions regarding the importance of level of racial threat in explaining policy adoption by local level officials, this finding had to be compared across all three cases.

Finally, I found that the city of Madison officially adopted all of the task force's recommendations. This was the first step in exerting a level of control of political actors, and to a lesser degree nongovernmental actors, in order to ensure task force recommendations were actually adopted in their respective organizations. I found that the city of Madison made a requirement that all city agencies (most prominently, the EOC) and administrative heads give reports on the progress they were making in the implementation of the task force recommendations. In addition, the requirement that any funds to be used for implementation of the recommendations must be approved by the Common Council was another important feature of political control used by the city.

The next chapter, Chapter Five, is a case study of the Columbia Mayor's Race Relations Task Force. This case moves my discussion one step closer towards a cross-case examination that will allow for a thorough analysis of each the four major contentions. In Chapter Five, I give a brief background of the city of Columbia, an analysis of the impetus behind its creation of the mayor's race relations task force, and the dynamics of the task force itself. Finally, I analyze the findings relative to the surveys and interviews conducted.

Bibliography

Blake, C. N. (1998). If All the World Were Madison, Winsconsin." [Electronic Version] from http://www.culturefront.org/culturefront/magazine/98/fall/article.21.html.

Buhle, P. (Ed.). (1990). *History and the New Left: Madison, Wisconsin, 1950-1970.* Philadelphia: Temple University Press.

Campbell, G., and Martell, C. (1999). *Insider's Guide to Madison, Wisconsin* (3rd ed.): Globe Peguot Press.

Channel 3000.com News. (1999, March 30). Bauman vs. Parks: In Their Own Words. from http://www.channel3000.com/news/stories/news-990330-133026.html

City of Madison, WI. (2001). Welcome to the Official City of Madison, WI website. Retrieved May 1, 2001, from www.cityofmadison.com

Elazar, D. J., Gray, V., and Spano, W. (1999). *Minnesota Politics and Government (Politics and Governments of the American States).* Lincoln, NE: University of Nebraska Press.

Epstein, L. D. (1958). *Politics in Wisconsin.* Madison: University of Wisconsin Press.

Johnson, R. T. (1964). *Robert M. La Follette, Jr. and the Decline of the Progressive Party in Wisconsin.* Madison: State Historical Society of Wisconsin.

Krieger, J. (Ed.). (1993). *The Oxford Companion to Politics of the World.* New York: Oxford University Press.

Marguiles, H. F. (1968). *The Decline of the Progressive Movement in Wisconsin 1890-1920.* Madison, WI: State Historical Society of Wisconsin.

Miller, J. E. (1982). *Governor Philip F. La Follette, the Wisconsin Progressives, and the New Deal.* Columbia, MO: University of Missouri.

Moe, T. (1984). The New Economics of Organizations. *American Journal of Political Science, 28*(4), 739-777.

Nichols, J. (2001, September 14). Politics in Cities Across U.S. Take a Left Turn. *Common Dreams Newscenter,* from http://www.commondreams.org/views/060100.102.htm

Niskanen, W. (1971). *Bureaucracy and Representative Government.* Chicago: Aldine.

Stein, R. M. (1990). The Budgetary Effects of Municipal Service Contracting: A Principal-Agent Explanation. *American Journal of Political Science, 34*(2), 471-502.

Task Force on Race Relations. (1999). *Improving Race Relations in the Greater Madison Area: Final Report.* Madison, WI.

Unger, N. C. (2000). *Fighting Bob La Follette: The Righteous Reformer.* Chapel Hill, NC: University of North Carolina Press.

United States Census Bureau. (1990). *Census Data.*

Weingast, B. R. (1984). The Congressional Bureaucratic System: A Principal-Agent Perspective (with applications to the SEC). *Public Choice, 44*(1), 147-191.

Wood, B. D. (1988). Principals, Bureaucrats, and Responsiveness in Clean Air Enforcements. *American Political Science Review, 82*(1), 213-234.

Chapter Five: Columbia, Missouri Mayor's Race Relations Task Force

This chapter is a case-study analysis of the city of Columbia's Mayor's Race Relations Task Force. In this chapter, I provide a brief background of Columbia as well as the city's impetus behind the creation of its race relations task force. In doing so, special attention is paid to the major environmental shocks that serve as a catalyst for innovation by city officials and nongovernmental actors. The context of the discussion includes elaboration of the findings from the data generated by surveys and interviews. In this chapter, I also discuss findings specific to the major questions and contentions presented in this book. In this chapter, I find that two main factors best explain why local level policymakers in Columbia adopt fewer task force recommendation that those in Madison: 1) the political culture of Columbia, and 2) the lack of identification of an environmental shock. With the discovery of the importance of oversight in the case of Madison, I also investigate the role oversight in the adoption of the recommendations in Columbia. I find that there was a lack of oversight by the city, which may have consequently led to a lower level of policy adoption in Columbia.

City Background: Columbia, Missouri

The city of Columbia is the seat of state government for Boone County, Missouri. With a population around 70,000, Columbia is the home of the University of Missouri, and is a growing Midwestern city. The city is not a typical small, Mid-America town. Columbia is often noted for being one of America's best towns to live in (City of Columbia, 2001a). The city has a relatively low crime rate, low cost of living, a high number of college graduates per capita, and a high number of physicians per capita. Columbia provides the advantages that a college town has to offer, yet has a range of cultural and leisure opportunities not usually found in a small, Midwestern city.

In many respects, the lion's share of industry and commerce in Columbia emanates from the University of Missouri. Medical and insurance services also play a large role in the city's economy. According to Missouri politics scholar, David Luethold, maintaining the stability and livelihood of the university, as well as promoting economic growth and development, drives the political scene in the city (D. Luethold, Interview, January 1, 2002). In many respects, Columbia can be thought of a Madison in the making. Both cities are home to large public universities and have economies that are highly dependent upon services offered by their universities.

Columbia and Boone County have become Democratic Party strongholds—but not with the same level of consistency in support for the party as in Madison and Dane County (D. Luethold, Interview, January 1, 2002). Although there has not been a literature written on the politics on Columbia, there is a body of evidence to support this claim. Evidence from analysis of presidential election voting patterns in Boone County since 1980 supports this contention. Historically, voters in Boone County and Columbia have cast their ballots for Democratic Party candidates. One noticeable exception is the 1984 presidential race, in which Republican candidate Ronald Reagan won Boone County. Part of the explanation behind why a Republican like Ronald Reagan could win a traditionally pro-Democratic locale like Boone County stems from the "multi-polar" ideological structure that has evolved within the local party structure—particularly the diffuse interests of those affiliated with the Democratic Party (H. Tillema, Interview, December 17, 2001).

Political analysts and scholars, such as Herb Tillema, have found that the Democratic Party in Columbia and Boone County has grown into a party of individuals from quite diffuse ideological backgrounds. According to Tillema, the Democratic Party in Boone County has grown to include a class of liberal, young professionals from the city of Columbia and a larger class of traditionalist Democrats from the county "not quite different from Republicans . . . more like traditional dixiecrats . . . "(H. Tillema, Interview, December 17, 2001). The Democratic Party leadership in Columbia has stressed "yellow dog Democrat days" to keep the term alive and use it for the advantage of the party (H. Tillema, Interview, December 17, 2001). The difficulty for the liberal Democrats in Columbia has become putting aside the ideological differences between the Democrats in the city proper and those in the county. According to Tillema, "successful Democratic candidates have been those that appealed to the conservatives and the liberals. Successful candidates have come to realize that the traditional dixiecrats are socially conservative on race . . . as long as you do not place emphasis on race, gun control, abortion, and raising taxes, you can oppose social regulation of all areas of control" (H. Tillema, Interview, December 17, 2001).

Other scholars support the contention that the politics of Columbia and Boone County intermingle to create a unique political landscape. According to Missouri state politics scholar, Richard J. Hardy, the political landscape in Columbia has an eclectic mixture of traditionalistic and moralistic cultures

(Hardy, Interview, August 12, 2001). In addition to Hardy, Luethold argues that the older governing coalitions in Columbia have begun to face a new challenge to their power (D. Luethold, Interview, January 1, 2001). A small class of white-collar workers who are highly active in politics and affiliated with the university, local hospitals, and the insurance industry has begun to increase in size and pose a secondary voice in the politics of the city (R.J. Hardy, Interview, August 12, 2001, D. Luethold, Interview, January 1, 2002). These individuals, according to Luethold, are "new to the city and don't have the same ties to local politics as people who have lived in Columbia a long time. These people are not as strong cadre party supporters . . . they are more likely to be switch-ticket voters" (D. Luethold, Interview, January 1, 2001). As a matter of fact, Luethold finds empirical evidence that Columbia is more likely to have switch-ticket voters than most locales in the entire state of Missouri (D. Luethold, Interview, January 1, 2002).

The liberal philosophies of the newer class of political actors in Columbia, as compared to that of the older power structure, are quite different. The new camp has advocated philosophies similar to that of the social liberals in Madison. Like their counterparts in Wisconsin, these actors in Columbia have been more sensitive to social mores about race, gender, and social welfare. They have also been more likely to abandon traditional political ties and special party loyalties if such changes were thought to be for the betterment of public goals (D. Luethold, Interview, January 1, 2002). In many respects, a division between these two groups has evolved over time with the white collar, university, medical, and insurance affiliated groups disassociating themselves from the older Democrats (R.J. Hardy, Interview, August 12, 2001, H. Tillema, Interview, December 17, 2001). In general, the evolutionary process the city has undergone in its social capital has caused the exacerbation of this rift and change in power structure.

Columbia's political culture, over time, is becoming ever so slightly more moralistic due to the influx of a new breed of social capital moving to the city (R.J. Hardy, Interview, August 12, 2001.) These individuals are more affluent, more educated, and more open to different viewpoints. Consequently, the politics of innovation Columbia is interwoven in the evolutionary process the city is experiencing in its social and political culture and the maintenance of the traditional power structure by older Democrats hesitant to relinquish political power to new blood. The politics of innovation in Columbia are also affected by the desire of a small number of actors in the city's governing, social, and economic institutions to move the city away from the old school way of politics towards becoming a more progressive and liberally moral town. Whereas Madison claims to have arrived at this status, the city of Columbia is still seeking to achieve this level of notoriety. As such, Columbia is at a crossroads in the life of the city with respect to its political culture.

There are a small number of actors in Columbia who are trying to move the city away from the traditionalistic philosophies and power structures that have long dominated the town. The creation of the Columbia race relation's task force by Mayor Darwin Hindman is one piece of evidence to support this argument. Actors such as Mayor Hindman desire to promote a culture that is rooted in more moralistic ideals. Indeed the literature finds that public officials in communities that promote more moralistic ideals "will themselves seek to initiate new government activities in an effort to come to grips with problems as yet unperceived by a majority of the citizenry" (1999). This type of philosophy may have been part of the reality behind Columbia mayor Darwin Hindman's creation of a race relations task force. This contention, however, will be evaluated in the next section.

Summary of the Context of Politics in Columbia and Implications for Innovation

Whereas the politics of innovation in Madison are centered on fostering the city's image, the politics of innovation in Columbia are centered on a small number of actors in the city's economic, social, and governing institutions who are trying to create a new direction and new image for the city—an image more consistent with a liberal moralistic culture. In Madison, the possibilities for innovation in racial policies are higher than in Columbia because there is greater community articulation and belief in the notion that the town is liberal and moralistic. Consequently, local actors in Madison would be more expeditious in adopting policies that buttress this perceived reality. A division in the community about the importance of developing an image that the city is progressive and morally liberal, however, limits the possibilities for race-based innovations in Columbia. Consequently, potential shocks to the city's environment will not have the same effect on all local governmental and nongovernmental organizations. There will be those actors who feel the shocks effect the city's environment and will adopt policies in an effort to help create a new image for the city. There will also be a significantly large number of individuals (much larger than in Madison) who are not concerned with or agree about the direction the city's image should take and will not adopt policies addressed at resolving the environmental shock.

The Impetus Behind the Columbia Mayor's Race Relations Task Force

The Columbia mayor's race relations task force was created by Mayor Darwin Hindman under a cloud of suspicion. The mayor, on one hand, argued he created the task force to determine the history and current status of race relations in Columbia. He claimed that he had a genuine interest in studying race relations in an effort to make the city a better place for all its residents (Mayor's Columbia Race Relations Task Force, 1996). On the other hand, many locals felt the mayor was prompted to create the task force because the city had been recently affected by a number of events that were tarnishing the image he was trying to build for the city. Many actors in the city alleged that a confrontation involving a young female and the Columbia police department was the shock that led to the creation of the task force. Others alleged that a melee at a local black-owned establishment, Lou's Palace, where the Columbia police department was also involved led the mayor to create the task force. Interestingly, both of these events were quite similar to the events that took place in Madison. In addition, both cities ultimately created race relations task forces. The key difference, however, was that the shocks were recognized in Madison by the city's governing, social, and economic institutions as well as had noticeable effects on the environment of the city and its institutions. In Columbia, on the other hand, there was no formal recognition that these events led to the creation of the task force or that they had marked effects on the environment of the city and its institutions. In addition, local level governmental and nongovernmental policymakers, in general, did not indicate they noticed any effects of the events on their organization's environment.

Although both of these events in Columbia occurred prior to the creation of the task force, the mayor did not confirm that either of them were the catalyst for his creation of the task force. In an interview with Mayor Hindman, he reported that his impetus behind creating the task force stemmed from his feeling that "there was a considerable need for the task force . . . . there was something (in Columbia) that was not being tended to" (D. Hindman, Interview, March 28, 2001). Mayor Hindman argued, "no particular event sparked the creation of the task force, but a lot of people thought that there was some event that did. Some people alleged that it was an event involving the daughter of Mary Ratliff, but no, at the time I was working on it, it was not the Mary Ratliff daughter incident." The mayor also stated, "there were other people that alleged it to have something to do with an arrest at a bar called Lou's Palace. That is the event most people attribute it to. However, in reality, it was something that I wanted to do" (D. Hindman, Interview, March 28, 2001).

The case of Columbia is quite interesting in that under the surface, there appears to be some type of disruption to the city's environment that acted as a catalyst for the creation of the task force. According to one task force member, the mayor indicated before these two events occurred that he wanted to create such a task force. However, after these two incidents transpired, they may have led the mayor to take on a sense of urgency about creating the task force (survey response). The mayor, on the other hand, clearly denies that these two events actually led him to create the task force. He claims that the seed for the task force had already been planted by the time these two events took place.

Although this may be the case, these two events seemed to have spurred the mayor into action. Had these two events not taken place during the time frame when the mayor was contemplating creating the task force, it is doubtful that the group would have come to be created as soon as it was. This is not to say, however, that at some point in time the task force would not have come to fruition. But in reality, the two disruptions gave a sense of urgency, and perhaps legitimacy, to the creation of the task force—perhaps more so than it would have received if nothing had occurred.

The importance of these events for race-based innovations in Columbia cannot be overemphasized. In the case of Columbia, it could play out that focusing community attention on these two events and how detrimental such tensions could be for the city would have been in the best interest of Mayor Hindman if he truly wished to influence local level actors to adopt task force recommended policies. This contention is made by again turning to Elazar's analysis of politics in traditional political cultures. Elazar (Elazar et al., 1999) finds that change indicative in innovative policies may be hard to come by in communities with cultures such as Columbia. According to Elazar, political leaders in communities with traditionalistic political cultures, "play conservative and custodial rather than initiatory roles *unless pressed strongly from the outside* (emphasis added). Good government in [traditional] political culture involves the maintenance and encouragement of traditional patterns and, if necessary, their adjustment to changing conditions with the least possible upset" (Elazar et al., 1999). Implicit in Elazar's argument is that change in cities with such cultures is anything but innovative; change is slow and piecemeal—if at all. Only in cases where strongly pressed from the outside (perhaps by some environmental shock) would we expect to see policy adoptions that are changes from the status quo.

The Dynamics of the Columbia Mayor's Race Relations Task Force

The Columbia mayor's race relations task force was created on February 22, 1996 by Council Bill No. R 33-96. On February 28, 1996, the task force held its first meeting. The task force consisted of 30 members who were selected by Mayor Hindman. In staffing the task force, the mayor selected many of the members on his own inclination. Many of these individuals were people that the mayor knew and respected for their political activism, academic and professional background, and/or professional affiliations. Others were citizens nominated by individuals in the community or those who submitted their own names for candidacy to serve on the task force. The mayor subsequently contacted these people and inquired into their interest to serve. Some of these individuals declined participation while others chose to serve. From surveying task force members (see Table 5:1), I found that the task force included, among other participants, two university professors, an insurance agent, a minister, an employee of a state civil rights department, a university program director, and employee of the city Parks and Recreation Department. Mayor Hindman's process of selecting task force participants resulted in the selection of members whose professional affiliations were quite different from each other. The task force clearly was not composed of a group of individuals from the same level of professional and academic training.

Table 5:1

Columbia Mayor's Race Relations Task Force
Select Task Force Member's Profiles and Selected Responses

- Gender

5 Male
2 Female

- Political Affiliation

3 Democrat
1 Nonpartisan
1 Liberal
2 Moderate Republican
1 Non-Identifier

- Motivation to Serve on the Task Force

5 Asked by the mayor
1 Recommended to the mayor as a candidate
1 Civic Duty

- Expertise/Background

5 Professional/Academic Background
2 Personal Experiences

From surveying task force participants, I found that member's political affiliations ranged from moderate Democrat, nonpartisan liberal leaner, socially liberal, liberal democrat to moderate Republican. One task force member responded she was a "Republicrat . . . owing no allegiance to either party" (survey response). From the responses provided, the task force appeared to have a slight bend towards the liberal side in its membership composition—more so than the Madison task force. There was a level of variance in the party affiliations reported by task force members; however, the variance was not large. At best, the Columbia task force had a slightly bipartisan membership composition. From assessing the task force's full roster and utilizing my knowledge of the political and professional affiliations of most its members, it was more evident that the task force was largely made up of academic and professionals who were liberals. This discovery was quite interesting and in line with the contention made earlier in this chapter that many of the political leaders in the governing and social institutions of Columbia were trying to move the city towards becoming more of a progressive and liberal town. These findings concerning the political affiliations of the task force's membership support this contention—at least with regards to the office of the mayor. The staffing of a task force with mostly liberals demonstrates that Mayor Hindman had hoped to produce task force recommendations that had liberal overtones.

The data reveal that members of the Columbia task force included men, as well as women that were of African American and Caucasian American background. Noticeably absent from this group were Latinos, Asians, and other groups. This was not the case with the Madison task force. The Madison task force included individuals of various racial backgrounds. I thought perhaps that a more in-depth assessment of the Columbia task force's membership roster would reveal representation by other racial groups. However, from examining the task force's final report, as well as reading one task force member's survey response, I found that there were no other racial groups represented other than blacks and whites. The finding that the task force was composed of only blacks and whites could have something to do with Columbia not being a very diverse town. However, as one task force member noted, the mayor's focus in creating the task force was on black and white relations—not other racial and ethnic groups.

The importance of the power to nominate task force members was outlined in Chapter Three. I noted that I was interested in examining what type of role the mayor, city council, and other political principals played in the process of staffing the task force. When nominating individuals to serve on the task force, Mayor Hindman reported that he "effectively had sole discretion in selecting task force participants . . . . at best, the approval by the city council was a formality . . . it may have been the case that I had absolute sole discretion . . . people made applications, but people did not have to do that" (D. Hindman, Interview, March 28, 2001). The mayor indicated that he solicited various people to serve and the city council was only peripherally involved in the nominations. The mayor reported that he "really much put it (the task force) together by himself" (D. Hindman, Interview, March 28, 2001). He noted that it was possible that he asked the city council for input, but did not remember.

According to the mayor, in trying to design the task force and how it would work, the city was "plowing deep ground" (D. Hindman, Interview, March 28, 2001). Although this type of task force was a new endeavor for the city, Mayor Hindman noted that there was a predecessor that influenced the Columbia task force. Mayor Hindman reported, "we went and met with Mayor Cleaver (of Kansas City) . . . in Kansas City, they had already finished theirs (race relations task force). We met with him and the president of the Urban League and picked up some ideas" (D. Hindman, Interview, March 28, 2001). Mayor Hindman noted that he went about staffing the task force differently than how the mayor of Kansas City went about staffing his task force. According to Mayor Hindman, "we didn't do it in the same way . . . they (Kansas City) had a lot more people. We went about it in a different way" (D. Hindman, Interview, March 28, 2001).

Mayor Hindman reported that he wanted to pick people to represent different sects of the community. He felt it was important to do so because "as with every city commission, it does not work to appoint people who come from one point of view. They will parrot that one view . . . you need a system where people will bounce back ideas and test them . . . we are interested in a positive result" (D. Hindman, Interview, March 28, 2001). As far the political philosophies the mayor was looking for in members, he indicated that he did not want individuals who espoused views on the extremes of the political spectrum.

The contention was presented in Chapter Three that mayors would select task force members that they felt would have credibility and legitimacy in the eyes of local policy makers. This position was supported by the responses given by Mayor Hindman. According to Mayor Hindman, he was concerned about the perception local level officials would have about the task force members. He felt that if he had "picked people that other people could respect, they tend to respect the task force as a whole. This does not mean blue ribbon . . . just good people" (D. Hindman, Interview, March 28, 2001). The mayor said that he felt that this would lead to a greater likelihood of people adopting their recommendations. He hoped "that some bureaucrat would not just say 'oh, these are elected officials—I'm not going to pay attention, etc. (D. Hindman, Interview, March 28, 2001)."

There was a noticeable difference in the positions by Mayor Bauman and Mayor Hindman with regards to whether they felt local level officials would be concerned about the political agendas of the mayors in creating the task force and the credibility of task force appointees. Whereas Mayor Bauman reported that she was not influenced by what local level actors in Madison might think of her appointments, Mayor Hindman indicated that he was indeed concerned about what local officials in Columbia would think about his appointees.

Assuming Mayor Bauman and Mayor Hindman were expressing complete openness in their replies, one possible explanation for these finding points back to political culture. In cities with political cultures such as Madison, scholars have noted there to be typically less corruption in government and "less tolerance of those actions that are considered corrupt, so politics does not have the taint it so often bears in the individualistic environment" (Elazar et al., 1999). Perhaps in the city of Madison, there is more of an atmosphere of trust and integrity in the city's social and governing institutions. Thus, city constituents are less likely to be suspicious of policymaker's agendas. On the other hand, "traditionalistic political cultures tend to be anti-bureaucratic" (Elazar et al., 1999). It could be that Mayor Hindman is aware that local officials are not typically responsive to government-sponsored recommendations and actions. Thus, he would have to be much more careful about protecting the image of his task force than would Mayor Bauman with her task force.

One other possible explanation for why these mayors had different opinions on the importance of the credibility of their task force appointees stems from the process under which members were selected to serve. The contention was set forth that task forces staffed under a single-institutional construct would result in the selection of participants who shared similar political philosophies as the appointing principal. In Columbia, although the city council placed the legal seal of approval on the task force, they played no role in the selection of its members. In the case of Columbia, local level actors might have scrutinized mayoral appointments more closely due to the mayor's sole discretion in staffing the task force. It could have been the case that Mayor Hindman was aware of this possibility—despite the fact that he made no mention of it.

As evidenced by the case of Columbia, task forces staffed under a single-institutional construct can lead to the creation of task forces in which the political ideologies espoused by its members closely resembles that of the personal political philosophies of the appointing principal. This finding was consistent with principal-agent models. A liberal himself, Mayor Hindman created a task force with an ideological bend towards the left end of the political spectrum. The mayor admitted that he effectively had the sole discretion to select the task force's members. He also indicated that the city council was only peripherally involved. He stated, "I really pretty much put it together by myself" (D. Hindman, Interview, March 28, 2001). Interestingly, the mayor said that he wanted to select people who represented different sects (sic) of the community. He wanted individuals in academia, business, the working class, social leaders, and those in education. The mayor did not, however, report that he wanted individuals from a cross-section of ethnic or political backgrounds.

Task force members were asked a number of questions in order to generate data concerning different facets of the dynamics of race relations task forces. In the case of Columbia, seven of 15 task force members to whom I sent surveys responded. This represents a return rate of 48%. From assessing survey responses of task force members, I found that participants brought with them a diverse range of factors that motivated them to serve. In addition, I found that task force participants came to the force with varied training that they felt made them well suited to serve on the task force (recall Table 3).

The members of the Columbia task force provided insight into the general characteristics task force members bring with them to their job. With regards to factors that motivated the members to serve, the responses were similar to those in the case of Madison. Two Columbia task force members, both African American, reported they were motivated to serve because they held a degree of sensitivity to the issue of race relations. One of these members, a minister, noted that given his experiences with race relations in a more openly racial intolerant town in the South, he wanted the opportunity to investigate and compare the degree of racial hostility in Columbia to that of his hometown. The other member, a state equal rights agency employee, saw serving on the task force as a chance to promote racial harmony (survey responses).

Task force members also reported that they were motivated to serve due to the mayor requesting their participation. It was noted earlier that the mayor contacted some task force members on his own inclination. There were also those members who were initially recommended to the mayor and the mayor subsequently contacted these candidates to inquire about their desire to serve. Five task force members reported that they came to serve because the mayor made contact with them about serving. One source stated that he was first recommended to the mayor and subsequently contacted and asked to serve (survey responses). These responses provided me insight into some of the explicit reasons why task force members decided to serve on the force. Implicit in these task force members agreeing to serve upon the request of the mayor, however, could also be that the members held a sense of civic duty. Indeed, one task force participant noted that his civic mindedness was one of the reasons he agreed to serve on the task force. It also could have been the case that these members saw serving on the task force as a chance to participate in the political process, give back to the community, and/or engage in a dialogue with their fellow Columbia citizens.

The findings in this case regarding why citizens are motivated to serve on task explicitly and implicitly support the contention made in the previous chapter on the Madison task force. In that chapter, I note that among the motivating factors task force members cite for participating in the task force include personal attachment to the issue, civic-mindedness, social-awareness, and a desire to engage in social dialogue. The members of the Columbia task force provide similar reasons for why they agree to serve on their community's task force. Columbia task force members cite personal engagement to racial issues, personal desire to help improve the community, and civic-duty as their impetus behind serving on the force.

The argument that task force participants have some type of special training or background that makes them particularly well suited to serve on such forces was presented in Chapter Three. Task force participants were asked to cite reasons they felt made them adept at serving on the Columbia race relation's task force. One member reported that his academic background and research interests in the area of civil rights made him knowledgeable on the issue of race relations. This member, who was a university professor, also felt that having run for public office made him more aware of people's needs (survey response). One task force member, an employee of the state's equal opportunity agency, stated that he was particularly well suited to serve on the task force given his professional affiliation. This member had 23 years experience in civil rights enforcement. He also felt that his college years as an activist and serving in the military made him adept to serve on the force (survey response).

One interesting response came from one source that was an insurance agent. This member felt that having spent "forty-five years of being black" made him an "expert" on the issue of race relations (survey response). This individual obviously based his level of expertise on the issue of race relations through his cultural experiences throughout his lifetime. Only one respondent reported that they did not feel as though they had any special training or qualifications to serve on the force. This member felt that he did not have any particular training or background that made him well suited to serve on the task force. This source felt that no types of special skills were needed to serve on the task force other than the willingness to listen and learn (survey response). As with the case of Madison, however, task force participants in Columbia generally reported they felt that had some type of background or training that made them a good choice to serve on the task force. The responses provided by the task force participants indicate that they do have a level of training, knowledge, and/or experience proportionate with that necessary to serve on such a task force.

The data in this case with regards to task force member's background and training support the findings made in the previous chapter on Madison. I find in Chapter Four that Madison task force members feel that they have some type of special training or background that makes them particularly well suited to serve on a race relations task force. From assessing the backgrounds task force members in Columbia cited as evidence of the suitability for serving on a race relations task force, I find more support for the position that that race relations task forces have an eclectic mixture of individuals with varying degrees of backgrounds and trainings—some of which are more closely associated with experience and knowledge of race related issues than others. In having this type of diversity, the task force does not achieve the level of status associated with being blue ribbon. Nevertheless, such task forces have a fair representation of individuals whose backgrounds are commensurate with the level of specialization necessary to effectively and efficiently study the issue of race relations.

The position that task forces were often created as the result of an environmental shock was presented throughout this book. This was found to be the case in Madison. Shocks were manifested in Madison by their recognition in the city's governing, social, and economic institutions, as well as the noticeable effects of the shocks on the environment of the city and its institutions. In Columbia, on the other hand, there was no formal recognition that these events were affecting the city or even that they lead to the creation of the task force (according to responses provided by Mayor Hindman and other city leaders in the surveys I collected). In addition, there were no marked effects on the environment of the city and its institutions (according to responses provided by the Columbia Police Department and other governmental, civic and business leaders in the surveys I collected). For these reasons, Columbia was said to represent a case where it was not evident that an environmental shock existed. However, from analysis of the events surrounding the creation of the task force, underlying racial tensions in the city were found to be present. Because of this, I wanted to further probe the possibility that the events might have had an effect on the creation of the Columbia task force. As such, I probed task force members about their intuition about why the mayor might have created the task force.

In surveying task force members, I wanted to know if there might have been any agendas the mayor was promoting in creating this task force. In essence, I wanted to know if there was anything that he was not revealing about what could have prompted him to create the force. To address this, I utilized two methods. First, I investigated Mayor Hindman's campaign speeches and state of the city addresses. My analysis of these documents revealed that the mayor did not use the task force very much in his dialogue with the public and the media. I did not find a single mention of the task force in the State of the City statements (City of Columbia, 1996, 1997, 1998, 1999, 2000, 2001b). Part of the reason for this could have been that in Columbia, the City Manager, Raymond A. Beck, was responsible for formal presentation of the State of the City statements. In addition, only once did I find evidence of where the mayor mentioned the task force in a campaign speech. It should be noted that on many occasions, Mayor Hindman ran unopposed. Consequently, he did not have the same level of pressure placed upon him (as did Mayor Bauman) to utilize various accomplishments of his (e.g., the task force) in an effort to win reelection.

The second method of discovery I implemented towards probing this contention was to ask the task force participants to elaborate on why *they* felt the mayor created the task force. Two task force members indicated that they felt the mayor's reason for creating the task force was out of his genuine interest to see race relations improve in Columbia. One of these members also added that the mayor had mentioned during his campaign for office that he wanted to evaluate race relations in Columbia. This was quite some time before the aforementioned events had transpired. A source felt that the mayor created the task force because is was "aware of Columbia's problems and willing to work at them" (survey response). She also felt that the Columbia Police Department had problems long before and after the situation with [Mary Ratliff's] child . . . the task force idea had been talked about way before that dumb incident!" (survey response). This respondent noted that many incidents prior to the commissioning of the task force in the city were a result of problems with the Columbia Police Department.

Task force respondents in this case, however, also responded that a number of events centered upon race relations problems (in their opinion) was the reason why Mayor Hindman created the task force. One source noted that the events regarding the Columbia police's confrontation with a local youth and Lou's Palace may have spurred the mayor into action. This respondent also reported that the mayor's desire to see a community recreation center be built in the center may have prompted him to create the task force. Two task force members both reported that the aforementioned events likely had something to do with the mayor creation the task force. They felt the mayor may have had some genuine interest to address race relations in Columbia, but the disruptions likely affected his level of dedication to creating the force. In addition, one respondent felt that incidents with [a local department store], a [local black business proprietor] and the Columbia Police Department prompted the mayor to create the task force. These responses were quite different from those of the respondents who felt the mayor created the task force out of a genuine interest to study the problem of race relations.

The interview responses indicated that the creation of the race relations task force in Columbia had, in part, something to do with the mayor's own interest in examining race relations in Columbia. However, the responses also indicated that events involving a local youth, an African American business establishment and the Columbia police department could have acted as a catalyst for the creation of the task force. It is conceivable that Mayor Hindman saw a potential crisis arising and decided to create the task force to circumvent its occurrence. While his interview responses did not reveal that this was his motivation, this notion was not dismissed given the responses provided by task force participants.

In this book, I argue that innovation is related to the existence of an environmental shock. Recalling the earlier discussion of political culture, Elazar (Elazar et al., 1999) finds that political leaders in traditionalistic cultures seek to initiate new government activities in an effort to address problems *not yet perceived by a majority of the citizenry* (emphasis added). In the case of Columbia, I surmise that Mayor Hindman likely felt that building a new image for the city of Columbia would be undermined if such events continued to occur and be magnified. I also suggest that Mayor Hindman perceived that the events could effect the city's environment if he did not move quickly to address its smoldering racial tensions. However, I also argue that a majority of other key policy makers in the city of Columbia do not hold the same perception about the effects on the events on their internal or external organizational environments as a result of these events. Consequently, the possibilities for innovation in the city of Columbia are limited by a lack of a larger community feeling that race relations in the city are volatile.

Assessment of the Work of the Columbia Mayor's Race Relations Task Force

Mayor Hindman charged the task force with determining the history and current status of race relations in Columbia. He noted that in the city of Columbia, up until the 1960s, African Americans were not permitted to enter the Missouri Theater through the front entrance. Blacks had to enter the facility through a back entrance. According to the mayor, it was with the door in mind that the optimism for change in the community that the task force pursued its duties. In order to accomplish their responsibilities, the task force took several steps. At the outset, the force saw a need for an open discussion of race relations in Columbia. To accomplish this, the force circulated over 5,000 surveys at more than 60 locations and events, including publication of surveys in two local newspapers—the Columbia Missourian and the Columbia Daily Tribune. The response level was high, with over 3,000 written responses to the surveys being generated, including several hundred letters (Mayor's Columbia Race Relations Task Force, 1996).

The Columbia task force held a wide range of personal dialogues with the public, including phone calls to task force member's homes, contacts on the streets, and other one-on-one discussions. Consultation was made with a wide range of local public and civic officials, including a Boone County Circuit Court Judge, the Police Officers Association, the Black Police Officers Association, the Chief of the Columbia Police Department, various religious leaders, the mayor of Kansas City, and members of the Kansas City race relations task force. The task force also conducted and participated in group discussions and dialogues at various community events, including an NAACP dinner, a public forum at Earth Day, and Martin Luther King Memorial.

With regard to the work of the task force, the group divided itself into nine subject areas. Each subject area assessed the pulse of the community with regards to their own particular subject area. This process was carried out over the month of April. Upon their completion, each of the subject areas met once again and added a media subject area and combined community service with recreation. The groups then engaged in dialogue within their respective areas. This process was completed in May, and in June, the task force finalized their reports. In issuing their final report, the task force was careful to note that the sum of the parts (the final report) did not necessarily reflect the opinions and thoughts of all members. In other words, there was not necessarily a consensus among members with regards to the findings and recommendations. Nevertheless, the task force agreed to a number of fundamental principals and findings. The task force issued eight general findings in all. Upon the culmination of their 17-week endeavor, the task force produced a final report outlining a number of findings and recommendations.

A number of interesting similarities and differences between the work of the Madison task force and the Columbia task force stand out. First, both task forces relied heavily on public input as well as expert testimony in making their assessments and findings about the perceived reality of race relations in their respective cities. Secondly, both task force utilized a division of labor in going about fulfilling their responsibilities. In addition, both task forces also produced a final report that outlined specific findings and recommendations by policy area. There are, however, some noticeable differences between the two task forces. While it was the case that both task forces divided themselves into smaller groups to study the broad issue of race relations, the Madison task force utilized two groups that were specifically engaged in discussing a particular series of events regarding racial tension. The Columbia task force did not have any particular event to begin with as a point of departure. As such, they should have had a harder time than the Madison task force in knowing just where to start and what to investigate. Given that the Columbia task force was patterned after the Kansas City task force, however, its job was made a little easier.

In addition, the Columbia task force was larger in its membership composition than the Madison task force. This size difference, however, did not seem to have any noticeable effect on the task force to go about doing its job. Finally, the Columbia task force, unlike the Madison task force, did not have any city officials who were actual members of the task force. In Columbia, the mayor attended meetings of the task force but did not sit in on meetings in the capacity of a task force member. Given the findings in the chapter on Madison that task force members in that city felt they had complete discretion and were able to complete their tasks uninhibited, having the mayor and a council member sit on the task force likely had no effect on the task force's ability to carry out their perfunctory duties.

The contention was presented in Chapter Three that mayors and city councils might try to exert control over the recommendations task forces produce. In the case of Madison, task force members were found to have had complete discretion in going about carrying out their duties and forming their recommendations. To investigate this issue with regards to the Columbia task force, members were asked to describe and elaborate on the amount of discretion they had in completing the tasks charged to them, as well as producing final recommendations. In going about conducting their work, Columbia task force members by and large reported that they retained nearly complete discretion. One task force member noted that the group was "free to do what was needed and recommended as we saw fit" (survey response). Another member said the mayor and city council were "pretty much hands off . . . I cannot recall the mayor or city council being there until the very end" (survey response).

A response of noteworthiness was made by one of the task force members. This member said he saw little of the city council and the mayor sat in only on a few of the meetings. In general, he felt that the task force had a free hand to do what it wanted. This member did note, however, that what the mayor "did do was narrowed it (the focus of the discussion) to race (blacks). He also put a time deadline for the final report "(survey response). This task force member also responded that the mayor narrowed the discussion to race—specifically black versus white. The use of issue framing in public policy was noted to be a common practice (Baumgartner and Jones, 1993). These scholars argue that politicians attempt to frame issues in an effort to shape the way issues are discussed. It could have been the case that Mayor Hindman felt the underlying tensions in the community of Columbia centered on issues of black versus white. Perhaps he did not want the task force to stray away from this focus.

These findings support the discovery made previously in the chapter on Madison regarding task force discretion. The evidence in the case of Columbia points to the fact that task forces can and do retain a great deal of discretion in going about fulfilling their responsibilities. Even in cases where political principals, such as mayors and council members, minimally participate in the task force's discussions, members are given a large amount of discretion to complete their duties. One reason for this, especially in the case of Columbia (given the city's political culture), is that mayors and council members do not want to damage the credibility of the task forces recommendations by having its members reveal the final product was made under pressure from government institutions and is laden with political agendas. Additionally, mayors and council members, particularly in the case of Madison (and perhaps Columbia) may feel that task force members, due to their level of training and educational background, are better skilled to address the issue and make associated recommendations.

Columbia task force members who participated in this study were asked to report their personal assessment of race relations in Columbia before and after the implementation of the force. The responses were very poignant, to say the least. One task force member stated that his overall assessment was that minimal change within Columbia had occurred as a result of the task force. This member also noted that because the task force only had the power to make recommendations, their prescriptions were not legal mandates. He reported that he did not know of any recommendations that went to the city that were implemented. Those committees who issued recommendations that did not have to do with city implementation, in his perception, had more success than those that needed a city council vote. According to this source, the task force was concerned about how the recommendations would be received by the mayor, city council, agencies, and businesses that would be affected by its report. He felt that the task force was "somewhat prophetic in thinking not much would change" (survey response).

Other task force respondents reported that the major change that occurred in the city was a heightened awareness of the problems that existed in Columbia. One of these sources felt that some of Columbia's citizens had made more of an effort towards inclusion of blacks into the city's social structure. He also felt that any changes that had been made with respect to race relations had occurred because of demands by those in the city's governing and social institutions. This task force member felt the key aspect to task force recommendations being adopted was backing (emphasis added) (survey response). Task force respondents also reported that finding any changes as a direct result of the task force's work were hard to pinpoint. One task force respondent felt as though things might have gotten better, but was not sure. He noted that while the task force had not put into effect any changes in terms of local policies, he felt the task force had created a dialogue. Another task force respondent echoed this sentiment. He reported that the major difference he had notice was that the police had become more race conscious on how policing was done.

Data Analysis of Task Force Recommendations Adopted

Five major contentions were presented in Chapter Three. The underlying thesis was that policymakers in cities where an environmental shock existed would adopt more task force recommendations that would policymakers in cities where there was no environmental shock. The case of Columbia, as discussed in the previous sections, illustrated an instance where an environmental shock was not recognized to have existed. However, it was noted that a number of events could have come to serve as a shock. Because there was not articulation of the events having the effect of an environmental shock, I expected to find that local governmental and civic leaders would adopt fewer task force recommendations than policymakers in Madison.

To investigate these inquiries with respect to the case of Columbia, I surveyed a random sample of governmental and nongovernmental actors in the city of Columbia. These surveys facilitated the generation of a body of data by which policy innovation could be measured. As with the case of Madison, potential survey participants were contacted initially on February 14, 2001. I made five different follow-ups, one a month, to encourage participation of all initially contacted. After a five-month period, I decided to conclude my data collection. These efforts resulted in ten surveys being returned. This represented a return rate of 18%. Of these actors, six were government and four were non-governmental. The analysis of data generated by these surveys is presented in the next section.

Findings

The respondents in the data set included five governmental officials who worked in the city's Public Works Department, Office of Community Services, Department of Economic Development, and Columbia Police Department. One actor did not indicate his specific office, but his responses indicated that he worked with some aspect of the city's housing department. Also, one additional governmental actor included an official in Boone County government. The four nongovernmental actors who participated in the study included a realtor with a local realty company, a minister, an official with the city's Chamber of Commerce, and a member of a Democratic Party organization called Muleskinners.

Of the ten policymakers who responded, only one reported that he adopted policies recommended by the Columbia race relations task force. In addition, the one official who did adopt such a policy was the only one of these actors who reported that his office felt affected by race relations problems in Columbia (see Table 5:2). This official, who reported that he was a liberal, worked in the city's office of community service—which had as a part of its organizational responsibilities the duty to focus on equity issues with regards to the funding of social services for low-income and at risk populations. Given his office's responsibility to make policies sensitive to minorities, it was not surprising that his organization had adopted task force recommendations.

The types of policies adopted by this official are interesting to note. One policymaker reported that the city of Columbia's Human Rights Commission had focused on and/or implemented the following activities:

1. Planning for the implementation of a Community Study Circles Program,
2. Development and distribution of a packet of information on all city boards and commission's to promote diversity on these boards and commissions,
3. Revision and improvement of investigation into processes and procedures,
4. Collaboration on a community-based Fair Housing Education and Outreach Program,
5. Development of a partnership with the Columbia Public Schools' Office of Multicultural Education through the Partners in Education program,
6. Focusing on improving public relations about filing complaints of discrimination, and
7. Increasing funding for the Human Rights Investigator position and adding community education responsibilities (survey response).

When asked about the effects on race relations problems on policy adoption in his organization, this respondent indicated that his "organization has always focused on equity issues with regard to the funding of social services for low-income, at-risk populations. The organization has also always focused on race, equality, and diversity issues as a high priority (survey response)." This response led me to suspect that this policymaker, due to the nature of his job, was more actively engaged in handling issues of a race sensitive nature. Because his office was directly responsible for addressing complaints of inequitable treatment of blacks in the provision of city services, this policy maker would be more aware of racial problems in the city of Columbia. He would also have a greater propensity to adopt task force recommendations aimed ad addressing race relations.

The responses provided by the nine actors who reported they did not adopt task force recommended policies echoed many of the reasons officials in Madison provided for their not adopting task force recommendations. What is noticeably different, however, is that in the case of Madison, the majority of actors who reported they were liberals adopted task force recommendations. In Columbia, however, 8 of 10 actors reported they were closer to the Democratic/moderate Democratic end of the political spectrum—yet they did not adopt task force recommendations.

Some of the responses provided insight into reasons why these actors did not adopt task force recommendations. One policymaker, a realtor, argued that as a realtor, he served anyone who wanted to purchase a home, "regardless of their race, creed, color, marital status, etc." (survey response). In addition, this respondent felt that the "task force was uninformed about the realtor community's dedication to fair housing in the recommendations made" (survey response). The responses given by the realtor are indicative of the larger body of responses provided by local policy makers in Columbia. In general, the data revealed that local level officials in Columbia did not perceive there were race relations problem in Columbia, nor did they feel that their traditional departmental policies impacted blacks disproportionately as compared to whites. Local officials in Columbia also did not feel that the external or internal environments were threatened by any type of race relations problems in Columbia.

In response to the task force's recommendation that the city should make a concerted effort to recruit more minority owned businesses and minority workers, one source, a moderate Democrat who worked in the city's Department of Economic Development, felt that the city of Columbia "should be recruiting businesses to fill a gap in the community regardless of who owns them" (survey response). In addition, this actor refuted a task force finding regarding a lack of qualified blacks for employment positions by saying, "I've never heard any of the companies state there aren't enough qualified blacks" (survey response).

One policymaker was a member of the Democratic Party's Muleskinners organization. This political group is made up mostly of the professional class of liberals in the city of Columbia. This respondent refuted a task force finding that efforts needed to be made to increase political participation by blacks in Columbia. This respondent argued that he did not feel the city's government "should spend money on voter registration" (survey response). As a method of providing evidence that spending resources towards recruiting blacks to be political active could be wasteful and does not necessarily mean they will participate, this respondent noted that "two members of the central committee are African American, but neither are active" (survey response). He went on to say that "it is all well and good to have a cross section of the population involved in city government, but we should only have persons who are interested in serving and not just pew fillers" (survey response).

Of particular interest were responses provided by an official with the city of Columbia Police Department. As noted previously, this department had a number of confrontations that involved blacks in the city of Columbia. It was alleged by many that these events prompted Mayor Hindman to create the race relations task force. One policymaker who responded was a high ranking official in the Columbia Police Department. He noted that he was a moderate Democrat with some Republican favorites. In response to a task force recommendation arguing that the Columbia police should do a better job of informing blacks on police policies and practices, this actor said that the city's police department informed "all citizens, not just minorities" (survey response). In addition, he did not really feel that race relations in Columbia were problematic. He noted that in his personal assessment of race relations in Columbia, communication was "better that it ever was—not everybody agrees, but there [was] a dialogue" (survey response).

Table 5:2

Columbia Mayor's Race Relations Task Force
Select Local Level Policymaker's Profiles And Select Responses

- Organization/Department among Respondents/Size of Constituencies

6 Governmental
4 Nongovernmental

1 No response
3 > 60,000
6 < 15,000

- Profile of Respondents—Political Affiliation

1 No response
1 Moderate Independent
6 Moderate Democrat
1 Yellow Dog Democrat
1 Moderate Republican

- Profile of Respondents—Gender

2 Female
6 Male
1 No response

One source, a top official with the city of Columbia Chamber of Commerce and a moderate Republican, was surprisingly the only other official who felt there were problems with race relations in the city of Columbia. In response to why his department had not adopted any task force recommendations, this policymaker reported that with no minorities currently employed in his office, there were no issues internally regarding race related problems. He did not feel, however, that there was anything prohibitive in his department's policies that would not allow anyone to succeed (survey response). This actor reported that his personal assessment of race relations in Columbia was that there was "benign neglect—until some unpleasant event occurs, some people don't seem to work on the situation" (survey response). This argument made by this respondent echoed the major thesis of this paper. In essence, this policymaker agreed with the position that race conscious policies would not be adopted unless some event (an environmental shock) occurred that personally affected the environment of an organization. Clearly, in the case of Columbia, the articulation of some major shock was not present. Subsequently, local level officials did not feel any type of reverberations surrounding race related problems in the city.

One of the possible consequences of Mayor Hindman downplaying the significance of the two events that occurred in the city was that he did influence others to become aware of the environmental shock. An event does not become a significant factor until those in positions of power and decision-making in a community's governing, business, and social institutions recognize it. In the case of Madison, the mayor, common council, as well as other city agencies (especially the Madison Police Department), civic leaders, and business owners (particularly minority business owners) expressed a sense of urgency about the volatile nature of race relations in their city. In Columbia, not only did Mayor Hindman fail to place emphasis on the disruptions that took place in the city, the city council failed to do so as well. The lack of articulating the event as a shock could have the effect of downplaying the seriousness of the race relations task force and its recommendations. As the survey responses indicated, many actors in Columbia's social and business sector did not recognize an environmental shock. It was likely that a lack of articulation by the decision-making elite in the city of Columbia (with the mayor being a powerful leader in this group) that the events had affected the environment of the community, these actors did not take notice of the events either.

There are many events that have the potential to become shocks; however, they must be transformed into reality by a recognition or feeling of them. An event will not become a shock if the event does not have a marked affect on the internal environment of an organization (complaints, demands for services, etc.) In the case of Columbia, Mayor Hindman did not create a sense of crisis that could have provoked a period of punctuated equilibrium. Instead, he glossed over the seriousness of the issues. In Madison, it would be much easier to restore the city's image as a liberal and progressive town because locals and outsiders would be more likely to chalk up the events to being an anomaly. In Columbia, on the other hand, such events could have acted to foster an older, more deeply rooted image of the city. Locals and outsiders would not likely have given Columbia the benefit of the doubt that the events were uncharacteristic of the city's political culture. Consequently, political and civic leaders in Columbia would find it more important to engage in damage control to the city's image than those in Madison.

Additional Factors Assessed to Explain Policy Innovation

For assessment of other factors that could have had an impact on the policy adoption by these officials in Columbia, I measured a number of other variables. These variables included personal political stance, constituency size, and personal view on the nature of race relations in Columbia. I found that with regards to political stance, most of the respondents indicated they were liberal or moderate Democrats. Although most respondents in Columbia indicated they were Democrats, on average they tended to be more moderate than the Democrats in Madison. Noticeably, the only actor who reported he was a liberal was also the only actor who reported his department adopted task force recommendations. Just as a note, one respondent, an official in the county's government, reported that he was a "yellow dog democrat" (survey response). This official gave no responses on any of the substantive questions asked with regards to his organization's policy adoption of task force recommendations.

With regards to constituency size, one source, whose organization adopted task force recommendations, reported that the size of his department's constituency was the entire city. In general, the respondents indicated that their constituencies ranged in size from the entire city of Columbia to a small, more concentrated population. This was also the case with respondents in the case of Madison. Actors who did not adopt task force recommendations had constituencies that varied in size. One of these officials, a minister who was a moderate democrat with some nonpartisan leanings, reported that his church had six full time personnel, 8 part-time and a membership of 550 parishioners. One source reported that he was a policymaker with the Democratic Party's Muleskinners. He noted that all Democrats in Boone County made up his constituency. The finding that this actor did not adopted any task force recommendations regarding increasing minority participation in the political process was particularly interesting given that Democrats have typically be sensitive to issues regarding race. However, recalling the earlier discussion on the traditionalist political culture prevalent in the older governing coalitions of Democrats in Columbia, this finding becomes significantly less surprising.

The respondent's views on race relations in Columbia were, by and large, feelings and attitudes of disinterest and a lack of seriousness. Responses concerning race relations in Columbia ranged from the perception that things were "o.k., but could be much better," to "the problems I have seen seemed to be in the black neighborhoods" (survey responses). The respondent who reported that he was a minister said that race relations in Columbia were "in some ways good, other ways not" (survey response). He noted that churches were segregated and most low-income areas are black neighborhoods and closer to industrial areas (survey response).

Part of the explanation behind why Columbians hold such benign views on race relations in the city is that most residents do not come in contact with blacks that are not affiliated with the university, they do not travel to lower-income, black neighborhoods, nor do they have any type of social interaction with these individuals (survey response). Census data supports this contention in that it indicates Columbia is a city with housing segregated by race (United States Census Bureau, 1990). As such, most white Columbians live in their own world isolated from the problems of race relations. Outside of the problems located in the black neighborhoods, so to speak, most Columbians feel the city is the ideal place to live and raise a family—as well as retire (Mayor's Columbia Race Relations Task Force, 1996). Even though Columbia has more blacks as a percentage of the city's population than does Madison, the problems centered on race relations in Madison were much more magnified than in Columbia. The events that began to unfold were more troubling for the social, political, and business institutions in the city. Couple this with the more socially liberal and moralistic culture in Madison, the issue of race relations provokes a much more responsive attitude by the city's policy makers.

To support the argument that most Columbians do not perceive race relations to be problematic, I analyzed survey data generated by the Columbia race relations task force regarding the views of Columbia residents on the nature of race relations in the city. As discussed earlier in this chapter, the surveys consisted of 17 questions that explored attitudes and experiences. Several of the questions were deliberately phrased in a manner that could be considered hostile towards blacks. The task force did this so that they could determine the degree to which white respondents would exhibit racism by agreeing with the questions.

Respondents were 82 percent white, 13 percent black, and 5 percent other races. Six out of 10 were women. There were a range of four possible responses, but the task force collapsed these into two categories—"agree" and "disagree" (Mayor's Columbia Race Relations Task Force, 1996). The survey results indicated that most Columbians were not overtly racist and were willing to try to improve race relations. However, with regards to the perceptions of the equal treatment of blacks versus whites by many of the social, governmental, and economic institutions in Columbia, the findings proved there was clearly nothing close to a level of agreement between blacks and whites. With regards to the perceptions of equal police treatment of blacks and whites, 60% of whites agreed that both groups were treated equally, while nearly 90% of black respondents disagreed that their was equal treatment.

With regards to attitudes towards equal treatment of blacks and whites in schools and job markets, approximately 71% of whites in Columbia agreed that there was equal treatment, while 81% of blacks disagreed. Nearly 80% of white Columbians felt that white people treated blacks well while only about 47% of blacks agreed with this statement. The polemic views continue across nearly all survey questions. About 48% of whites in Columbia agreed discrimination against blacks was not a problem while nearly 82% of blacks disagreed. Lastly, 50% of white Columbians agreed that there was too much exposure about black problems whereas nearly 77% of blacks disagreed. These findings suggest that in most instances (but not all), white citizens in Columbia do not feel affected by any problems regarding race relations in the city. However, blacks in Columbia indeed feel that there is a disparity in the way blacks and whites are viewed and treated by the city's governing and social institutions.

There were additional factors that were investigated to determine if they seemed to have explanatory value in policy adoption. Of these variables, only one appeared to have a relationship to innovation—personal assessment of race relations in Columbia. There was variance among the personal political affiliations reported by respondents. Actors ranged from liberal, moderate liberal, moderate independent, moderate Democrat, yellow dog Democrat, to moderate Republican. The vast majority of these actors, however, reported that they did not adopt any task force recommendations. Consequently, there appeared to be no relationship between political ideology and policy adoption.

With regards to constituency size, there was also variance present. Respondents indicated a wide-range of constituency sizes. However, there was no pattern of policy adoption that could be explained by the size of the respondent's constituencies. Lastly, personal assessment of race relations in Columbia held by the policymaker appeared to have some connection with policy adoption by these respondents. In the case of Columbia, nine of ten respondents indicated task force recommended policies were not adopted. Of these nine actors, only three noted that there was anything remotely close to a problem with race relations. Taken as a whole, these nine actors did not feel that race relations in Columbia were very troubling at all. Respondent used phrases such as "benign neglect" and "o.k., but could be much better" (survey responses). Even the one policy actor who did adopt task force recommendations reported that race relations in Columbia were "constantly improving" but there was "room for improvement" (survey response). These findings suggested that in cases where policy makers in Columbia did not view race relations in they city to be of a serious nature, their departments did not adopt task force recommendations.

Findings on the Impact of an Environmental Shock and Other Factors in Policy Innovation

In Chapter Three, I argued that local level policymakers would adopt more task force recommendations in cases where an environmental shock(s) was present in their organizational environment than would policymakers in instances where there was no environmental shock present in their organization's environment. I noted in Chapter Three that the case of Madison illustrated an instance where an environmental shock was present. I also discussed that in the case of Columbia, there were a number of events that could have been identified but as environmental shocks, but they were not recognized as such. Given the findings with regards to the number of Columbia policymakers that adopted task force recommendations, my contention about the role of the presence of an environmental shock on innovation was supported. Clearly, more policymakers in Madison adopted task force recommendations that in the case of Columbia.

The contention that the credibility of task force recommendations would have an effect on the number of task force recommendations adopted by local level policymakers was made in Chapter Three. This argument was based upon the expectation that task forces whose membership composition were partisan in nature would be viewed by local level actors as driven by partisan political agendas of task force members. Task forces recommendations would be seen as espousing the ideologies and philosophies of a group of like-minded individuals and not a broader section of the community. As such, partisan task forces produced non-credible recommendations. As a consequence of this, local officials would have adopted fewer task force recommendations. I also argued that task forces whose membership composition was bipartisan in nature would be less likely viewed by local level actors as driven by partisan political agendas of task force members. As such, bipartisan task forces were said to have produced credible recommendations. As a consequence of this, local officials would have adopted more task force recommendations.

In the case of Columbia, the task force had a slightly bipartisan membership composition—but less than that of the Madison task force. It was argued in Chapter Three that local level policymakers would adopt more task force recommendations the greater the bipartisan nature of the task force. As indicated earlier, only one local level governmental and nongovernmental actor in Columbia adopted task force recommended policies. Compared to the findings in the chapter on Madison, it appeared that in cases where a task force had greater bipartisanship, the more recommendations policymakers adopted. However, to more accurately assess this relationship, the analysis would have to be extended to include Kansas City.

Of note, one policymaker reported that the "task force was uninformed about the realtor community's dedication to fair housing in the recommendations made" (survey response). This statement indicated that this policy maker felt the task force was not very knowledgeable about the complex issues regarding how realtors implement fair housing policies. This respondent's argument also illustrated that for at least him, the task force was not credible. However, this source noted that his opinion had little to do with political party affiliation. He argued that it had more to do with the knowledge of task force members compared to that of realtors in the particular area of concern. This policymaker felt that realtors would have been better adept at addressing this issue.

In Chapter Three, I purported that there would be a relationship between the influence of task force members and the number of task force recommended policies adopted by local level governmental and nongovernmental actors. This contention was based upon the expectation that task forces served as policy experts and reference points for local level officials. I argued that in where task forces members were more influential, local level officials would adopt more task force recommendations. In the case of Madison, I found that survey respondents provided no indication that task force members were or were not influential in their adoption of policies. Local level actors gave no response as to whether they adopted recommended policies as a result of the influence of task force members or whether they did so for other reasons. The case of Columbia produced similar results as Madison—with one exception. The local official in Columbia who adopted task force recommendations stated, "The task force recommendations assisted by focusing additional efforts in the areas recommended" (survey response). This actor's statement provided the only evidence of the two cases examined thus far that where task force members exerted a level of influence over policymakers were task force recommendations adopted. However, it was found earlier that this official's department was officially engaged in the making of policies that were sensitive to race relations. As such, the relationship between the influence of the task force members on policy adoption by this policy maker was, at best, spuriously related to his job duties and policy area.

As stated previously, nine of ten respondents in the case of Columbia stated they did not adopt task force recommendations. As with Madison, survey respondents in Columbia provided no indication that task force members were or were not influential in their adoption of policies. The survey participants gave no response as to whether they adopted recommended policies as a result of the influence of task force members or whether they did so for other reasons. Coupled with the findings in the case of Madison, these findings led me to suspect that task force members did not hold a level of influence that was strong enough such that policy makes would cite it as having been important factor in whether or not they adopted task force recommended policies.

The role of the level of racial threat in the city and the number of local level governmental and nongovernmental actors who adopted task force recommended policies was presented in Chapter Three. I noted that theories on racial threat predict policymakers would adopt more task force recommendations the lower the level of racial threat in that community. The level of racial threat in the city of Columbia was found to be higher than in Madison but lower than in Kansas City. As such, I postulated that local level governmental and nongovernmental actors would adopt fewer task force recommendations than actors in Madison but more than those in Kansas City.

The finding that only one of ten (10%) local level officials in Columbia who responded said they adopted task force recommended policies was an important discovery. This finding, when compared to Madison, indicated that as the level of racial threat increased across these two cases, the number of local officials who adopted task force recommendations decreased. As such, a higher level of racial threat pointed to a decrease in the number of actors who adopted task force recommendations. This finding must be placed in light of the findings for Kansas City before any conclusions can be drawn.

In Chapter Three, I presented Elazar's formulation of political culture. I argued that political culture served as a key variable to explain the variance in race-based policy innovations. I noted that I used pre-existing analyses of the political cultures of each of my three cases done by scholars who studied the politics in each of those three cases. Earlier in this chapter, I found that Columbia illustrated a case of a community with more of a traditionalistic political culture. With regards to my expectations of the role of the political culture of Columbia on race-based innovations, I expected to find that because Columbia was a community at the median on a continuum indicating the number of actors who held public-centered values, it would be less innovative with respect to polices benefiting the community as a whole than Madison but more innovative than Kansas City. Again, the finding that one of ten (10%) local level officials in Columbia who responded said they adopted task force recommended policies was an important discovery. However, as with the racial threat argument, this early finding on political culture and the number of actors who adopted task force recommendations must be placed in the context of a discussion of the findings across all cases before any conclusions can be drawn.

In Chapter Four, I noted that although I did not predict oversight would play a role in the number of actors who adopted task force recommendations, there was, however, a control mechanism built into the substantive portion of the Madison task force's final report. I noted that the city of Madison officially adopted all of the task force's recommendations. The city also required reports and used budgeting as a means to control whether policymakers adopted task force recommendations. Even nongovernmental actors were monitored in an effort to exert a level of control over their adoption of the task force recommendations.

The city of Columbia, unlike Madison, did not build in any mechanism of political control over agents in an effort to ensure they adopted task force recommendations. As discussed in Chapter Two, I found that political influence, or political control, theories, predicted elected officials would enjoy a significant amount of control over their administrative agencies. Principal-agent models, I noted, posited that political principals were able to control bureaucratic agents by creating a structure of dependency. Despite being at a disadvantage in information on how the bureaucracy went about performing its tasks, principal-agent models predicted elected officials would use various incentives to control bureaucratic performance (Moe, 1984; Niskanen, 1971; Stein, 1990; Weingast, 1984; Wood, 1988). Clearly, the mayor and the city council did not create a structure whereby they would have formal monitoring of policymakers—governmental nor nongovernmental. Columbia might have been better served to model this feature of the Madison task force and have had the city official adopt the task force recommendations.

Summary

The preliminary findings in the case of Columbia revealed a number of different items. First, the findings demonstrated that where there was no articulation of an environmental shock, local level policymakers adopted fewer task force recommendations than did policymakers in the case where a shock existed. Local level officials indicated that their organizations had not been directly affected by any type of race relations problems. In fact, most respondents reported that they did not think race relations in Columbia were very problematic.

The politics of innovation in Columbia, as with Madison, were found to be connected to the city's political culture. I found that the politics of innovation in Columbia were centered on a small number of actors in the city's economic, social, and governing institutions that were attempting to create a new direction and new image for the city—an image more consistent with a liberal moralistic culture. In Madison, the possibilities for innovation in racial policies were said to be higher than in Columbia because there was greater community articulation and belief in the notion that the town was morally liberal. Consequently, local actors in Madison were quick to adopt policies that buttressed this perceived reality.

A division in the community about the importance of developing an image that the city was progressive and morally liberal, however, limited the possibilities for race-based innovations in Columbia. Consequently, any shocks to the city's environment (the effort to create a new image) would not have the same affect on all local governmental and nongovernmental organizations in Columbia as they would in Madison. There would be those actors who felt the shocks affected the city's environment and would consequently adopt policies in an effort to help build a new image for the city. There would also be those individuals who were not concerned with or who agreed about the direction the city's image should take. As such, these actors would not adopt policies addressed at resolving the environmental shock.

Other variables were assessed, including personal political stance, constituency size, and personal view on the nature of race relations in Columbia, to discover if any other factors had an affect of policy adoption by the respondents. I found that with regards to political stance, most of the respondents indicated they were liberal or Moderate Democrats. Although most respondent indicated they were Democrats, on average they tended to be more moderate than the Democrats in Madison. Noticeably, the only actor who reported he was a liberal was also the only actor who reported his department adopted task force recommendations. With regards to constituency size, there was also variance present. Respondents indicated a wide-range of constituency sizes. However, there was no pattern of policy adoption that could be explained by the size of the respondent's constituencies.

Lastly, personal assessment of race relations in Columbia held by the policymaker appeared to have some connection with policy adoption by these respondents. In the case of Columbia, nine of ten respondents indicated task force recommended policies were not adopted. Of these nine actors, only three noted that there was anything remotely close to a problem with race relations. Taken as a whole, these nine actors did not feel that race relations in Columbia were very troubling at all. Respondent used phrases such as "benign neglect" and "o.k., but could be much better" (survey responses). Even the one policy actor who did adopt task force recommendations reported that race relations in Columbia were "constantly improving" but there was "room for improvement (survey response)." These findings suggested that in cases where policy makers in Columbia did not view race relations in they city to be of a serious nature, their departments did not adopt task force recommendations.

It was argued that part of the explanation behind why Columbians held such benign views on race relations in the city was that most residents did not come in contact with blacks who were not affiliated with the university, they did not travel to lower-income, black neighborhoods, nor did they have any type of social interaction with these individuals. As such, most white Columbians lived in their own world isolated from the problems of race relations. It was argued that outside of the problems located in the black neighborhoods most Columbians felt that the city was an ideal place to live, raise a family, and retire. Even though Columbia had more blacks as a percentage of the city's population than Madison, the problems centered on race relations in Madison were much more magnified than in Columbia. The events that began to unfold were more troubling for the social, political, and business institutions in the city. Coupled with the more socially liberal and moralistic culture in Madison, the issue of race relations provoked a much more serious-minded attitude by the city's policy makers.

To support the argument that most Columbians did not perceive race relations to be problematic, I analyzed survey data generated by the Columbia race relations task force regarding the views of Columbia residents on the nature of race relations in the city. I found that with regards to the perceptions of the equal treatment of blacks versus whites by many of the social, governmental, and economic institutions in Columbia, local residents demonstrated there was clearly nothing close to a level of agreement. One such finding by the Columbia task force that illustrates this is their finding that about 48% of whites in Columbia agreed discrimination against blacks was not a problem while nearly 82% of blacks disagreed.

The findings in Columbia suggested that in most instances (but not all), Columbians, including governmental and nongovernmental actors, did not feel affected by any problems regarding race relations in the city. In addition, survey respondents made no mention of any types of events that affected the internal or external environment of their organizations. In the one case where a policy maker reported task force recommendations were adopted, this official noted that it was his department's job to make policies that were sensitive to the equal treatment of blacks versus whites. Consequently, this policy maker had a greater propensity for innovation given his job responsibilities. It was argued that any other factors examined that might have had some relationship to policy adoption by this actor were spuriously related to his organization's policy responsibilities.

In cases such as Columbia, where the task force was slightly bipartisan in its membership composition, it was argued that local level policymakers would adopt more task force recommendations than in cases where the task force was partisan due to a credibility factor. As in the case of Madison, it was found that local level actors in Columbia provided no information that allowed for discussion of the explanatory power of this variable. Respondents did not mention if they felt the task force's political nature had an affect on how they view the recommendations produced by the force. One official, however, did state that he felt the task force was not knowledgeable about his policy area (housing policy with regards to real estate sales). This finding led to a hunch that policy makers focused more on the knowledge task force members had on the issues they debated in determining the credibility of their recommendations.

With regards to the influence of the task force on the policy adoption by local level officials, it was argued that where task forces members were influential, local level officials would adopt more task force recommendations. In the case of Columbia, one survey respondent provided an indication that the task force was influential in their adoption of policies. The remaining policy makers gave no response as to whether they adopted recommended policies as a result of the influence of task force members or if they adopted such policies for other reasons. These findings suggested that, although it could not be stated with any certainty, task force members did not hold a level of influence that was strong enough such that policy makes would cite it as having been important in whether or not they adopted task force recommended policies.

The role of the level of racial threat by African Americans in the city and the number of local level governmental and nongovernmental actors who adopted task force recommended policies was analyzed. The level of racial threat by African Americans in the city of Columbia was found to be higher than in Madison but lower than in Kansas City. As such, I postulated that local level governmental and nongovernmental actors would adopt fewer task force recommendations than actors in Madison but more than those in Kansas City. The finding that only one of ten (10%) local level officials in Columbia who responded said they adopted task force recommended policies was an important discovery. This finding, when compared to Madison, indicated that as the level of racial threat increased across these two cases, the number of local officials who adopted task force recommendations decreased. As such, a higher level of racial threat pointed to a decrease in the number of actors who adopted task force recommendations. This finding must be placed in light of the findings for Kansas City before any conclusions can be drawn.

In Chapter Three, I presented Elazar's formulation of political culture. I argued that political culture served as a key variable to explain the variance in race-based policy innovations. I noted that I used pre-existing analyses of the political cultures of each of my three cases done by leading scholars who study the politics in each of those three cases. I found that Columbia illustrated a case of a community with a traditionalistic political culture. With regards to my expectations of the role of the political culture of Columbia on race-based innovations, I expected to find that because Columbia was a community at the median on a continuum indicating the number of actors who held public-centered values, it would be less innovative with respect to polices benefiting the community as a whole than Madison but more innovative than Kansas City. Again, the finding that one of ten (10%) local level officials in Columbia who responded said they adopted task force recommended policies was an important discovery. However, as with the racial threat argument, this early finding on political culture and the number of actors who adopted task force recommendations must be placed in the context of a discussion of the findings across all cases before any conclusions can be drawn.

The next chapter, Chapter Six, is a case study of the Kansas City Mayor's Race Relations Task Force. This case moves my discussion to the final step towards a cross-case examination that will allow for a thorough analysis of each the four major contentions. In Chapter Six, I give a brief background of the city of Kansas City, an analysis of the impetus behind its creation of the mayor's race relations task force, and the dynamics of the task force itself. Finally, I analyze the findings relative to the surveys and interviews conducted.

Bibliography

Baumgartner, F. R., and Jones, B. D. (1993). *Agendas and Instability in American Politics*. Chicago: University of Chicago Press.
City of Columbia, MO. (1996). *State of the City*. Columbia: City of Columbia, MO.
City of Columbia, MO. (1997). *State of the City*. Columbia: City of Columbia, MO.
City of Columbia, MO. (1998). *State of the City*. Columbia: City of Columbia, MO.
City of Columbia, MO. (1999). *State of the City*. Columbia: City of Columbia, MO.
City of Columbia, MO. (2000). *State of the City*. Columbia: City of Columbia, MO.
City of Columbia, MO. (2001a). City of Columbia, MO. Retrieved May, 1, 2001, from www.gocolumbiamo.com
City of Columbia, MO. (2001b). *State of the City*. Columbia: City of Columbia, MO.
Elazar, D. J., Gray, V., and Spano, W. (1999). *Minnesota Politics and Government (Politics and Governments of the American States)*. Lincoln, NE: University of Nebraska Press.
Mayor's Columbia Race Relations Task Force. (1996). *Report to the Mayor*. City of Columbia, MO.
Moe, T. (1984). The New Economics of Organizations. *American Journal of Political Science, 28*(4), 739-777.
Niskanen, W. (1971). *Bureaucracy and Representative Government*. Chicago: Aldine.
Stein, R. M. (1990). The Budgetary Effects of Municipal Service Contracting: A Principal-Agent Explanation. *American Journal of Political Science, 34*(2), 471-502.
United States Census Bureau. (1990). *Census Data*.
Weingast, B. R. (1984). The Congressional Bureaucratic System: A Principal-Agent Perspective (with applications to the SEC). *Public Choice, 44*(1), 147-191.
Wood, B. D. (1988). Principals, Bureaucrats, and Responsiveness in Clean Air Enforcements. *American Political Science Review, 82*(1), 213-234.

Chapter Six: Kansas City, Missouri Mayor's Race Relations Task Force

This chapter is a case-study analysis of the city of Kansas City's Mayor's Race Relations Task Force. In this chapter, I provide a brief background of Kansas City as well as the impetus behind the creation of its race relations task force. In doing so, special attention is paid to the major environmental shocks that serve as a catalyst for innovation by city officials and nongovernmental actors. The context of the discussion includes elaboration of the findings from the data generated by surveys and interviews. I also discuss findings specific to the major questions and contentions presented in this book. I find that three main factors best explain why local level policymakers in Kansas City adopted fewer task force recommendation than those in Madison and Columbia: 1) the political culture of Kansas City, 2) the lack of an environmental shock and 3) the level of racial threat by African Americans. With the discovery of the importance of the oversight of the adoption of task force recommendations in the cases of Madison and Columbia, I also investigate the role oversight plays in the adoption of task force recommendations in Kansas City. I find that a lack of oversight by the city also contributes to a lower level of policy adoption in Kansas City.

City Background: Kansas City, Missouri

Kansas City began as a small trading post in 1821 and has grown into the nation's 25th largest city in population and the eighth largest in land area. The city is located near the geographic and population centers of the country and is often referred to as the Heart of America. Its metropolitan area is on the state line of Kansas and Missouri and encompasses approximately 140 cities and 11 counties. The consolidated city spans four counties—Jackson, Cass, Clay, and Platte. In addition, there are approximately 13 school districts that serve the city.

Kansas City prides itself on its range of culture outlets and amenities. The city boasts that it has more fountains than any city except Rome and more boulevards than any city except Paris. The city celebrates it African American presence through the Kansas City Jazz Museum and the Negro Leagues Baseball Museum. The city is also an economic center in that it is serves as the headquarters for Sprint Communications, H&R Block, the National Collegiate Athletic Association (NCAA), Hallmark Cards, and Vanguard Airlines. Kansas City is home to a federal reserve bank and ranks first in the country in inland foreign trade zone space.

With regards to the politics of Kansas City, the city has experienced a somewhat unique evolution in the development of its power structure. The city has undergone many structural reforms in its government in the post-Tom Pendergast years (Dishman, 1940; Dorsett, 1968; Hartmann, 1999; Larsen, 1997; Milligan, 1948). Pendergast ran an office dominated by machine politics and was accused of practicing corruption in the use of political power for personal gain and benefit for those who were in cahoots with his office (Dorsett, 1968; Hartmann, 1999; Milligan, 1948). The city of Kansas City saw much more equitable growth in wealth throughout the community in the years following Pendergast. The development of a large middle class in Kansas City was one of the major triumphs of the anti-Pendergast reforms (Reddig, 1986).

Although Kansas City has developed a mostly white middle class and a small African American class (29% in 1990), it has supported a small number of African Americans in their bids to win key positions of decision-making power and leadership in the city (this has also been seen in cities such as Seattle, Baltimore, Pittsburgh, and a few others). Most cities of the size of Kansas City have not seen African Americans win key citywide or district-wide elected offices until the percentage of blacks in the city has reached near a majority. Kansas City's proclivity to support black candidates has been, in large part, due to it being a solid Democratic town. In addition, the city's individualistic political culture (as discussed in the next section) lends itself to strong identification to political actors based upon party ties.

In addition to its modest support of blacks for elected offices, the city of Kansas City has made efforts to confront its de facto racial segregation that has evolved within its city limits. Urban politics scholars have noted that Kansas City, unlike many cities of comparable size, has achieved large white middle-class within its consolidated limits (Pierce and Hagstrom, 1984). To explain how Kansas City has achieved this, scholars have cited the major accomplishments made by Kansas City since World War II. The city has: 1) annexed suburban areas to keep a substantial portion of the areas middle class within the city limits, 2) undertaken beautification projects if the 1960s and 1970s that were designed to make the city more comfortable for middle class residents, commuters, and businesses, and 3) built a convention center and other projects to attract residents and business to the city's downtown area (Pierce and Hagstrom, 1984). The masses of middle-class whites have not fled Kansas City to the degree in which they have in other major cities—partly because of the aforementioned reasons. In addition, the has annexed all of the land it could that was in the path of urban development and growth sprawl in order to keep a large number of whites within the city limits.

Kansas Citians, much like Madisonians, are conscious of the image of their city. Locals do not want to be viewed by other locals or outsiders as racists. The city wants to promote an image that it is a racially tolerant city and one working hard towards achieving racial harmony. At the same time, Kansas Citians do not acquiesce to political demands laden with racial overtones. As characteristic of communities with individualistic political cultures, policymakers in Kansas City consistently demonstrate they will not be beholden to politicians who decry racism and advocate special treatment of blacks versus whites. The city's history with federally mandated busing is just one such example (Reid, 2001). Kansas Citians have shown resistance to outside efforts by the State of Missouri and the federal government that are aimed at integrating the city's public schools. Consequently, injecting the issue of race in Kansas City politics typically results in negative political consequences for non-whites (Smith, 1993).

Kansas City has not demonstrated strong support for African American candidates who have run for elected offices. The politics of racial threat have played a major role in sustaining this reality. African American candidates who have run for office in Kansas City have faced the reality that white Kansas Citians were fearful that if elected, a black leader would neglect the interests of the white community in favor of those of the black community. Consequently, black candidates have found it necessary to find the right balance of de-emphasizing race in an effort to capture the white vote yet giving enough attention to issues important to African Americans in order to capture their vote.

Three historical examples have come to best illustrate how the politics of race has affected leadership in Kansas City. First, the 1979 election of Republican Richard Berkley, a white Republican, over Democrat Bruce Watkins, an African American, as the city's first Republican mayor in fifty years. Berkley's election was particularly surprising given that Kansas City has long been a stronghold of the Democratic Party. Second, the 1982 landslide election of then state senator Alan Wheat to Congress further illustrated the role of race in Kansas City politics. Kansas Citians helped Wheat defeat his white, liberal Republican opponent, John Sharp, only three years after they had rejected a black Democrat for mayor. Finally, the 1991 election of Emanuel Cleaver to the office of mayor exemplified that Kansas City would elect a black mayor. Kansas Citians elected city councilman Emmanuel Cleaver, an African American Democrat, over the election's favored candidates (Dick King and Brice Harris) as well as the low-key white councilman Robert Llewellen, as the city's first black mayor. Given the 1979 legacy and its large white population base, Kansas City's election of Wheat and Cleaver was surprising.

In the 1979 mayoral election, both Berkley and Watkins used race to their advantage. Berkley made campaign promises that were designed to appease the city's white middle class. Promises, such as building public housing only "where it's needed" and consulting with neighborhood organizations before planning any public housing construction in their neighborhoods, were the kinds of things white Kansas Citians wanted to hear ("Watkins Seemed to Sense Defeat," 1979). What they did not want to hear, on the other hand, were all the things being said by Watkins. As the founder and organizer of Freedom, Incorporated—then Kansas City's preeminent black neighborhood organization—Watkins brought with him many of the organizations goals of black empowerment and mobilization to the campaign. Whites in Kansas City feared that Watkins would use the office of the mayor to advance his political goals of increasing black political power. This was particularly unpleasant to white Kansas Citians given the black power movement flourishing at that time. Ultimately, whites in Kansas City rejected supporting Watkins, even though he was a Democrat and pro-labor union. After the election, some Democrats noted the negative impact that race played on the election by saying, "We're good Democrats, but we're better racists" ("Labor's Missing Muscle," 1979), meaning that even though Watkins had all the characteristics of the type of candidate Kansas City would normally support, it rejected him in his bid for mayor (Smith, 1993).

Three years after their rejection of Watkins, Kansas Citians would do an about-face and support a black candidate for elective office. Alan Wheat, who many felt was fingered by former Kansas City Congressman, Richard Bolling, was elected to the office of United States Congressman. Alan Wheat, like Watkins, was a black Democrat who was pro-labor union. His opponent, John Sharp, too was pro-labor union, but was a Republican. The key difference between Wheat and Watkins, however, was that Wheat downplayed the issue of race—much to the favor of Kansas Citians. During the 1991 Congressional race, John Sharp refused to place emphasis on Wheat's race up until the eleventh hour ("Wheat," 1982). Sharp recommended a constitutional amendment to prohibit the busing of schoolchildren across district lines. Wheat responded that he also opposed busing, but did not want to "clutter up the [state] Constitution with such amendments" ("Wheat," 1982). What Wheat did was to portray himself as an anti-busing moderate (which white Kansas Citians liked) and allay any fears whites may have had about Wheat becoming a militant advocate for black issues (Smith, 1993).

Negative campaigning marked the 1991 mayoral election in Kansas City. Favored candidates, Dick King and Brice Harris, attacked each other vigorously in the primary. Political insiders and strategists argued that Kansas Citians had became fed up with the negative ads used by these two candidates and thus rejected both of them in favor of Emmanuel Cleaver and Robert Llewellen for the runoff ("Lewellen 'So Close' But Couldn't Match Cleaver," 1991). Presumably, the defeat of King and Harris demonstrated that negative campaigning in Kansas City would have negative consequences. Thus Llewellen strayed away from focusing on any form of negative campaigning, including playing the race card, in the runoff election against Cleaver ("Lewellen 'So Close' But Couldn't Match Cleaver," 1991). The Cleaver campaign tried to downplay their candidate as one whose focus would be only black issues in favor of one who would bring the city together. Cleaver stressed his reputation throughout the city as an effective leader. Cleaver's ultimate campaign goal was to convince voters that he could build racial harmony among all peoples in Kansas City (Smith, 1993).

Summary of the Context of Politics in Kansas City and Implications for Innovation

The politics of innovation in Kansas City are rooted in promoting the collective self-interests of the community as articulated by the community's large white middle class. This is characteristic of the individualistic political culture. In communities with such a culture, there is a general feeling that government should not have any concern with questions of the good society, except insofar as it may be used to advance some common view formulated outside the political arena (Elazar, Gray, and Spano, 1999). This is quite different from the city of Madison. Kansas Citians feel that the city's large white middle class, and not governmental actors, should articulate notions of the good society. Kansas Citians are first and foremost concerned about government policy decisions that are first untainted by political corruption (Reddig, 1986; Smith, 1993). Secondly, Kansas City's large white middle class favors policies that are race neutral and that do not tend to point fingers or lay blame on white Americans for the social, economic, and political conditions of the city's small black population.

The possibilities for race-based innovations in Kansas City are also contingent upon how race-based policy recommendations are couched. The literature on deracialization emphasizes how shifting emphasis away from race instead of using it as a divisive issue can win the appeal of a large number of white Americans (Hamilton, 1978, 1997). The use of deracialization in Kansas City politics is important because Kansas Citians have demonstrated that they will not be responsive to race-based policy recommendations that are laden with blame placing and overtly geared towards promoting black issues—even in instances where an environmental shock might exist. In addition, local level policymakers are likely to be reluctant to adopt task force recommendations that are advocated by actors who are associated with promoting the proverbial "black" agenda. A black mayor who creates a race relations task force is bound to be more suspect in his intentions than a white mayor who does the same because the black mayor would be seen as a sufficient representation of black-only interests.

The prescription of race-based initiatives in Kansas City, in many ways, creates a paradox. In attempting to influence actors to adopt race-based policies, advocates must downplay the issue of race and convince policymakers that they, themselves, will receive some personal benefit by adopting them. Given that much of what race relations task forces do is to indulge upon the root of race relations problems in a community and assign responsibility for improvements in specific areas to various city actors, policymakers in Kansas City are less likely than those in Columbia and Madison to be responsive to adopting such policies. The very nature of policies centered on improving race relations creates a tenuous relationship between those who aim to make the recommendations for improving race relations and those who they hope to influence to adopt them.

The Impetus Behind the Kansas City Mayor's Race Relations Task Force

Mayor Emanuel Cleaver announced late in 1995 that he was creating a task force to study the nature of race relations in Kansas City. He argued that he was creating the task force to produce a report card of how well the races were relating to each other in the city. His ultimate goal, in his own words, was to create a "harmony" among the races in Kansas City (Mayor's Task Force on Race Relations, 1996). Although I was not able to ascertain Mayor Cleaver's participation, I discovered in an interview with William Whitcomb, a mediator with the Department of Justice's Community Relations Service, that that mayor's intentions behind creation of the task force came from his historical awareness to "racial disparity and in racial disharmony in Kansas City. The city had been designated as one of the most racially divided communities when Cleaver was with the SCLC and a city councilman. It had always been on his mind how to bring harmony to the city. This is why he put together Kansas City Harmony in a World of Difference (W. Whitcomb, Interview, November 1, 2001).

The Dynamics of the Kansas City Mayor's Race Relations Task Force

The Kansas City mayor's race relations task force was created in January of 1996 by Mayor Emanuel Cleaver. The task force consisted of over 300 participants—making it the largest of the three task forces studied in this book. The core membership of the task force was much smaller in scope than the actual membership size of the task force. Mayor Cleaver appointed approximately 20 key individuals to serve as the task force's leaders. In going about staffing the task force's top-level members, the mayor selected many individuals on his prerogative. Many of these individuals were people that the mayor knew and respected for their political activism, academic and professional background, and/or professional affiliations. Others were citizens nominated by individuals in the community or those who submitted their own names for candidacy to serve on the task force. The mayor subsequently contacted these people and inquired into their interest to serve. Some of these individuals declined participation while others chose to serve.

I wanted to gather Mayor Cleaver's insight into the dynamics he took into consideration when creating the task force. Because I was not able to ascertain his participation, I turned to an assessment of the list of members of the task force to rationally draw conclusions about what the mayor must have been trying to do in creating the task force. My concern for doing so stemmed from a number of contentions I presented earlier in the book. In Chapter Three, I outlined the importance of the power of mayors to select task force members at their sole discretion. I noted that I was interested in examining what type of role the mayor, city council, and other political principals played in the process of staffing the task force.

In Chapter Four, I found that in the case of Madison, Mayor Bauman was required by city ordinance to have her nominees approved by the common council. Despite this requirement, I found that Mayor Bauman was given a great deal of latitude to select the task forces members on her own. Her process of selecting members ultimately resulted in the creation of a task force whose membership composition was still very diverse. In the case of Columbia, Mayor Hindman reported that he too had sole discretion in selecting task force participants. He felt that having to have his nominees approved by the city council was a mere formality. Mayor Hindman felt that he had absolute sole discretion to create the task force. Given this power, however, Mayor Hindman did not select a task force with as diverse racial and partisan backgrounds as the Madison task force. In the case of Kansas City, Mayor Cleaver was not required by ordinance to have his nominees approved by the city council (unlike in Columbia and Madison). Mayor Cleaver had total discretion as to whom he could appoint to serve on the task force. Given the discretion afforded to him, I expected to find that Mayor Cleaver would select members whose social, political, and economic backgrounds were similar to his own.

From surveying task force members (see Table 6:1), I found that the task force included individuals who worked in community nonprofit organizations, actors from the legal profession, employees from large corporations, actors from federal agencies, and clergy members. Mayor Cleaver's process of selecting task force participants resulted in the selection of members whose professional affiliations were quite different from each other. The Kansas City task force, as with the other two task forces studied here, clearly was not composed of a group of individuals from the same level of professional and academic training. Mayor Cleaver did not abuse his power to select task force members at his discretion by naming individuals solely affiliated with one or two types of organizations and academic backgrounds.

With regards to the political backgrounds of the task force members selected by Mayor Cleaver, I found that member's political affiliations ranged from Democrat (4 members), non-partisan (2 members), to liberal Republican (1 member). From the responses provided, I found the task force was bipartisan in nature; however, its level of partisanship was not as diverse as that of the

Table 6:1

Kansas City Mayor's Race Relations Task Force
Select Task Force Member's Profiles and Responses

- Gender

5 Male
2 Female

- Political Affiliation

4 Democrat
2 Non-partisan
1 Liberal Republican

- Motivation to Serve on the Task Force

3 Civic Duty
1 To Offer Expertise
1 Interest in the Topic
2 Asked by the Mayor

- Expertise/Background

6 Professional and Academic Background
1 No response

Madison task force. I found that there was a moderate level of variance in the party affiliations reported by task force members in Kansas City. Given this finding, it was clear that the Madison task force was most bipartisan, with the Kansas City task force coming in second. It could have been the case, however, given that the Kansas City task force consisted of over 300 members, the task force did indeed have a very diverse level partisanship. My sample was based largely on the task forces core power structure—which was approximately 20 members. I was able to assess who these 20 members were, and as such, made my assessment based upon the partisan backgrounds of these individuals. Of note, I found that one task force member felt that Mayor Cleaver did not take into concern partisan identification when he created the task force. This member noted that he felt the Mayor was more concerned about getting "good people" than trying to create a task force with a fair representation of individuals from various political backgrounds (survey response).

The data I collected on the task force's membership revealed that its members included men, as well as women, that were of varied racial backgrounds. As with the Madison task force, the Kansas City task force included whites, African Americans, Latinos, Asians, and other racial groups. The Kansas City task force was noticeably more racially diverse than the Columbia task force. The staffing of the Kansas City task force appeared to have clearly been rooted in bringing together diverse groups of individuals in the effort to study race relations in the community. The diversity in the task force could have been, in large part, due to Mayor Cleaver's goal of creating a task force that spanned various sectors of the community in an effort to build his goal of racial harmony.

Task force members were asked a number of questions in order to generate data concerning different facets of the dynamics of race relations task forces. In the case of Kansas City, seven of 10 task force members to whom I sent surveys responded. This represented a return rate of 70%. From assessing survey responses of task force members, I found that participants brought with them a diverse range of factors that motivated them to serve. In addition, I found that task force participants came to the force with varied training that they felt made them well suited to serve on the task force (recall Table 6:1).

The members of the Kansas City task force provided insight into the general characteristics task force members bring with them to their job. With regards to factors that motivated the members to serve, the responses were similar to those in the cases of Madison and Columbia. Four respondents stated that their desire to help improve race relations in Kansas City motivated them to serve on the task force. These respondents each had different professional backgrounds, yet they shared a similar concern about helping the community improve upon its race relations. There were other factors task force participants cited as their motivation for deciding to serve on the force. One source whose professional affiliation was closely associated with the issue of race relations, stated that the level of expertise he could offer to the force motivated him to serve. Another source mentioned that she not only came to serve on the task force to help improve Kansas City, but because she wanted to be a part of the group. Likewise, another source stated that he came to serve on the task force because Mayor Cleaver requested his service. Implicit in the responses of both these respondents was an indication of a level of civic engagement displayed by several task force members across all three cases.

The findings in this case regarding why citizens were motivated to serve on task explicitly and implicitly supported the contentions made in Chapters Four and Five. In those chapters, I noted that among the motivating factors task force members cited for participating in the task force included personal attachment to the issue, civic-mindedness, social-awareness, and a desire to engage in social dialogue. The members of the Kansas City task force provided similar reasons for why they agreed to serve on their community's task force. Kansas City task force members cited personal engagement to racial issues, personal desire to help improve the community, and civic-duty as their impetus behind serving on the force.

The argument that task force participants have some type of special training or background that makes them particularly well suited to serve on such forces was presented in Chapter Three. Task force participants were asked to cite reasons they felt made them adept at serving on the Kansas City race relation's task force. Unlike in the cases of Columbia and Madison, the majority of Kansas City task force members did not respond that their academic training made them a good choice for the task force. Only one member noted that his educational background made him an attractive candidate to serve on the task force. The bulk of the responses from the task force members revealed that they felt the professions in which they were employed gave them the skills necessary to serve on such a task force.

Clearly, the respondent who reported that he worked in the community justice sector, had a professional background that closely tied him to the issue of race relations. The other members, at first glance, did not appear to have professions that made them good choices to serve on a race relations task force. However, given that the Kansas City task force was designed to study race relations through the lens of specific policy areas, each member's profession became more clearly associated. One source, who worked with the Boy's and Girl's Club, was responsible working with the youth cluster portion of the task force. One respondent, who worked in the legal profession, was responsible for helping assess the status of race relations as it applied to aspects of justice in the community. Likewise, other respondents worked with issue-groups that were specific to their professional training and experiences.

The data in this case with regards to task force member's background and training supported the findings made in the previous chapters on Madison and Columbia. I found in Chapter Four that Madison task force members, and in Chapter Five, Columbia task force members, felt that they have some type of special training or background that made them particularly well suited to serve on a race relations task force. I found that many of the task force members did indeed have skills that were commensurate with those desirable to study a topic such as race relations. From assessing the backgrounds task force members in Kansas City cited as evidence of the suitability for serving on a race relations task force, I was not immediately convinced that these members were particularly good choices to serve on a race relations task force. I did not find that these members, except for one, had any particular training or background in studying the issue of race.

My understanding of the scope of race relations was broadened given further contemplation of how each of these members could have been a valuable asset to a force created to study the issue of race relations. I realized that studying race relations did not necessarily mean a task force member was required to have studied, practiced, or trained in areas that specifically dealt with African Americans or other races. Because issues pertinent to race relations spanned a myriad of policy areas (as evidenced by the task force being divided into issue area working groups), I realized it was vital to have individuals who were trained in these various areas for such a task force to be effective. Given the training of its members, the task force was an aggregate of individual level specialists, so to speak, who brought with them knowledge about how their particular professions affected and were affected by race relations.

The position that task forces were often created as the result of an environmental shock in a community was presented in Chapter One. This was found to be the case in Madison. I noted that shocks were manifested in Madison through their recognition by top-level policymakers in the city's governing, social, and economic institutions, as well as the noticeable effects they had on the environment of the city and its institutions. In Columbia, on the other hand, there was no formal recognition that these events had affected the city or that they lead to the creation of the task force (according to responses provided by Mayor Hindman and other city leaders in the surveys I collected). In addition, there were no marked effects on the environment of the city and its institutions (according to responses provided by the Columbia Police Department and other governmental, civic and business leaders in the surveys I collected). In Chapter Two, I noted that in the case of Kansas City, there were no events recognized as environmental shocks by the city's top level policymakers in the city's governing, social, and economic institutions. I also noted that there were no noticeable effects of the events on the environment of the city and its institutions. Despite having made this assessment going into my analysis of the Kansas City task force, I wanted to investigate whether or not my contentions were accurate.

To discover if the Kansas City task force was created as a result of some other agenda or reason (specifically, electoral motives) that went unidentified by Mayor Cleaver, I utilized two methods. First, I analyzed Mayor Cleaver's campaign speeches and state of the city addresses. I found no mention of the specific idea of a task force in Mayor Cleaver's campaign speeches—only his usual discourse about promoting racial harmony in Kansas City. Because Mayor Cleaver was not a candidate for mayor in the election following the culmination of the task force, there were of course no campaign speeches made. I did find, however, that Mayor Cleaver talked a great deal about the task force. When he did so, it was usually in the context of roundtables, discussions, and lectures. The local media and civic organizations in Kansas City focused heavily on the nature of race relations in Kansas City and devoted a great deal of airtime towards focusing on the work of the task force. I found that Mayor Cleaver was more reactive than proactive in mentioning the task force. In those instances where he was asked to talk about race relations in Kansas City, the mayor was quite expansive in discussing the task force and how it related to his long-term goals for improving the quality of life in Kansas City. He did not, on the other hand, actively pursue avenues for bragging about his record on race relations and his having created the task force.

The second method of discovery I implemented towards probing the contention that the Kansas City task force might have been created for hidden reasons was to ask the task force participants to elaborate on why *they* felt the mayor created the task force. The interview responses indicated that most members felt that the creation of the race relations task force in Kansas City was due to Mayor Cleaver's concern about improving the community. Two respondents indicated that they felt the mayor sincerely wanted to see Kansas City have better race relations (survey response). When asked if there could have been any other reasons why Mayor Cleaver created the task force, one source stated that he did not think there were any specific events that acted as a catalyst for the task force (survey response).

A number of respondents, however, indicated that there were possibly some events that may have led the mayor to create the task force. When asked what these events were, two respondents indicated that they were not sure but that they felt there "must have been something" (survey response). One task force member in particular delved more deeply into other possible reasons why Mayor Cleaver may have created the task force. This respondent noted that the mayor, first and foremost, had a compassion for equal justice (survey response). He also noted, however, that a number of other things, specifically the historically tenuous relationship between the Kansas City police department and the community, were part of the thinking behind Mayor Cleaver's creation of the task force. This respondent also noted that the mayor felt the city historically had race related problems in education and housing and wanted to shed some light on these disparities. But, most importantly, he argued that it "was not one specific event or catalyst, but from a historical perspective, a number of things that came to fruition" (survey response). Another respondent corroborated this position in arguing "there was a misconception the task force was created due to racial profiling by the police. The whole purpose of creating the task force was to shine light on the circumstances then [in 1996]" (survey response). Given these findings, it was evident that there were no particular events that were identified as the catalyst for the creation of the Kansas City race relations task force.

Assessment of the Work of the Kansas City Mayor's Race Relations Task Force

Mayor Cleaver charged his race relations task force with determining the status of race relations in Kansas City and where the city needed to "go" [to improve upon them] (Mayor's Task Force on Race Relations, 1996). He also charged the task force to look at a number of issues through the lens of race relations—specifically, business, housing, law enforcement, media, religion, and more ((Mayor's Task Force on Race Relations, 1996). According to the mayor, his primary concern was that race relations in Kansas City were stagnant and in need of drastic improvement. The city's chapter of the Urban League agreed to work with the city in coordinating meetings, conducting facilitator training, and managing the day-to-day operations of the task force. In organizing the task force, the mayor named two general co-chairs, four vice-chairs, and chairs and co-chairs of thirteen issue working groups. Each working group subsequently developed its own "scope of work, vision and time lines" (Mayor's Task Force on Race Relations, 1996).

At the outset, the force saw a need for an open discussion of race relations in Kansas City. To accomplish this, the task force utilized a number of different strategies. First, the force held a number of workshops. One workshop of note was a youth summit. This workshop involved the input of over 100 local youth who voiced their opinions about what path they felt race relations should take in the community. Other working groups conducted workshops pertinent to the specific issue they were studying. These workshops involved not only the issue group chairs and co-chairs, but also local residents who wanted to participate for a variety of reasons. The task force relied on widespread participation by local residents to engage in a dialogue about race relations in the community.

The task force then set out to assess the perceptions held by local residents about the nature of race relations in Kansas City. To do so, the force developed a questionnaire to survey citizens in the community, interviewed locals, and corroborated with the Kansas City Star newspaper to conduct touchtone telephone polls. The task force found that the majority of African Americans and Hispanic Americans in Kansas City felt that race relations in the city were either stagnant or had not improved at all (Mayor's Task Force on Race Relations, 1996). The task force then hosted three community input sessions to further assess the community's feelings about the nature of race relations in the community. During these community input sessions, the task force involved some 300 members of the community. Again, local residents were afforded the opportunity to serve on various committees and clusters. Widespread community participation allowed the task force to gauge many disparate perceptions and voices on the nature of race relations in Kansas City.

The task force relied on a division of labor to complete its tasks. This structure, however, was not created at the discretion of the task force itself. Mayor Cleaver identified specific issue areas that he wanted the task force to study and subsequently appointed individuals to serve as chairs and co-chairs of these smaller units such that they would direct the discussions of each working group. Consequently, the force was divided into 13 working groups, or what some task force participants referred to as "clusters" (Mayor's Task Force on Race Relations, 1996). Each working group assessed the pulse of the community with regards to their own particular subject area. This process was carried out over the months of February and March 1996. Upon the culmination of their work, the individual clusters did not issue in aggregate form what was referred to as a final report by the Madison and Columbia task forces; rather, the Kansas City task force issued an "interim report" (Mayor's Task Force on Race Relations, 1996). In the interim report, the findings and recommendations of each of the clusters were listed. The report was issued on April 4, 1996, as mandated by Mayor Cleaver, in recognition of the 28th anniversary of the assassination of Dr. Martin Luther King, Jr.

A number of interesting similarities and differences between the work of the Kansas City task force and the Madison and Columbia task force stood out. First, each task force was similar in that it relied heavily on public input in making its assessments and findings about the perceived reality of race relations in their respective cities. Each task force engaged in dialogue with the public and held open discussions in which local residents could voice their opinions and perceptions about race relations in their respective cities. The Kansas City task force, however, did not rely on expert testimony as heavily as the Columbia and Madison task forces. Another similarity between the task forces was that each utilized a division of labor in going about fulfilling their responsibilities. Each task force divided itself into small units that were responsible for addressing specific issues as they applied to race relations. The mayor in the case of Madison allowed her task force more latitude in determining how it would go about completing the tasks charged to it. Although she specifically directed the task force to study two issues relative to racial profiling, the task force was not otherwise told what issues it should study in assessing race relations in Madison. Consequently, the Madison task force was forced to turn to an older report on race relations previously issued in that community in which specific subject areas pertinent to race relations had been identified. In Kansas City and Columbia, however, the mayor set the agenda of the task forces with regards to the issue areas the task forces would study—thus indirectly mandating a specific structure for the force.

Each task force, upon completing its work, outlined specific findings and recommendations by policy area. In general, each task force identified nine policy areas of concern and associated recommendation courses of action. The Madison task force issued recommendations on additional policy areas. The reason for this, as noted in Chapter Four, was that the Madison task force had created two additional sub-groups that were specifically engaged in discussing a particular series of events regarding racial profiling in that community. In the cases of Columbia and Kansas City, the task force was given a specific time frame in which to complete their work. By comparison, the Kansas City race relations task force had the shortest life span—having been given approximately four months to complete its job. The Columbia task force was given slightly more time—it had approximately five months to complete its work. The Madison task force, on the other hand, was not given a time restriction to finish its jobs. Consequently, the Madison task force took over a year to complete its work.

The Kansas City task force was considerably larger in its membership composition than both the Columbia and Madison task forces. This size difference may have had some effect on the Kansas City task force's ability to go about doing its job in a timely and organized manner. One task force participant stated that when the deadline for issuing their findings came around, the task force began scrambling to produce a reasonable set of conclusions—even thought they did not have enough time to study the issues efficiently (survey response). Finally, the Kansas City and Columbia task forces, unlike the Madison task force, did not have any city officials who were actual members of the task force. In Columbia and Kansas City, the mayor attended meetings of the task force but did not sit in on meetings in the capacity of a task force member. The mayor in Madison, although she allowed the task force a large degree of discretion, seemed to be a much more visible actor with regards to the daily work of the task force.

The contention was presented in Chapter Three that mayors and city councils might try to exert control over the recommendations produced by task forces. In the case of Madison and Columbia, task force members were found to have had complete discretion in going about carrying out their duties and forming their recommendations. To investigate this issue with regards to the Kansas City task force, members were asked to describe and elaborate on the amount of discretion they had in completing the tasks charged to them, as well as producing final recommendations. In going about conducting their work, each of the Kansas City task force members who responded reported that their working groups had complete discretion. One task force member noted that the group had "total discretion, he [the mayor] did not handicap what we did" (survey response). Another member said the mayor and city council did not interfere with the task forces work. He noted that he "would not have responded well to being bullied" (survey response). In general, the task force members who participated in this study felt that there were no reigns placed on them as they went about completing their work.

These findings support the discovery made previously in the chapters on Madison and Columbia regarding task force discretion. The evidence in each of these cases points to the fact that task forces can and do retain a great deal of discretion in going about fulfilling their responsibilities. One reason for this, as I discussed in Chapters Four and Five, is that mayors and council members probably do not want to damage the credibility of the task forces recommendations by having its members reveal the final products are made under pressure from government institutions and are laden with political agendas. Additionally, mayors and council members may feel that task force members, due to their level of training and educational background, are better skilled to address the issue and make associated recommendations.

Kansas City task force members who participated in this study were asked to report their personal assessment of race relations in Kansas City before and after the implementation of the force. This question was asked so that I could garner an indication of whether or not task force members felt their work had made an impact on race relations in the community. The responses of Kansas City task force members provided relative to this question were strikingly similar to the responses given by task force members in the cases of Madison and Columbia. In general, task force members responded that the major changes that occurred as a result of the task force were either the heightening of awareness and creation of a dialogue about race relations in the community or the self-enlightenment of task force members about the nature of race relations in Kansas City.

Task force member's responses demonstrated that most task force members (5 of 7) did not feel that the invocation of the force had any substantive affect on race relations in Kansas City. A source stated, "by and large, I don't think anything has changed. Maybe some changes on an individual basis...you may find some personal enlightenment, but I don't know that there is a significant change" (survey response). One respondent echoed this sentiment by stating "the task force was important mainly to the members of the force" (survey response). A task force respondent reported that she felt race relations in Kansas City before and after the implementation of the task force were tolerable (survey response). This task force member felt that even today, some 5 years after the task force, things had not changed much. She felt the problem was that people do not know how to address the problems rooted in race relations. This member argued, "it will take someone with a lot of creativity to come up with a way to make a real change" (survey response).

Two task force members were slightly more positive than the others about the effects of the task force on race relations in Kansas City after it disbanded. Two respondents felt as though there was a general level of maturation in race relations in Kansas City in the post-task force years. One of these respondents noted that the gap between blacks and whites in Kansas City had narrowed over time and was continuing to get smaller. This source also felt as though after the task force there was a "more keen awareness of race relations problems and how various aspects of race relations affected our community from both a behavioral and structural aspect than before" (survey response). It should be noted, however, that both respondents also noted that although there had been a level of improvement in race relations given the work of the task force, there were still serious problems with race relations in the city (survey responses).

Data Analysis of Task Force Recommendations Adopted

Five major contentions were presented in Chapter Three. The underlying thesis was that policymakers in cities where an environmental shock existed would adopt more task force recommendations than would policymakers in cities where there was no environmental shock. The case of Kansas City, as discussed in the previous sections, illustrated an instance where events that could have been recognized as environmental shocks were not articulated. I noted there was no recognition by Mayor Cleaver of any events having affected the city's environment nor having led to his creation of the race relations task force. In Chapter Three, I argued that unless local level policymakers felt affected by some type of environmental shock, they would not adopt task force recommendations. In the case of Kansas City, I expected to find that local governmental and civic leaders adopted fewer task force recommendations than policymakers in Madison (where an environmental shock existed) and in Columbia (where a number of events had occurred despite not being articulated as shocks).

To investigate these inquiries with respect to the case of Kansas City, I surveyed a random sample of governmental and nongovernmental actors in the city of Kansas City. These surveys facilitated the generation of a body of data by which policy innovation could be measured. As with each of the previous cases, potential survey participants were contacted initially on February 14, 2001. I made several different follow-ups to encourage participation of all initially contacted. Kansas City proved to be the most difficult of all three cases in which to generate survey responses. After an eight-month period, I decided to conclude my data collection. These efforts resulted in eight surveys being returned (see Table 6:2). This represented a return rate of 15%. Of the policymakers that responded, seven were government and one was non-governmental. The analysis of data generated by these surveys is presented in the next section.

Findings

The respondents in the data set included policymakers in the Kansas City Department of Human Relations, Department of Human Resources, Department of Neighborhood and Community Services, North Kansas City School District, City Attorney's Office, City Auditor's Office, and the Kansas City Council. Of the eight policymakers who responded, none reported that they adopted policies recommended by the Kansas City race relations task force. The responses provided by these eight actors provided insight into why policymakers in Kansas City did indeed adopt fewer task force recommendations than those in Madison and Columbia. Most survey participant's responses seemed as though they were trying to circumvent addressing whether or not they had adopted any recommendations issued by the task force. They were, however, very expansive

Table 6:2

Kansas City Mayor's Race Relations Task Force
Select Local Level Policymaker's Profiles And Select Responses

- Organization/Department among Respondents/Size of Constituencies

6 Governmental
2 Nongovernmental
1 No response

- Profile of Respondents—Political Affiliation

1 No response
3 Liberal
2 Nonpartisan
2 Independent

- Profile of Respondents—Gender

4 Female
4 Male

with providing information on how their departments already addressed race relations in Kansas City. Through my assessment of their responses, I found that the policymakers were providing details of policies that were already incorporated into their departmental policies and were not anything in the way of innovations. Consequently, I found it implicit in their responses that they had not adopted any policies, directly or indirectly, as a result of the recommendations of the task force.

Only a small number of policymakers in Kansas City who participated in this study provided explicit information for why they did not adopt task force recommendations. In general, their reasons echoed the explanations given by policymakers in Madison and Columbia. One source reported that the reason his department had not adopted many of the recommendations of the task force was because his office did not have "formal jurisdiction" over the recommendations (survey response). He did not, however, indicate which department did have jurisdiction over the specific recommendations that he was referring to. A source noted that he agreed with many of the findings of the task force regarding law enforcement in Kansas City, but he disagreed with many of the recommendations. He also noted that policies within his department that affected race relations were not adopted because of the work of the task force, but because his office "served all communities" (survey response). This policymaker's response had undertones that supported my earlier discussion of the role of focusing on race at its implications in Kansas City politics.

In some instances, policymakers argued that their organizations were not the intended target of the task forces recommendations. There were two such examples. One source noted that he felt none of the recommendations listed in his survey related to his department. Upon investigation of his contention, I found that at least one recommendation indirectly involved his department. He did elaborate on that recommendation by arguing that it was more properly aimed at other city departments. In particular, a recommendation was made that the city should create an agency to monitor fair housing. This respondent argued that he did not think the idea was feasible. He felt that "while a noble idea, it seems to be adding an additional level of bureaucratic oversight...that is not necessary. If current ordinances, laws, etc., are rigidly enforced with significant legal and monetary consequences for abusers, new or revised agencies would probably not be needed" (survey response).

A source, who worked in the city attorney's office, noted that her office did not work with in the area of criminal justice regarding those that were made in the findings of the task force. What was interesting was that most of the findings and recommendations listed in her survey dealt with the justice system and the Kansas City police department. She did not feel, however, that there was any relationship-even indirectly-between the recommendations that affected the Kansas City police department and the city attorney's office. In an effort to distance herself from the task force recommendations relative to the justice system and the Kansas City police department, she noted that "the Kansas City,

Missouri, Policy Department is an entity separate from the city, so [the] law department has not adopted any new policy.

This finding demonstrated that in some instances, task force recommendations were clearly outside the jurisdiction and scope of the policymaker being surveyed. However, in some instances, the recommendations proved to be of such a complex nature that no one organization/department would have had or wanted to take on the sole authority and/or responsibility for its adoption and implementation. Clearly, task force recommendations in many instances would have involved the coordination of several different departments in a concerted effort to adopt the recommendations—something that most actors did not demonstrate a propensity to do.

Earlier in this chapter, I noted that there was a strong individualistic culture in Kansas City that limited the possibilities for innovation. I argued that policymakers in Kansas City felt strongly about policymaking autonomy—that they did not want mandates to be handed down by government or other outside actors. Rather, policymakers felt that policy decisions should come from notions of what the community wanted. One response provided in this case fully illustrated this position. A respondent with the North Kansas City School District, reported that in her department there was "great reluctance to create an inter-district committee (as recommended by the task force) because there [was] great reluctance to get too closely involved in the myriad of problems of the Kansas City School District" (survey response). Also, she noted there was reluctance to do so "because each school district has its own board and administration and its own demographics. This autonomy is at the core of education. Few want to have any curriculum offering dictated outside their own boundaries" (survey response). Given the history of the tenuous relationship between the Kansas City school district, the suburban schools districts, and the state of Missouri regarding the issue of segregation in its public schools, I surmised that this policymaker felt the creation of an inter-district committee would result in the emaciation of some of the Northern Kansas City School District's autonomy.

In addition to this respondent's comment on policymaking autonomy, I gathered that the issue of race probably played a factor in her feelings on many of the recommendations made by the task force. I surmised this given her implicit interjection of the issue of race. When this respondent noted, "Each school district has its own demographics," this led me to construe that she was referring to the racial demographics that existed within the public schools throughout the metropolitan Kansas City area. As I noted earlier in this chapter, politics in Kansas City has long been driven by concerns of race—specifically as it has been applied its local school systems. With the failure of court ordered busing and building of expensive magnets schools designed to lure suburban whites to the inner city schools, Kansas City demonstrated that it would not be beholden to mandates that were solely driven by concerns rooted in the issue of race. A 1999 article in "Education Reporter" prominently articulated this contention. The piece noted that, "a major obstacle to [success of the efforts to integrate the school] was the district's involvement in racial politics. Race [was] the first and foremost consideration in almost anything to do with the district...in almost any decision, it (race) [was] first and foremost, either formally or informally" (Forum, 1998).

Additional Factors Assessed to Explain Policy Innovation

For assessment of other factors that could have had an impact on the policy adoption by these officials in Kansas City, I included a number of other variables. These variables included the policymaker's personal political stance, constituency size, and personal view on the nature of race relations in Kansas City. I found that with regards to political stance, there was only a moderate amount of variance in the level of partisanship that policymakers reported. By and large, the responses indicated that the task force was composed mostly of Democrats and those as the median of the political spectrum. None of the respondents indicated that they identified with parties that were more to the extreme right wing.

With regards to the constituency size, there was variance present in the responses provided. Noticeably, the responses were relatively equal—with three respondents citing large constituencies and four respondents citing smaller constituencies. Specifically, three respondents indicated that their constituency size was greater than at least 300,000 citizens. Four respondents, on the other hand, indicated that their constituency size was less than 100,000. Only one respondent did not provide information on the size of his constituency.

The respondent's views on race relations in Kansas City demonstrated that there was variance present. Three respondents felt that race relations in Kansas City were problematic. Four respondents, on the other hand, felt that race relations in Kansas City were not terrible, but needed more attention. One policymaker did not respond to this question. In general, there was no consensus among policymakers regarding the nature of race relations in Kansas City.

These additional factors were investigated to determine if they seemed to have explanatory value in policy adoption. Because there was no variance present in the number of actors who adopted task force recommendations, however, I could only conclude that none of these factors had any relationship to whether or not policymakers adopted task force recommendations in the case of Kansas City. I found that regardless of the personal political stance of policymakers, they did not adopt task force recommendations. Likewise, no matter the constituency size of the policymakers, they did not adopt any task force recommendations. Finally, given the differences in views about the nature of race relations in Kansas City, policymakers still did not adopt task force recommendations.

Findings on the Impact of an Environmental Shock and Other Factors in Policy Innovation

In Chapter Three, I argued that local level policymakers would adopt more task force recommendations in cases where an environmental shock(s) was present in their organizational environment than would policymakers in instances where there was no environmental shock present in their organization's environment. I found that in the case of Madison, where an environmental shock was present, policymakers adopted more recommendations than in the case of Columbia—where race related events had occurred but were not articulated as environmental shocks. In the case of Kansas City, I found that neither Mayor Cleaver nor any of the respondents articulated an environmental shock. Three policymakers did note that they felt race relations affected their organization; however, they did not respond that there were any events that they considered to be significant enough factors to prompt them to make innovations in racial policies. Given the findings in the case of Kansas City that no policymakers reported they adopted task force recommendations, my contention about the role of the presence of an environmental shock on innovation was supported.

The contention that the credibility of task force recommendations would have an effect on the number of task force recommendations adopted by local level policymakers was made in Chapter Three. This argument was based upon the expectation that task forces whose membership composition were partisan in nature would be viewed by local level actors as driven by partisan political agendas of task force members. Task forces recommendations would be seen as espousing the ideologies and philosophies of a group of like-minded individuals and not a broader section of the community. As such, partisan task forces produced non-credible recommendations. As a consequence of this, local officials would not have adopted task force recommendations. I also argued that task forces whose membership composition were more bipartisan in nature would less likely be viewed by local level policymakers as having been driven by partisan political agendas. As such, bipartisan task forces were said to have produced credible recommendations. As a consequence of this, local officials would adopt more task force recommendations.

In the case of Kansas City, the task force had a slightly bipartisan membership composition. It was hypothesized that local level policymakers would adopt more task force recommendations the more bipartisan the membership of the task force. As indicated earlier, however, local level governmental and nongovernmental actors in Kansas City did not adopt task force recommended policies. Given the theoretical expectations for this variable, I expected to find that Kansas City policymakers would adopt fewer task force recommendations that in Madison, but more than in Columbia. As such, the findings in the case of Kansas City went counter to the expectation for the relationship between the credibility of task force recommendations and policy innovation. Given these findings, I surmised that the credibility of the task force's recommendations did not have a relationship to policy adoption as I expected. In addition, although it was found that the task force was slightly bipartisan in nature, policymakers did not provide any responses that indicated whether or not the task force held any credibility due to the nature of its partisanship.

In Chapter Three, I argued that there would be a relationship between the influence of task force members and the number of task force recommended policies adopted by local level governmental and nongovernmental actors. This contention was based upon the expectation that task forces served as policy experts and reference points for local level officials. I argued that in cases where task forces members were more influential, local level officials would adopt more task force recommendations. I found that in Kansas City, the task force was the least influential of the three cases. Given these findings, my contentions regarding the influence of task forces was on target.

The role of the level of racial threat by African Americans in the city and the number of local level governmental and nongovernmental actors who adopted task force recommended policies was presented in Chapter Three. I noted that theories on racial threat predicted policymakers would adopt more task force recommendations the lower the level of racial threat by African Americans was in that community. The level of racial threat by African Americans in the city of Kansas City was found to be higher than in Madison and Columbia. I found that not only did statistical figures confirm this, but also the political history and context of politics in Kansas City as well. As such, I postulated that local level governmental and nongovernmental actors would adopt fewer task force recommendations than actors in Columbia and Kansas City.

The finding that no local level officials in Kansas City who responded said they adopted task force recommended policies was an important discovery. This finding, when compared to Madison and Columbia, indicated that as the level of racial threat increased across these three cases, the number of local officials who adopted task force recommendations indeed decreased. As such, a higher level of racial threat pointed to a decrease in the number of actors who adopted task force recommendations.

In Chapter Three, I presented Elazar's formulation of political culture. I argued that political culture served as a key variable to explain the variance in race-based policy innovations. I noted that I used pre-existing analyses of the political cultures of each of my three cases done by leading scholars who study the politics in each of those three cases. Earlier in this chapter, I found that Kansas City illustrated a case of a community with an individualistic political culture. With regards to my expectations of the role of the political culture of Kansas City on race-based innovations, I expected to find that because Kansas City was a community with private centered values, it would be less innovative with respect to polices benefiting the community as a whole than Madison and Columbia.

In Chapter Four, I noted that although I did not predict oversight would play a role in the number of actors who adopted task force recommendations, the control mechanism built into the substantive portion of the Madison task force's final report had a significant impact on why policymakers adopted task force recommendations. I noted that the city of Madison officially adopted all of the task force's recommendations. The city also required reports and used budgeting as a means to control whether policymakers adopted task force recommendations. Even nongovernmental actors were monitored in an effort to exert a level of control over their adoption of the task force recommendations.

I found in Chapter Five that the city of Columbia, unlike Madison, did not build in any mechanism of political control over agents in an effort to ensure they adopted task force recommendations. Neither the mayor nor the city council created a structure whereby they would have formal monitoring of policymakers—governmental or nongovernmental. I argued that Columbia would have been wise to model this feature of the Madison task force recommendations and have it officially adopted by the city and incorporated into city policy.

In the case of Kansas City, task force members corroborated my argument about the importance of oversight on whether or not policymakers adopted task force recommendations. A number of task force members felt as though the primary limitation of the task force was that no follow-up or oversight mechanism was created by the city to ensure the recommendations would be adopted. One task force member reported that he was very disappointed that the city of Kansas City created the task force without planning to engage in oversight of local level departments and organizations to ensure the adoption of the recommendations. This respondent felt that "the major weakness of the task force idea was the lack of creating accountability for heeding the task force's recommendations" (survey response). Another respondent supported this contention by noting that he "would never serve on another task force unless there was some type of follow-up or oversight" in the adoption of the task force's recommendations (survey response). He felt that the city should not have realistically expected anyone to adopt any task force recommendations if it did not monitor who was making an effort towards doing so (survey response).

In the case of Kansas City, the lack of oversight by the city was also a function of a change in the city's administration. Unlike in Madison and Columbia, where both mayors held on to their office after the task force was disbanded, Kansas City saw a change in its governmental leadership structure soon after its task force disbanded in 1996. Mayor Cleaver left office after his term in 1999 and Mayor Kay Barnes took the helm as the city's top executive. In surveying top-level executives with the Kansas City Urban League and Kansas City Harmony, I found that the drive behind the race relations task force had died significantly since its founder, Mayor Cleaver, had left office. According to a top official at the Urban League, many citizens in Kansas City looked to the Urban League to continue the initiatives begun in 1996 due to it having facilitated the task force's operation. However, this official noted that it was not the Urban League's responsibility to take on the adoption and implementation of the recommendations. Consequently, there was community-wide confusion about the status of the recommendations made by the task force (survey responses).

I also interviewed a top-level official with a local faith-oriented civic organization called the "Kansas City Harmony." This official reported that her department was trying to champion the call for improving race relations that was begun with the race relations task force in 1996. She noted, however, that it was difficult to get local level policymakers to be responsive to her organization's efforts because of two main reasons: 1) a lack of emphasis being placed on the recommendations by the city's administration in the post-Cleaver years and, 2) local level policymakers not feeling as though the issue of race relations affected their organizations. This official with the Kansas City Harmony argued that in Kansas City, unless policymakers felt as though race relations personally affected their departments, her organization had a very difficult time in getting them to be responsive to opening their minds and ears to a even dialogue on race—much less the idea to adopt the recommendations. Given these findings, I surmised that having had a change in administrations to one that did not focus on oversight of the adoption of task force recommendations only decreased the likelihood that policymakers in Kansas City would adopt the task force's recommendations. Clearly, the new administration could have improved upon the effort begun under the Cleaver administration by engaging itself in oversight of the adoption of task forces recommendations by local level policymakers. It failed, however, to do so.

The discovery that there was no oversight over the adoption of task force recommendations in Kansas City was critical to this study. Placed in the context of my analysis across all three cases, I found that were oversight existed (Madison), policymakers adopted more task force recommendations. On the other hand, in cases where there was no oversight (Columbia and Kansas City), policymakers adopted fewer task force recommendations. Going into my analysis, I did contend that oversight would be a key factor in whether or not policymakers adopted task force recommendations. However, my discovery regarding this relationship led me to believe that principal-agent theories were vital to understanding why policymakers innovate.

Summary

The preliminary findings in the case of Kansas City revealed a number of different items. First, the findings demonstrated that where there was no articulation of an environmental shock, local level policymakers adopted fewer task force recommendations than did policymakers in a case where a shock existed. The majority of local level officials in Kansas City indicated that their organizations had not been directly affected by any type of race relations problems. In addition, the minority of respondents reported that they did not think race relations in Kansas City were very problematic.

The politics of innovation in Kansas City, as with my other two cases, were found to be connected to the city's political culture. I found that the politics of innovation in Kansas City were centered on the individualistic promotion of goals as articulated by the community's large white middle class. Kansas Citians, I noted, did not want to be told how they should go about running their organizations—especially when they come in the form of mandates from actors outside of their own organizations. I argued that in Kansas City, the possibilities for innovation in racial policies were contingent upon the imagery associated with the policies. I noted that race-based policies that tended to point fingers or place blame on specific government and non-governmental actors, these policymakers in turn would not be responsive to adopting the recommendations. In essence, playing the race card in Kansas City typically works to the disadvantage of those who employ its use.

Other variables were assessed, including personal political stance, constituency size, and personal view on the nature of race relations in Kansas City, to discover if any other factors had an effect of policy adoption by the respondents. I found that with regards to political stance, I found there was a modest amount of variance present in the responses—most of the respondents indicated they were liberal or non-partisan. With regards to constituency size, there was also variance present. Respondents indicated a wide-range of constituency sizes. Likewise, respondents varied in their opinions about the nature of race relations in Kansas City. Some policymakers felt that race relations in the community were not troubling but needed more work while others felt race relations were problematic. Overall, however, there was no pattern of policy adoption that could be explained by either of these variables because there was no variance in the number of actors who adopted task force recommendations.

In the case of Kansas City, there was no event articulated as an environmental shock by any key policymakers in the city's governing, business, and civic institutions. In addition, policymakers in Kansas City who responded in this study made no mention of any types of events that affected the internal or external environment of their organizations. I found that in Kansas City, where there was no environmental shock present, policymakers indeed adopted fewer task force recommendations that actors in cases where a shock was present (Madison) and where there was a potential shock (Columbia).

In the case of Kansas City, where the task force was moderately bipartisan in its membership composition, it was argued that local level policymakers would adopt more task force recommendations that in cases where the task force was less bipartisan due to a credibility factor. Across my three cases, I found that the more partisan the task force was, the fewer the number of actors who adopted task force recommendations. However, respondents in the case of Kansas City, however, did not mention if they felt the task force's partisan nature had an affect on how they view the recommendations produced by the force.

Consequently, I could only surmise that the partisan nature of the task force had some type of bearing on the number of actors who adopted the task force's recommendations.

With regards to the influence of the task force on the policy adoption by local level officials, it was argued that where task forces members were more influential, local level officials would adopt more task force recommendations. In the case of Kansas City, three survey respondents provided an indication that the task force was not influential in whether or not they adopted task force recommendations. The remaining policy makers gave no response as to whether they adopted recommended policies as a result of the influence of task force members or if they adopted such policies for other reasons. In comparison to my other two cases, Kansas City represented the case where the task force had the least amount of influence on policymakers. These findings suggested that the less influential task force members were, the fewer the number of policymakers that adopted task force recommended policies.

The role of the level of racial threat by African Americans in the city and the number of local level governmental and nongovernmental actors who adopted task force recommended policies was analyzed. The level of racial threat by African Americans in Kansas City was found to be the highest across all three cases. As such, I postulated that local level governmental and nongovernmental actors would adopt fewer task force recommendations than actors in Madison and Columbia. The finding that none of the eight local level officials in Kansas City who responded said they adopted task force recommended policies was an important discovery. This finding, when compared to my other two cases, indicated that as the level of racial threat increased across these cases, the number of local officials who adopted task force recommendations decreased. As such, a higher level of racial threat pointed to a decrease in the number of actors who adopted task force recommendations.

In Chapter Three, I presented Elazar's formulation of political culture. I argued that political culture served as a key variable to explain the variance in race-based policy innovations. I noted that I used pre-existing analyses of the political cultures of each of my three cases done by leading scholars who study the politics in each of those three cases. I found that Kansas City illustrated a case of a community with an individualistic political culture. With regards to my expectations of the role of the political culture of Kansas City on race-based innovations, I expected to find that because Kansas City was a community whose actors held private-centered values, its policymakers would be the least likely to innovative with respect to polices benefiting the community as a whole. Again, the finding that none of the local level officials in Kansas City who responded said they adopted task force recommended policies was an important discovery. Given the findings across all three cases, I found that my contention was correct regarding racial threat. As the level of racial threat by African Americans increased across my three cases, the number of policymakers who adopted task force recommendations decreased.

The next chapter, Chapter Seven, is a comparison/contrast of all three case studies. This analysis allows me to investigate my major questions and contentions in the context of an aggregate body of data. In Chapter Seven, I pool the data where appropriate in order to provide a more robust explanation of my findings across all three cases. Following Chapter Seven, I conclude my study in Chapter Eight by providing a summary of the major arguments and findings presented throughout this book.

Bibliography

Dishman, R. B. (1940). *Machine Politics - Kansas City Model.* Columbia, MO: University of Missouri Press.
Dorsett, L. W. (1968). *The Pendergast Machine.* Lincoln, NE: University of Nebraska Press.
Elazar, D. J., Gray, V., and Spano, W. (1999). *Minnesota Politics and Government (Politics and Governments of the American States).* Lincoln, NE: University of Nebraska Press.
Forum, E. (1998). Historic Desegregation Case Proves a Failure [Electronic Version]. *EducationReporter*
Hamilton, C. V. (1978). Blacks and Electoral Politics. *Social Policy, 9,* 26.
———. (1997). Deracialization. *First World, 1,* 3-5.
Hartmann, R. H. (1999). *The Kansas City Investigation: Pendergast's Downfall, 1938-1939.* Columbia, MO: University of Missouri Press.
Labor's Missing Muscle. (1979, March 28). *Kansas City Star,* p. 3AA.
Larsen, L. H. (1997). *Pendergast!* Columbia, MO: University of Missouri Press.
Lewellen 'So Close' But Couldn't Match Cleaver. (1991, March 27). *Kansas City Star.*
Mayor's Task Force on Race Relations. (1996). *Interim Report to the Mayor.* Kansas City, MO: City of Kansas City (MO).
Milligan, M. M. (1948). *Missouri Waltz: The Inside Story of the Pendergast Machine by the Man Who Smashed It.* New York: C. Scribner's Sons.
Pierce, N., and Hagstrom, J. (1984). *The Book of America.* New York: Warner Books.
Reddig, W. M. (1986). *Tom's Town: Kansas City and the Pendergast Legend.* Columbia, MO: University of Missouri Press.
Reid, K. S. (2001). Rift Between Board, Chief has K.C. in Turmoil. *Education Week on the Web* March 28.
Smith, M. (1993). Does Race Matter: The Unusual Case of Kansas City. Unpublished manuscript. Ohio State University.
Watkins Seemed to Sense Defeat. (1979, March 28). *Kansas City Star,* p. 3AA.
Wheat. (1982, November 3). *Kansas City Star,* p. A7.

Chapter Seven:
Analysis of Findings Across Cases

This chapter is an analysis of the findings across all three case studies. In this analysis, I expand on my findings relative to the major questions presented throughout this book. In this chapter, I also discuss my findings relative to my contentions in the context of an aggregate body of data. To facilitate this discussion, I pool the data where appropriate in order to provide a more robust explanation of my findings across all three cases. Following Chapter Seven, I conclude my study in Chapter Eight by providing a summary of the major arguments and findings presented throughout this book.

In Chapter One, I made a number of observations about task forces that I wanted to investigate in order to discover if my contentions were on target. I argued that task forces were collections of citizens whose main purpose it was to assess a given issue, contemplate remedies, and produce policy recommendations directed towards addressing the problem at hand. I argued that task forces did not come together on a whim. I surmised that many were created because of some event(s) that had a dramatic effect on the environment of governmental and nongovernmental organizations. These events, I argued, had the ability to induce marked changes in continuous, stable organizational environmental conditions. I referred to such events as *environmental shocks*. Shocks to an organization's environment, in my assessment, created a period of organizational instability, change, and innovation—or what I referred to as *punctuated equilibria*. Punctuated equilibria, I noted, were temporary periods of instability sandwiched between periods of organizational stability.

With respect to the dynamics of task forces, I argued that task forces were similar to traditional governmental and nongovernmental agencies, but that they also had distinctive characteristics that differentiated them from the more traditional types of bureaucracies. I argued that as with governmental and nongovernmental bureaucracies, task forces were made up of aggregations of individuals that assessed fairly well defined issues and went about doing so by relying on a division of labor. What made them different from traditional bureaucracies, I noted, was that they came together for a short span of time. I argued that task forces typically did not become permanent institutions of government. Once they fulfilled their assigned responsibilities, they disbanded.

I noted that task forces could be community based or government created institutions. In my analysis, I argued that they were collections of individuals who typically were non-elected officials, but who held some level of qualification (knowledge of the subject, educational training, etc.) to serve on the force. I surmised that it may not have always been the case that all individuals on task forces were highly knowledgeable and/or had a background of expertise to serve on that particular task force. I felt that in some instances, it could be the case that individuals were interested in serving on the task force simply to fulfill a sense of civic duty, get involved in politics, or gain public exposure. In most cases, however, I felt that the appointing executive or assemblies sought to select members based on their acuity in studying the issue at hand.

In Chapter One, I made a number of additional observations about the characteristics of task forces. I argued that because task force members were not popularly elected to serve on particular task forces, coupled with the fact that task forces generally disbanded fairly quickly, it was virtually impossible to hold them accountable for the recommendations they produced. In addition, I noted that task force members did not get a chance to reevaluate and reformulate their recommendations unless they reconvened.

These aforementioned contentions were proffered so that they might serve as a foundation for my investigation into the general dynamics of task forces. To investigate these tenets, I chose a specific type of task force—mayoral race relations task forces—and selected three such cases for examination. The findings relative to the contentions I formulated across the three cases are presented in the next section.

Findings Relative to the Dynamics of Task Forces

In general, I found that the contentions I presented in this book regarding task forces were correct. There were several issues I was interested in studying. First, I wanted to discover if task forces were created as a result of some event(s) that I referred to as environmental shocks. I argued that shocks to an organization's environment were critical because they had the ability to create a period of organizational instability, change, and innovation. With regards to identifying whether events were indeed environmental shocks, I argued that it was important that those policymakers in positions of power and decision-making in a community's governing, business, and social institutions recognized the events as being shocks. Until they did so, the events, in my assessment, were not actual shocks. The events, in those instances, were only potential environmental shocks.

In my analysis, I found that in some cases, task forces were indeed created as the result of an environmental shock, whereas others were instituted even where no shock existed. From conducting interviews and surveys, I found that shocks (particularly, the alleged racial profiling in traffic stops and alcohol licensing, as well as claims that the city's EOC was racist) were manifested in Madison through their recognition by top-level policymakers in the city's governing, social, and economic institutions, as well as the noticeable effects they had on the environment of the city and its institutions. Mayor Bauman recognized that these events did indeed lead her to create the race relation task force in her community.

In Columbia, on the other hand, the data illustrated that there was generally no formal recognition by key policymakers that any events having affected the city or that any events lead to the creation of the task force. In addition, very few policymakers in Columbia reported that there were any marked effects on the environment of the city, its institutions, or their own individual organizations. All of this was the case in Columbia despite the fact there were underlying tensions that could have been articulated as environmental shocks rooted in race relation problems. Mayor Hindman denied that he created the task force as a result of any events that had taken place in the community. He argued that the impetus behind creating the task force was his genuine interest to assess the state of race relations in Columbia. With regards to driving force behind the creation of the Kansas City race relations task force, I found that there were no events recognized as environmental shocks by the top level policymakers in the city's governing, social, and economic institutions. I also found that there were no noticeable effects of any events on the environment of the city and its institutions.

Going into my study, I surmised that politicians might have had agendas that were not articulated to be associated with their creation of the task force. To assess this contention, I analyzed campaign speeches and state of the city addresses given by each of the three mayors in my cases. I also asked task force participants to elaborate on why they felt the mayors in their communities created the task force. In the case of Madison, I found that the task force was also a campaign tool used by the mayor. I found that in her campaign speeches and state of the city addresses, she repeatedly mentioned the task force. Most notably, she focused on the city's success with the race relations task force during her 1999 reelection bid by boasting that the city had received national recognition for its efforts at addressing race relations.

In the case of Columbia, I did not find evidence that Mayor Hindman used the task force to a significant degree in his discourse with the public and the media. I could not find a single mention of the task force in the State of the City statements issued by the city. In addition, I was able to find only one mention of the task force by Mayor Hindman during a campaign speech. I surmised that because Mayor Hindman ran opposed for the office of mayor in the year election following the culmination of the task force, he did not have the same level of pressure to substantiate and solidify his accomplishments during his tenure as did Mayor Bauman. In the case of Kansas City, I found that Mayor Cleaver talked a great deal about the task force; however, it was usually in the context of roundtables, discussions, and lectures. The local media and civic organizations in Kansas City focused heavily on the nature of race relations in Kansas City and devoted a great deal of airtime towards focusing on the work of the task force. I found that Mayor Cleaver was more reactive than proactive in mentioning the task force. In those instances where he was asked to talk about race relations in Kansas City, the mayor was quite expansive in discussing the task force and how it related to his long-term goals for improving the quality of life in Kansas City. He did not, on the other hand, actively pursue avenues for bragging about his record on race relations and his having created the task force. The reason for this was likely due to a number of factors, including the mayor's understanding of: (1) a lack of community consensus regarding the need for a race relations task force, and (2) the importance of de-emphasizing race for political success in Kansas City.

I wanted to analyze the importance of the power of mayors to select task force members at their sole discretion. Among the reasons I wanted to study this issue was to discover if the institutional rules associated with the creation of task forces resulted in the creation of task force with certain types of characteristics. I also wanted to know if the rules had any effect on the amount of discretion mayors retained after they created their task forces. First, with regards to the institutional rules for creating task forces, I found that in the case of Madison, Mayor Bauman was required by city ordinance to have her nominees approved by the common council. Despite this requirement, I found that Mayor Bauman was given a great deal of latitude to select the task forces members on her own. Her process of selecting members ultimately resulted in the creation of a task force whose membership composition was still very diverse across racial, gender, partisan, academic, and professional backgrounds.

In the case of Columbia, Mayor Hindman reported that he too had sole discretion in selecting task force participants. He felt that the requirement to have his nominees approved by the city council was a mere formality. Mayor Hindman felt that he had absolute discretion to create the task force. I found that given this power, however, Mayor Hindman did not create a task force as diverse as that in Madison. The Columbia task force, of the three cases, was the least diverse in terms of the racial and partisan backgrounds of its members. The Columbia task force was, however, diverse in the gender, academic, and professional backgrounds of its members.

In the case of Kansas City, Mayor Cleaver was not required by ordinance to have his nominees approved by the city council (unlike in Columbia and Madison). Mayor Cleaver had total discretion as to whom he could appoint to serve on the task force. I found that given the discretion afforded to him, Mayor Cleaver selected a moderately diverse task force in terms of its racial and partisan backgrounds—more so than the Columbia task force but less so than the Madison task force. The Kansas City task force was, however, just as diverse as the Columbia and Madison task forces with regards to its gender, academic, and professional backgrounds of its members.

With regards to the importance of the amount of discretion afforded to mayors in selecting task force members on the level of control the mayors retained over the task force, I found that discretion in the selection process resulted in ceremonial control over the task force but no explicit efforts to dictate their activities. The mayors in each of the cases retained full control over the task forces throughout their lifespan. In the cases of Columbia and Kansas City, both task forces were given a requisite time frame to fulfill their tasks. The mayors of all three cities appointed a general leadership structure to the task force and exerted control over what the task force would study. The part of the dynamics of task forces that I called "delegation of responsibility" was where mayors framed the issues so they would be discussed in a certain light. In framing the issues, the mayors also indirectly affected the substance and form of the task force recommendations. In general, however, the task force members in all three cases stated that they retained full discretion in fulfilling their perfunctory duties as well as formulating their final recommendations. I found that the evidence in each of these cases pointed to the reality that task forces did retain a great deal of discretion in completing their assigned tasks.

In my analysis, I wanted to shed light on the range of factors that motivated individuals to serve on task forces. I also wanted to uncover the varied levels of training task force members had that they felt made them well suited to serve. The responses task force members provided regarding the motivation to serve on the force were similar across all three cases. In general, task force participants stated that they came to serve on the force for reasons of 1) civic duty, 2) interest in the topic of race relations, or 3) their desire to help improve their community. There were other more unique responses cited—such as members feeling they could offer a level of expertise on the topic or their desire to be a part of the group.

I assessed the background of task force members in order to discover if they were indeed well trained to serve on such a task force. Given that the task force was designed to study the issue of race relations, its members (as with any task force designed to study an issue of a specific nature) should have been better choices than other individuals to serve on the task force. Initially, I posited that task force members should have had some type of special training, be it academic or professional, which was specifically tied to the issue of race in order for them to be considered well-suited to serve on a race relations task force. As my analysis progressed, however, I grew to understand that it was not necessary for task force members to have been particularly trained or experienced on the issue of race, per se. I surmised that having had some type of experience dealing with racial issues might have certainly put task force members in a more comfortable position to handle their tasks. However, I concluded that because issues pertinent to race relations spanned a myriad of policy areas (as evidenced by the task force being divided into issue area working groups), it was vital to have individuals who were trained in these various areas for such a task force to be effective.

Given the task force members responses on their training, professional and academic backgrounds, and other experiences, I found that the members that were selected to serve on all three task forces were indeed suited to serve on the task force. I found that the task force as a whole was an aggregate of individual level specialists who brought with them knowledge about how their particular professions affected and were affected by race relations. Within the task forces, members focused on various issue areas using a division of labor that allowed for specialization. In areas where the task force studied race relations through the lens of educations, the task force members who had training in the area of education self-selected to participate on that topic. Likewise, task force members congregated themselves into their respective issue areas that were most closely associated with their professional and academic backgrounds.

Each task force, upon completing its work, outlined specific findings and recommendations by policy area. In general, each task force identified nine policy areas of concern and associated recommendation courses of action. The Madison task force, however, issued recommendations on additional policy areas. The reason for this, as noted in Chapter Four, was that the Madison task force had two additional sub-groups that were specifically engaged in discussing particular events regarding racial profiling in that community.

The lifespan of the task forces varied according to whether or not deadlines were imposed for the completion of their work. In the cases of Columbia and Kansas City, the task force issued its final report in about 2 months after convening. The reason for this was that Mayor Hindman gave the force a specific time frame in which to complete its work. Likewise, Mayor Cleaver issued a deadline for the issuance of its recommendations. In contrast, the Madison race relations task force was not given a time restriction to finish its job. Consequently, the Madison task force took over a year to complete its work. The deadlines imposed on the Columbia task force did not seem to have an effect on its ability to produce recommendations. However, I found that the Kansas City task force scrambled to put together a report as its deadline approached. Consequently, it was not able to piece together recommendations that the majority of its members felt were well thought out.

These findings led me to conclude that requiring task forces to complete their tasks within a certain time frame can have positive and negative results. Some task forces will use their time efficiently and get the job done on time. On the other hand, some task forces will not make good use of their time and ultimately have to piece together recommendations in an effort to produce results. Similarly, giving task forces unlimited time can have positive and negative consequences. Presumably, having ample time to study an issue is a must for a task force if it hopes to probe deeply into the context of the problem. However, leaders who create task forces and do not give them a time frame for completion of its tasks run the risk that the task force will not be efficient in the use of their time. Consequently, it is important that task forces are given a window of time they have to complete their tasks that can be opened or closed based upon an assessment of how they are progressing.

I found that the task forces varied in the size and the number of governmental officials who sat on the task force. The Kansas City task force was considerably larger in its membership composition than both the Columbia and Madison task forces. The Kansas City task force had over 300 members compared to Madison's 14 and Columbia's 30. The Columbia and Madison task forces were able to effectively complete their tasks. The large size of the Kansas City task force may have had some effect on its ability to go about doing its job in a timely and efficient manner. In having such a large membership, the Kansas City task force likely became unwieldy in its level of coordination.

The Madison task force was unique in that the Mayor and a Councilmember sat on the task force in the capacity as a member. The Kansas City and Columbia task forces were different from the Madison task force in that they did not have any city officials who were actual members of the task force. Although not official members of their respective task forces, Mayors Hindman and Cleaver still attended meetings of the task force. I found that they did not, however, bully or use undue influence on task force members as they went about doing their work. In the case of Madison, on the other hand, Mayor Bauman and Councilman Ken Golden were official members of the task force. Because of their status as members of the force, I found that Mayor Bauman and Councilman Golden were more visible during the work of the Madison task force than were the mayors of Columbia and Kansas City. Of interesting note is that unlike in Madison, no city council members participated in an official capacity on the Columbia and Kansas City task forces. Having had city officials play such an interested role in the work of the task force in Madison likely provided a level of leadership and direction necessary to get the task force through the entire process.

In the next section, I discuss my findings relative to the contentions I presented in Chapter Three. Because of the relatively low number of responses I received on an individual case level, I aggregate the data where appropriate to provide a more robust explanation of my findings across all three cases. In this section, I analyze my contentions in the context of my findings across cases in order to provide broader generalizations about the relationship between task forces and policy innovation.

Analysis of Findings Relative to the Contentions Presented in the Study

Environmental Shock

In Chapter Three, I noted that this book's central thesis was that local level governmental, business, and civic policymakers would adopt more task force recommendations in cases where an environmental shock(s) was present in their organizational environment than would policymakers in instances where there was no environmental shock present in their organization's environment. As discussed in the literature review, a number of scholars have emphasized the role of shocks internal or external to an organization on the types of policies an organization adopts. To analyze this argument, I analyzed a case where an environmental shock was found to exist (Madison) and two cases where no environmental shock was found to be present (Columbia and Kansas City). For the cases of Kansas City and Columbia, I pooled the data to yield a total of 18 respondents. In the case of Madison, I had a total of 9 respondents. In assessing the findings, I found that in the case where an environmental shock was present, policymakers indeed adopted more recommendations than in cases were there were no environmental shock(s). A total of eight out of nine policymakers indicated they adopted task force recommendations in Madison whereas only one out of 18 in Kansas City and Columbia responded they adopted task force recommendations. Given the findings, I felt that local level governmental, business, and civic policymakers would adopt more task force recommendations in cases where an environmental shock(s) was present in their organizational environment than would policymakers in instances where there was no environmental shock present in their organization's environment.

Credibility of Task Force Recommendations

The contention that the credibility of task force recommendations would have an effect on the number of task force recommendations adopted by local level policymakers was made in Chapter Three. This argument was based upon the expectation that task forces whose membership composition were partisan in nature would be viewed by local level actors as driven by partisan political agendas of task force members. Task forces recommendations would be seen as espousing the ideologies and philosophies of a group of like-minded individuals and not a broader section of the community. As such, partisan task forces produced non-credible recommendations. I also argued that task forces whose membership composition were more bipartisan in nature would less likely be viewed by local level policymakers as having been driven by partisan political agendas. As such, bipartisan task forces were said to have produced credible recommendations. My argument regarding the relationship between the credibility of task force recommendations and the number of policymakers who adopted task force recommendations was that greater bipartisanship in task force membership will not induce policymakers to adopt more task force recommendations.

For analysis of this argument, I could not aggregate the data because each task force had a varying degree of partisanship in its membership composition. I found that the Madison task force was the most bipartisan, the Kansas City task force moderately bipartisan, and the Columbia task force limitedly bipartisan. This did not, however, limit my ability to analyze this argument. From analysis of the data, I found the Madison task force was most bipartisan and had the highest number of policymakers who adopted task force recommendations. However, the number of actors who adopted task force recommendations in

Kansas City as compared to Columbia was lower, despite the fact that the Kansas City task force was more bipartisan in its membership composition. Consequently, I could not reject this argument given the fact that as the level of bipartisanship in the task forces increased, the number of policymakers who adopted task force recommendations did not increase across all three cases. On the contrary, the numbers decreased (from 1 to 0) across the cases of Kansas City to Columbia

Additional insight into this relationship came from my analysis of the responses provided by policymakers. I found that, in general, policymakers gave no indication that the credibility of the task force recommendations, as a function of the partisanship in the task force's membership composition, made a difference on their policymaking decisions. In fact, most policymakers did not respond that they even knew anything about the individuals who served on the task force and those individual's partisan identification. Taken together, the evidence lead me to surmise that the credibility of the task force's recommendations had little impact on the number of policymakers who adopted task force recommendations.

Task Force Influence

In Chapter Three, I hypothesized that there would be a relationship between the influence of task force members and the number of task force recommended policies adopted by local level governmental and nongovernmental actors. This contention was based upon the expectation that task forces served as policy experts and reference points for local level officials. The argument for the relationship between the influence of task force members and the number of local level policymakers who adopted task force recommendations was that as the level of influence of task force members increased, the number of local level officials who adopted task force recommendations would not increase.

As with my previous argument, I could not aggregate the data for this argument because each task force had a varying degree of influence on local level policymakers. In my analysis, I found that policymakers in Madison did not give any indication that the task force had any influence on whether or not they adopted task force recommendations. However, in the case of Kansas City, a small number of policymakers indicated that the task force did not have any influence on whether they adopted any of the force's recommendations. In the case of Columbia, I found that two policymakers responded that the task force did indeed have an influence on whether they adopted task force recommendations. Given these findings, it was difficult to draw any conclusions regarding the argument. Because none of the respondents in the case of Madison indicated whether or not the task force had any influence on their policy adoption, there was a lack of a range of data that would have allowed for analysis of this relationship. Consequently, I was not comfortable with rejecting this argument.

In analyzing just Columbia and Kansas City, where data was yielded, the numbers point to the fact that as the influence of the task force increased, the number of local level officials who adopted task force recommendations also increased—however, only by 1 (from 0 to 1). Overall, I surmised that the purported relationship between the influence of the task force on the number of actors who adopted task force recommendations was not vital. I did not draw this conclusion based solely on the fact that a number of respondents in Madison did not provide any indication on whether or not the task force had any influence. I based this on the fact that each policymaker was specifically asked, twice, to indicate that amount on influence the task force had on their policy adoption. If the task force had any type of significant influence, I felt as though these policymakers would have responded in kind.

Racial Threat

The role of the level of racial threat by African Americans in the city and the number of local level governmental and nongovernmental actors who adopted task force recommended policies was presented in Chapter Three. I noted that theories on racial threat predicted policymakers would adopt more task force recommendations the lower the level of racial threat by African Americans was in that community. Consequently, the argument for the relationship between racial threat and the number of policymakers who adopted task force recommendations was that as the level of racial threat in a community increased, the number of local level policymakers who adopted task force recommendations would not decrease. Each case in my analysis had varying degrees of racial threat by African American in their respective community. As such, I did not aggregate the data for this argument. On the other hand, I was interested in discovering how the relationship between these two variables would play out given variance in one of the factors—the level of racial threat by African Americans in the community. In my analysis, I found that the case of Madison had the lowest level of racial threat. The city of Kansas City, on the other hand, had the highest level of racial threat. Finally, the case of Columbia was at the median of the three cases with regards to the level of racial threat.

The data illustrated that the argument regarding the relationship between level of racial threat and the number of policymakers who adopted task force recommendations was in line with reality. I found that as the level of racial threat by African Americans increased, the number of policymakers who adopted task force recommendations did indeed decrease. Specifically, the number of actors who adopted task force recommendations ranged from 8 in Madison (which had the lowest level of racial threat), to 1 in Columbia (which was at the median in terms of racial threat) to 0 in Kansas City (which had the highest level of racial threat). Given the clear connection between the nature of the task force's recommendations and the issue of race, it should have come as no surprise that the level of racial threat would have had an impact on the number of local level actors who adopted task force recommendations.

Political Culture

In Chapter Three, I presented Elazar's formulation of political culture. I argued that political culture served as a key variable to explain the variance in race-based policy innovations. The literature on political culture pointed to the reality that communities with public centered values would be more innovative than communities with private centered values in respect to polices benefiting the community as a whole. Given this contention, my argument was that communities with public centered values would not be more innovative (measured by the number of actors who adopted task force recommendations) than communities with private centered values.

In my analysis, I noted that I used pre-existing analyses of the political cultures of each of my three cases done by leading scholars who study the politics in each of those three cases. I found that Madison illustrated a case of a community with the strongest level of public centered values. The case of Kansas City, on the other hand, demonstrated a community with the weakest level of public centered values. I found Kansas City to have strong private centered values. The case of Columbia was at the median of the three cases in terms on the strength of public versus private centered values. Given these findings, I expected to find that more actors in Madison would adopt task force recommendations than in Columbia, and more in Columbia than Kansas City.

My findings demonstrated that this argument was in line with reality. Across the cases, I found that more actors in Madison did indeed adopt task force recommendations than in Columbia, and more policymakers in Columbia adopted task force recommendations than in Kansas City. I devoted extensive discussion about the political culture of each community in my analyses throughout Chapters Four, Five and Six. This discussion supported the findings relative to the number of actors who adopted task force recommendations. In addition, I found Elazar's characterization of political culture in moralistic, traditionalistic, and individualistic political cultures to be of use in applying each to the cities of Madison, Columbia, and Kansas City, respectfully. Due to limitations in availability of other conventional methods to measure political culture, I could not say with a high level of confidence that my measures of culture were actually anything more than political ideology. Despite this shortcoming, I surmised that political culture, along with the presence of an environmental shock and level of racial threat, provided the most explanatory power regarding the variance in the number of actors who adopted task force recommendations across the communities studied in this book.

The next chapter, Chapter Eight, is the conclusion of my study. In this chapter, I discuss the major questions and contentions presented an analyzed in this book. I discuss my findings relative to each case and compare the findings across all three cases. Finally, I expand upon my findings and discuss how the findings are relevant for a broader understanding of the role of mayoral task forces in governance, policymaking, and the betterment of race relations in communities. I also provide my assessment of future research in this tradition and the types of significant research questions that can be developed from this study.

Chapter Eight:
Task Forces as Agents of Policy Innovations - Analysis and Conclusions

In this study, the factors that contribute to the successful influencing of policy innovation by local level governmental, business, and civic policymakers were identified, investigated and discussed. This was done in order to assist elected officials, civic leaders, grassroots activists, and scholars of government, public policy, and race, in building a framework to understand how task forces fit into the bigger scheme of the political process. This study was based on the premise that task forces would only come to serve as agents of policy innovation in the communities that invoked their use under conditions where an environmental shock existed. Through an empirical analysis of three cases, I found that the presence of an environmental shock, or lack thereof, did indeed contribute to the innovativeness of policymakers in three communities. I also found, however, that other additional factors played a major role in whether or not these actors innovated. The most prominent of these factors included the political culture of the community, the level of racial threat by African Americans, and oversight of the adoption of task force recommendations.

The purpose of this chapter is to summarize the findings of the study and provide recommendations for governmental, business, and civic leaders to consider if they hope to effectively influence the adoption of policies that are produced by the task forces they create. In this chapter, I first provide a summary of the findings of this study. In doing so, I reiterate the major questions and contentions presented in this book and the findings relative to each. Next, I devote attention to the connections between policy innovation and task forces and how this study illuminates the implications of this relationship. I pay special attention to how this study broadens scholarly knowledge of task forces and their role in the political process. Finally, I discuss how this study contributes towards its major focus—a broadening of the understanding of how task forces can make a significant impact in the policy making process. In order to accomplish this, recommendations are provided based on the findings from Chapters Four, Five and Six, and on the cross case comparison done in Chapter Seven.

Summary of Major Questions and Contentions Presented in the Book

At this juncture, it is appropriate to revisit the major research questions and contentions that guided this study. In this study, I made a number of observations about task forces that I wanted to investigate in order to discover if my contentions were on target. My assessments and contentions about task forces were developed from an analysis of the scholarly literature on federal executive level task forces. I found that although the literature on task forces was scant, there was a body of knowledge concerning task forces that had its roots in analysis of task forces created by the federal executive and Congress. Given my analysis of this literature, I found it appropriate to use federal level commissions as a point of departure for my analysis.

In this book, I argued that task forces were collections of citizens whose main purpose it was to assess a given issue, contemplate remedies, and produce policy recommendations directed towards addressing the problem at hand. I argued that task forces did not come together on a whim. I surmised that many were created because of some event(s) that had a dramatic effect on the environment of governmental and nongovernmental organizations. These events, I argued, had the ability to induce marked changes in continuous, stable organizational environmental conditions. I referred to such events as *environmental shocks.* Shocks to an organization's environment, in my assessment, created a period of organizational instability, change, and innovation—or what I referred to as *punctuated equilibria.* Puncutated equilibria, I noted, were temporary periods of instability sandwiched between periods of organizational stability.

With respect to the dynamics of task forces, I argued that task forces were similar to traditional governmental and nongovernmental agencies, but that they also had distinctive characteristics that differentiated them from the more traditional types of bureaucracies. I argued that as with governmental and nongovernmental bureaucracies, task forces were made up of aggregations of individuals that assessed fairly well defined issues and went about doing so by relying on a division of labor. What made them different from traditional bureaucracies, I noted, was that they came together for a *temporary* span of time. I argued that task forces typically did not become permanent institutions of government. Once they had fulfilled their assigned responsibilities, they disbanded.

I noted that task force could be community based or government created institutions. In my analysis, I argued that task forces were collections of individuals who were typically non-elected officials, but who held some level of qualification (knowledge of the subject, educational training, etc.) to serve on the force. I surmised that it may not have always been the case that all individuals on task forces were highly knowledgeable and/or had a background of expertise to serve on that particular task force. I felt that in some instances, it could be the case that individuals were interested in serving on the task force simply to fulfill a sense of civic duty, get involved in politics, or gain public exposure. In most cases, however, I felt that the appointing executive or assemblies sought to select members based on their acuity in studying the issue at hand.

In Chapter One, I made a number of additional observations about the characteristics of task forces. I argued that because task force members were not popularly elected to serve on particular task forces, coupled with the fact that task forces generally disbanded fairly quickly, it was virtually impossible to hold task forces accountable for the recommendations they produced. In addition, I noted that task force members did not get a chance to reevaluate and reformulate their recommendations unless they reconvened.

With regards to the major contentions presented in this book, I developed five main variables to explain the variance in race-based policy innovation. The five key variables used in this book to explain the variation in the impact of mayoral task force on policy innovation in local communities were: One) presence of an environmental shock, 2) the credibility of task force recommendations, 3) task force influence, 4) level of racial threat, and 5) political culture. I developed a number of hypothetical relationships that I wanted to analyze in order to explain variance in the number of local level policymakers who adopted task force recommendations.

In this book, my central thesis was that local level governmental, business, and civic policymakers would adopt more task force recommendations in cases where an environmental shock(s) was present in their organizational environment than would policymakers in instances where there was no environmental shock present in their organization's environment. I posited this relationship based upon my assessment of the literature on policy innovation, organizational behavior, and international conflict. In my analysis, I discussed how the literature underscores the importance of shocks in the innovation process. In a review of the literature, I noted that scholars, such as Roger D. Schroeder, argued that innovation evolves, shapes, and is shaped, by the organization. According to Schroeder, the innovation process was stimulated by shocks . . . [things such as] "new leadership, product failure, a budget crisis, and an impeding loss of market share" . . . "either internal or external to the organization" (Schroeder, Van de Ven, Scudder, and Polly, 1989). Also, Aaron Wildavsky, in a study of organizational behavior, discovered that although incremental behavior was the norm in bureaucracies, agencies sometimes underwent dramatic changes as a result of shocks, such as changes in the organizations leadership structure (Wildavsky, 1975).

The contention that the credibility of task force recommendations would have an effect on the number of task force recommendations adopted by local level policymakers was also presented in this study. This argument was developed from an analysis of the Hoover Commission as articulated by Ferell Heady. Heady found that the commission's appointment power (which was divided three-ways) had an impact on the credibility of the commission's recommendations. Of the twelve total members on the Hoover Commission, each appointing officer was guided to make selections in such a way that only six members would come from "official life" and six who were "private citizens" at the time of appointment (Heady, 1949). The implications of this, as Heady notes, were threefold: 1) divisions along party lines did not occur, 2) partisanship was not an important factor in the reception given to the Commissions recommendations, and 3) the Commission's bipartisan nature lent weight to its recommendations (Heady, 1949).

Heady's argument, though not couched in theoretical language, was found to be in line with the new institutionalist school of thought. Such a framework, as it was applied to task forces, was said to have guided the prediction that task forces whose membership composition were partisan in nature would be viewed by local level actors as driven by partisan political agendas of task force members. Task forces recommendations would be seen as espousing the ideologies and philosophies of a group of like-minded individuals and not a broader section of the community. As such, partisan task forces produced non-credible recommendations. I also argued that task forces whose membership composition were more bipartisan in nature would less likely be viewed by local level policymakers as having been driven by partisan political agendas. As such, bipartisan task forces were said to have produced credible recommendations. I hypothesized that the more bipartisan the task force's membership composition, the more the number of local level policymakers who adopted task force recommendations would be.

In this study, I hypothesized that there would be a relationship between the influence of task force members and the number of task force recommended policies adopted by local level governmental and nongovernmental actors. As articulated throughout my analysis, and as evidenced by the title of this book, I felt that task forces could come to serve as important agents of policy innovation at the local levels. This contention was based the bureaucratic influence literature as it applied to policy innovation (Gray, 1973; Grupp and Richards, 1975; Walker, 1969). I found that several scholars have articulated the importance of policy experts and commissions as agents of policy innovation in local government and the business sector. I noted that Virginia Gray found that states served as key reference points for other states when they were contemplating the adoption of new policies. Implicit in her analysis, I argued, was a finding that the policy decisions of state bureaucrats serve as a reference point for bureaucrats in other states.

I found that also of importance were the analyses of Fred Grupp and Alan Richards, as well as Jack Walker. In my analysis, I discovered that Grupp and Richards argued that states were influenced by the recommendations of policy elites about the effectiveness of policy innovations in nearby states. As a result of these elite perceptions, policy makers in innovating states tended to emulate other state's policies when confronted with local problems. Also corroborating the finding that commissions and policy experts played a role in influencing the innovation process was Jack Walker. Walker found there were specialized communication networks of "federal and local officials, journalists, academic experts, and administrative consultants . . . [that were] . . . sources of information and policy cues" (Walker, 1969). Walker found that these actors engaged in activities similar to those of task forces—convening at conferences, exchanging ideas and knowledge, and publishing policy opinions and recommendations, etc. Given the analysis of this literature, I expected to find that the more influence a task force had, the more task force recommendations local level policymakers would adopt.

The role of the level of racial threat by African Americans in the city and the number of local level governmental and nongovernmental actors who adopted task force recommended policies was presented in this study. I noted that scholars, such as V. O. Key, argued that racial context could come to have an impact of the policy decisions made by local level officials (Key, 1949). I found Key's "racial threat hypothesis" held that large black populations were often seen as a threat to whites and lead to distinct political attitudes and behaviors among whites. As such, I postulated that as the level of racial threat by African Americans in community increased, the number of local level policymakers who adopted task force recommendations decreased.

In this book, I argued that political culture could come to play a prominent role in explaining the occurrence of innovation across my three cases. I presented Elazar's formulation of political culture, which argued that communities with public centered values would be more innovative than communities with private centered values respect to polices benefiting the community as a whole (Elazar, 1984; Elazar, Gray, and Spano, 1999). Given this contention, I expected to find that communities with public centered values would be more innovative than communities with private centered values.

To address the major questions and contentions I developed, I utilized an exploratory study conducted through the use of a case study approach with multiple-cases. I analyzed three communities that invoked the use of mayoral race relations task forces—Madison, Wisconsin, Columbia, Missouri, and Kansas City, Missouri. The data generated came from surveys, task force final reports, and interviews. The surveys and interviews I created were designed to elicit responses that would measure all variables. I selected participants for this study based upon a design that targeted key policymakers whom I needed to study.

Summary of the Findings of the Book

In general, I found that the contentions I presented in this book regarding task forces were correct. I presented a summary of my findings in Table Seven of Chapter Seven. Among the major points of my findings was the discovery that task forces were often created as the result of an articulated environmental shock and sometimes created when there was no shock that had been identified. I found that task forces did indeed go about their work through a division of labor—typically dividing themselves into what was called working groups or issue groups (clusters). Most members of the task forces were adequately skilled to serve on their respective task forces having had life and work experiences that made them adept at studying the issues at hand. Task force participants had a variety of factors that motivated them to serve on task forces; however, three main factors could be identified—civic duty, desire to help improve the community, and interest in the topic. Finally, I found that task forces did not always share similar qualities in terms of the types of individuals that were selected to serve on the task force. Some task forces were more diverse than others in terms of their racial, gender, and partisan membership composition. However, most task forces were quite diverse when it came to the professional and academic backgrounds of the task force members.

With regards to the contentions presented in this book, I found evidence that supported three of the five relationships I posited would exist. I found that the presence of an environmental shock, level of racial threat, and political culture, each had an impact on variance in policy innovation. Specifically, I discovered that in cases where an environmental shock existed (Madison), policymakers adopted more task force recommendations in cases where no environmental shock was present (Kansas City and Columbia). In terms of measuring policy innovation, I found that in the case of Madison, eight of nine policymakers who responded said they adopted task force recommendations. On the other hand, only one of ten policymakers in Columbia reported they adopted task recommendations, while none of the eight who responded in the case of Kansas City said they adopted task force recommendations.

With regards to level of racial threat, I found that as the level of racial threat increased (measured as the percentage of the total population that was African American), the number of local level policymakers who adopted task force recommendations decreased. Madison, which had the lowest level of racial threat, had the highest number of actors who adopted task force recommendations. Columbia, which was at the median of the three cases in terms of racial threat, was at the median in terms of the number of actor who adopted task force recommendations. Finally, Kansas City, which had the highest level of racial threat, had the lowest number of actors who adopted task force recommendations.

Political culture was found to have a significant impact on the possibilities for innovation in each of these three communities. In my analysis, I discussed in detail how the political culture of each of these communities either limited or promoted the likelihood that policymakers who innovate. I paid particular attention to how each community's political culture could have an impact on innovations that were specific to the issue of race relations. I found that communities with public centered values were indeed more innovative than communities with private centered values. Specifically, the city of Madison, with its moralistic culture, was most innovative and had the most publicly centered values. The community of Columbia, with its traditionalistic political culture, was found to be at the median of the three cases in terms of value placed on public versus private interests. Likewise, Columbia was at the median of the three cases in terms of the number of actors who adopted task force recommendations. Lastly, the city of Kansas City was found to have an individualistic political culture and the highest level of private centered values. In line with the expectations for the role of culture in innovation, Kansas City was the least innovative of the three cases.

Implications of the Study for Understanding the Role of Task Forces in the Innovation Process

To understand the role of task forces in the innovation process, as illustrated by this study, it is necessary to assess the findings relative to the body of knowledge that preexists concerning task forces and commissions. As previously stated, the universe of literature that exists on task forces emanates most prominently from studies of federal executive and Congressional level commissions. I note in Chapter One that federal executive and Congressional level commissions can be traced back as early as the Progressive Era's governmental reform movement. In that chapter, I analyze three important federal level commissions from the time period of 1905 to about 1950: 1) the Keep Commission (1905), 2) the Commission of Economy and Efficiency (1911), and 3) the Hoover Commission (1947). It is from the analysis of these commissions, as well as the three cases in this book, that I make my assessment of the overall role of task forces in the innovation process.

It is important to understand that task forces can serve as important tools in the governing process. The historical use of task forces at the federal level, as well as their modern day use in local communities, demonstrates that task forces are politically attractive tools for leaders to use in an effort to affect policy change. The reason for this is because of the main strength of task forces—their members. Task forces are staffed with individuals who are thought to be skilled, if not experts, in studying the issue at hand. In creating a body of individuals who are adept in studying some type of issue and making recommendations on how to improve upon a given problem, leaders can promote policy changes based upon sound judgments and analysis and what also appears to be unattached, untainted, and unbiased information. Task forces, in having such a chemistry, serve as a valuable resource for political, civic, and business leaders to use.

Federal level commissions have provided evidence of how task forces get their strength from the skill level of their members. Recalling the Keep Commission, President Roosevelt appointed Charles Keep, Assistant Secretary of the Treasury, to head a task force responsible for studying how to decrease government spending and waste. The connection between Keep's position in the

Treasury and knowledge on government spending could not have been clearer. Likewise, the Commission and Economy and Efficiency, created by President Taft, was created to study how to decrease government spending and waste. As such, Taft staffed with the commission with individuals who were experts on the issue of controlling waste in spending. As stated in Chapter One, the task force's members were thought to be efficiency experts. The professions of the force's members, which included auditing and administrative law, supported this label given to them.

The task forces studied here also provided evidence that task forces are composed of individuals knowledgeable about the problems they study. As with their federal level predecessors, the task forces invoked by the communities in this book were composed of individuals who had professional and academic training, and in some cases, life experiences, that provided them with the skills necessary to effectively study the problems and issues they were charged to investigate. In cases where the task force members wanted to probe more deeply into issues, they were savvy enough to know where and who to turn to in order obtain the most effective results. The know-how of task force members in going about studying the problem and making associated recommendations was found to be perhaps the key attribute of the three forces investigated in this book.

Despite the finding that task forces have this positive aspect, my general finding is that they are not one of the key factors that influence policymakers to innovate. Task forces, alone, are not agents of policy innovation. As demonstrated in this book, very rarely do policymakers innovate due to the influence of the task force itself. Task forces are limited in their potential influence largely by whether or not policymakers are motivated to innovate. Clearly, the literature on innovation notes the importance that the innovation process is limited by the presence of the motivation to innovate by policymakers (Mohr, 1969). The findings of this study illustrate this reality in that where policymakers are not required by city ordinance or other mandates to adopt task force recommendations, they only do so in instances where, primarily, they are pre-inclined to do so, and secondarily, the obstacles are low, and the resources present. Given this reality, it becomes clear that given a lack of oversight, task forces are only effective when policymakers are motivated to innovate and it makes economic and practical sense for the organization to innovate.

Limitations of the Research

Future research in this tradition faces a number of challenges that must be discussed here. First, the use of a case study approach, although an appropriate method of investigation, proves to yield a low response rate in terms of the number of governmental and nongovernmental policymakers. In general, such a low response rate limits the ability to generalize the findings to a larger body of actors. As such, I could not base my conclusions on any level of statistical significance. Couple this with the reality that going into such a project, it is difficult to know exactly who are the real decision makers in an organization (it could be the case that the individuals from which I sampled were not the true policymakers in the organization) and also, the range of actors who should have been surveyed. To yield a more robust analysis of this topic, these obstacles must be confronted. In addition to these limitations in the research, I also find that conducting a case-study analysis of local level politics proves to be a real challenge when it becomes necessary to generate a body of data—particularly when measuring variables such as political culture. In this book, I find that a body of literature exists on the city of Madison, and to a lesser degree, Kansas City. However, scant attention has been given to the city of Columbia—thus limiting the amount of data available to utilize more conventional measures of indicators such as political culture.

Recommendations and Conclusion

All is not lost for leaders who desire to create task forces and hope to influence policy innovation. What the literature on innovation neglects to mention, and what is extremely important, is the reality that policy makers can stimulate innovation through oversight. In this book, I add a very important contribution to the literature on innovation by nothing that there is an additional factor that is often necessary to be used if leaders hope to influence policymakers to innovate. Oversight is a form of monitoring that acts as a compensatory measure so as to counterbalance the loss likely where self-motivation does not exist. In this book, I find that task forces can indeed become agents of policy innovation when the principals that create the task forces require policymakers to take concerted action towards adopting the recommendations produces by these forces. In other words, policymakers can be motivated to innovate, so to speak, by political principals requiring them to innovate. This was evidenced by the case of Madison—which used oversight as a method to coerce policymakers to adopt task force recommendations. Kansas City and Columbia, on the other hand, failed to do so.

Given the findings in this book, I make the following recommendations for the creation of effective task forces and how to promote their influence over policymakers. First, leaders that create task forces must articulate the rationale behind the creation of the task force itself. The creation of a task force with the articulation of an understanding that there is a problem that the task force will address and provide substantive remedies that policymakers should adopt is vital. If there exists some type of event that creating principals can articulate as a shock, it is too their advantage that they do so if they hope to influence policy adoption. There must be an attempt to demonstrate a clear relationship between some event(s) and the problems that affect or could affect an organization. It is important to do so because if an organization does not feel that some event affects the internal or external portion of their environment, the first piece of the puzzle to innovations is lacking. It is the job of the creating principal(s) to make policymakers feel as though the events affect their organization—even in instances where making the connection between the events and the livelihood of the organization might otherwise be a stretch.

As discussed throughout this book, authorizing principals are in a position of leadership and power to articulate certain issues, events, problems, etc., and meriting serious attention by actors who they hope to influence. In doing so, these leaders transform what are otherwise "events" into environmental "shocks." Recognition by key leaders, such as mayors, governors, CEOs of business, etc., that events have or can have a marked effect on the environment of an organization acts to expand the scope of attention and conflict to other key policymakers who are in positions to adopt changes to their organizational policies. This is a politics of expansion of the scope of conflict (Schattschneider, 1960).

Task forces should take on the following basic characteristics to ensure that they will operate efficiently and effectively: 1) diversity in terms of the gender, racial, ethnic, professional and academic backgrounds of its members, 2) bipartisanship in the members political backgrounds (so that ideas and opinions will not be reinforced), 3) mandated time frame for completion of tasks, yet flexible enough to allow for the task force to complete its tasks effectively and efficiently, 4) membership size small enough so that the task force does not become unwieldy and clear channels of communication and identification of roles and responsibilities do not become clouded, 5) clearly identified responsibilities should be provided to the task force and power delegated to key individuals so that a hierarchy of control and responsibility is clear, and 6) receptivity given to the recommendations produced by the task force in the form of adoption of the recommendations by the organization (e.g., city's government, business) and requirement that targeted policymakers adopt the associated recommendations. This should be done with oversight that involves rewards and punishments, as well as the provisioning of appropriate resources so that policymakers can effectively implement the recommendations.

In the final analysis, there are a number of measures that political, business, and civic leaders can take to increase the likelihood that their task forces will influence innovation in organizations. These leaders must not, however, overlook the importance of the context of the politics in their communities. This is something that leaders cannot do anything about. Leaders must remember that not all communities will have as strong as a proclivity to innovate as others. Because all politics are local, leaders in communities must gauge how the community is likely to respond to the invocation of a task force—be it one whose job is to study race relations or any other topic. Overall, task forces face many challenges in the effort to influence the innovation process in governance.

Bibliography

Elazar, D. J. (1984). *American Federalism: A View from the States*. New York: Crowell.

Elazar, D. J., Gray, V., and Spano, W. (1999). *Minnesota Politics and Government (Politics and Governments of the American States)*. Lincoln, NE: University of Nebraska Press.

Gray, V. (1973). Innovation in the States: A Diffusion Study. *American Political Science Review, 67*(4), 1174-1185.

Grupp, F. W., Jr., and Richards, A. R. (1975). Variations in Elite Perceptions of American States as Referents for Public Policy Making. *American Political Science Review, 69*(3), 850-858.

Heady, F. (1949). The Operation of a Mixed Commission. *American Political Science Review, 43*(5), 940-952.

Key, V. O. (1949). *Southern Politics in State and Nation*. New York: A. A. Knopf.

Mohr, L. B. (1969). Determinants of Innovation in Organizations. *American Political Science Review, 63*(1), 111-126.

Schattschneider, E. E. (1960). *The Semisovereign People: A Realist's View of Democracy in America*. New York: Holt, Rinehart and Winston.

Schroeder, R. D., Van de Ven, A. H., Scudder, G. D., and Polly, D. (1989). The Development of Innovation Ideas. In A. H. Van de Ven, H. L. Angle and M. Scott Poole (Eds.), *Research on the Management of Innovation: The Minnesota Studies*. Chicago: Ballinger Pub.

Walker, J. L. (1969). The Diffusion of Innovations Among the American States. *American Political Science Review, 63*(3), 880-899.

Wildavsky, A. B. (1975). *Budgeting: A Comparative Theory of Budgetary Processes*. Boston: Little, Brown.

Index

Appropriations Act of 1912, 6
Arnold, Peri, 4, 6
Bauman, Sue, 39, 46, 65, 66, 68, 71
Baumgartner, F. R., 20
Berry, Frances Stokes, 18-19
Berry, William D., 18-19
Boone County, 90
bureaucratic influence, 22
Case study, 28, 61
Chicago Commission on Race Relations, 3
Classification Act of 1923, 6
Cleaver II, Emanuel, 36-37, 126-129, 131-136, 139, 144, 147, 158
Cleveland, Frederick, 5
Clinton, William, 3, 7
Columbia, Missouri, 28, 37-38, 43-44, 47, 53, 89-92
Commission on Economy and Efficiency, 4-6, 174
Commission on Organization of the Executive Branch of Government, 5
Czudnowski, M. M., 57
Diehl, Paul, 20
Elazar, Daniel, 25-28, 54, 63, 82, 94, 171
environmental shock, 2, 4, 36, 46, 47, 48, 70, 75-76, 77, 80, 100, 106, 113, 128, 133, 156-157, 161-162, 172
Fording, Richard, 53
Giles, Michael, 25, 52
Glaser, James, 25
Goertz, Gary, 20
Gray, Virginia, 22
Grupp, Fred, 23, 170
Hardy, Richard, 90-91
Heady, Ferrel, 5-6, 170
Hero, Rodney, 25, 27-28, 52
Hertz, Kaenan, 25, 52
Hindman, Darwin, 38, 92-93, 94, 96-98, 101-102, 110, 157-158
Hoover Commission, 5-6, 48, 170
innovation, 10-11
Johnson, Lyndon B., 3, 7
Jones, B. D., 20
Kansas City Harmony, 56, 146-147

Kansas City Urban League, 56, 135
Kansas City, Missouri, 28, 36, 40-41, 43, 45, 47, 51, 56, 128
Keep Commission, 4, 173
Kerner Commission, 3, 7
Key, V.O., 24-25, 51-52, 53, 171
Kinder, Donald, 52
Krause, George, 22
Luethold, David, 90
Lynn, Jr., Laurence, 16
Madison, Wisconsin, 28, 38-39, 47-48, 62-63
March, James G., 17
Mayor's Columbia Race Relations Task Force, 37-38, 44, 50, 89, 92-94
Mayor's Task Force on Race Relations (Kansas City), 36-37, 42, 43, 45, 50, 57, 123, 128
Mayor's Task Force on Race Relations (Madison), 38-40, 61, 64
Mendelberg, Tali, 52
Merriam, S. B., 34
Mesquita, Bruce Bueno, 20
Mohr, Lawrence, 11
nongovernmental organizations, 1-2, 9-11, 16-17, 19, 21-22
Pathways to One America in the 21st Century, 3
Patton, M. Q., 57
policy adoption. (*See* policy innovation)
policy innovation, 1, 10, 40, 41, 43, 47, 48, 50, 54, 55, 76, 77-78, 80, 82, 140, 143-144, 162, 165
political culture, 15, 25-28, 62, 63, 64, 146, 165
Progressive Dane Party, 62, 63
punctuated equilibria, 2, 21, 46, 168
race relations, 1, 3-4, 7-11, 24-25, 28, 35, 37, 38, 47, 51, 55, 64, 92, 128, 157
racial threat, 15, 24-25, 51,54, 58, 86, 115-116, 145, 164; racial threat hypothesis/thesis 25, 52-53, 171
Richards, Alan, 23, 170
Roosevelt, Theodore, 4
Schroeder, Roger D., 17, 169
Simon, Herbert A., 17
Steinberg, Stephen, 8

Taft, William, 4-6
task forces; 1-12, 15, 21-22, 24-25, 34-35, 174; task force influence 11, 15, 24, 48, 50, 81, 83, 115, 145, 149, 163-164; task force recommendations 2-4, 10-11, 15, 21-22, 43-44, 82, 104-106, 114-115, 136, 138-139, 174; credibility of 15, 21, 48, 50, 68, 75, 81, 97, 98, 105, 138, 162

Tillema, Herb, 90-91
Tolbert, C.J., 27-28
Walker, Jack, 23, 171
Warren Commission, 7
Waters, C.C., 7
Wildavsky, Aaron, 20, 169
Wilson, James Q., 18
Yin, R. K., 34

About the Author

Professor Middleton is an assistant professor of political science in the Department of Political Science at the University of Missouri-St. Louis (UMSL). He teaches courses in African American politics, minority group politics, introduction to law, and state and local government. His research focuses on the intersection of race and ethnicity in the evolution of political power, representation, public policy and law. His research has appeared in *Political Research Quarterly, Politics and Policy, National Political Science Review, The Jackson State University Researcher* as well as other peer-reviewed publication outlets. He has published numerous book-chapters, among them including entries titled, "Civil Rights of Hispanic Americans," "Rights of Immigrants," and "Civil Rights of Native Americans," in the Encyclopedia of American Civil Liberties and Rights (Greenwood Press). Prof. Middleton has conducted research in the Dominican Republic and the state of Mississippi where he studied African American and Afro-Latino attitudes towards black racial identity. Prof. Middleton's research also includes having investigated the interaction effects of immigrant culture and disability law, the emerging political allies and foes of immigrant Latinos in Mississippi politics, and the impact of Southern racial etiquette in the 2006 Tennessee U.S. Senate race.

In addition to teaching and research, Prof. Middleton is advisor for the UMSL chapter of Phi Alpha Delta Pre-Law fraternity. At the time of publication, Prof. Middleton was completing a Juris Doctor degree (J.D.) at the St. Louis University School of Law where he has been honored as a "Dean's Scholar" as well as "Theodore McMillian Scholar." He is also a member of the prestigious *Alpha Sigma Nu* Jesuit Honor Society. Professor Middleton volunteers for the Immigration Law Project of the law firm of Legal Services of Eastern Missouri (LSEM) where he works in the area of Immigration Law. At LSEM, Professor Middleton has assisted in drafting complaints to be filed in the Federal District Court for the Eastern District of Missouri, drafted motions to be filed with the Executive Office of Immigration Review, done intake and interviews of clients, and translated legal documents from Spanish to English.

Prof. Middleton also serves on the Editorial Board of the *Journal of Immigrant and Refugee Studies* and has served as the Chair of the Committee on the Status of Blacks in the Profession for the Western Political Science Association

CPSIA information can be obtained
at www.ICGtesting.com
Printed in the USA
BVHW032202130320
575046BV00001B/35